HD
7105.35
.U6
S38
1985b

Schulz, James H.

The economics of
aging

DATE DUE		
NOV 2 0 1989		
OCT 1 8 2007		

the economics of AGING

third edition

james h. schulz

florence heller graduate school
brandeis university

VAN NOSTRAND REINHOLD COMPANY
New York

Sociology Editor: Sheryl Fullerton
Production Editor: Jane Townsend
Designer: Paula Shuhert

Library of Congress Catalog Card Number: 84-23340
ISBN: 0-442-28132-3

Manufactured in the United States of America

Published by Van Nostrand Reinhold Company Inc.
135 West 50th Street
New York, New York 10020

Van Nostrand Reinhold Company Limited
Molly Millars Lane
Wokingham, Berkshire RG11 2PY, England

Van Nostrand Reinhold
480 Latrobe Street
Melbourne, Victoria 3000, Australia

Macmillan of Canada
Division of Gage Publishing Limited
164 Commander Boulevard
Agincourt, Ontario MIS 3C7, Canada

15 14 13 12 11 10 9 8 7 6 5 4 3 2 1

Library of Congress Cataloging in Publication Data

Schulz, James H.
  The economics of aging.

  Bibliography: p.
  Includes index.
  1. Old age pensions–United States. 2. Retirement income–United States. 3. Aged–United States–Economic conditions. I. Title.
HD7105.35.U6S38 1985b 330.973'0927'0880565 84-23340
ISBN 0-442-28132-3

Contents

Preface

Readers of the first two editions of *The Economics of Aging* will notice some changes in the third edition. Major portions of the book have been changed and updated. More attention is given to the growing economic impact of expenditures for elderly programs and to the so-called dependency burden. The frequently heard argument that the elderly are no longer poor is carefully examined in light of new data. Recent changes in the social security law are incorporated, including the major amendments of 1983, and changes in the social security pension age are discussed. A new chapter, "Health, Disability, and SSI Benefits" (Chapter 7), has been added, expanding the discussion of these topics. The chapter on social security financing has been updated to reflect recent developments, and both short-term and long-term financing receive extensive consideration.

There have also been considerable shifting of topics and changes in the organization of chapters. The new order of presentation groups complementary topics closer together and should make the material easier to follow. And each chapter now ends with a list of chapter highlights and suggested additional readings.

The glossary of terms has been expanded to assist readers unfamiliar with economic terminology. Glossary terms appear in bold face type upon first appearance in the text.

Policy makers and the elderly themselves generally agree that economic security in old age is one of the most important problems needing a solution. Yet, as in other areas of knowledge, misconceptions abound. Most aged are not poor; they are not the group most seriously hurt by inflation; they have not been *forced* to retire. Social Security is not bankrupt.

We do not know the answers to all the questions raised concerning the economic situation of the aged. However, this book attempts to present a wide range of existing knowledge, which permits a more sophisticated view of the many issues and which, in some cases, challenges the conventional wisdom.

I have tried to cover technical topics in a relatively nontechnical and concise manner. Inevitably, a lot of the complexities and much of the existing literature could not be discussed. However, the suggested readings at the end of each chapter will be useful to those readers seeking to extend their knowledge on particular issues. Again, however, I have tried to avoid highly technical works.

Some readers may be surprised by the proportion of the book devoted to pension issues (four chapters). To me, however, the key to understanding the current and future economic status of the aged is an understanding of private and public pension programs. Therefore, I have devoted considerable space in the book to describing these programs and, more importantly, to discussing their economic impact on the younger and older populations.

I first became interested in the economics of aging when some years ago I had the opportunity to ask one of the most knowledgeable persons in the aging field, Clark Tibbitts, "What have economists contributed to our knowledge about growing old?" His answer and challenge to a young graduate student who was then searching for a dissertation topic—"Why don't you find out?"— triggered a sequence of events of which this book is a product. It is appropriate then that the book begins again with an introduction by Clark Tibbitts, a person who has dedicated a major portion of his life to improving the social and economic welfare of older persons.

The number of people who have contributed to this book over the years with their suggested changes, corrections, and useful insights has now become too large to list each individually. I would, however, like to acknowledge the following third edition reviewers: Elizabeth Elmore, Stockton State College; Charles H. Hawkins, Central Washington University; Harold L. Orbach, Kansas State University; and Herbert S. Parnes, Emeritus, Ohio State University.

I also wish to explicitly thank my family for their support and understanding. As I pushed hard to finish the third edition before going off to Africa in 1983, it was their cooperation and enthusiasm that helped keep me going to meet the deadline.

Finally, my sincere thanks to Margaret Stubbs for her research and typing assistance for all three editions.

James H. Schulz
Waltham, Massachusetts

Introduction

by Clark Tibbitts

The appearance of three editions of *The Economics of Aging* within a period of eight years testifies to the dynamic nature of the subject and to its cogency for students, practitioners, policy makers, and researchers in the field of gerontology and its underlying disciplines. The invitation to contribute an introduction to this new and extensively revised edition affords me the opportunity to reflect on some of the principal developments that have taken place in the field during the more than half century of my working life.

My first awareness of the economics of aging came to me during my adolescent years in Chicago. The United Charities of Chicago used to conduct an annual "tag day" to raise funds for needy older people in the Chicago area and help support the county home for the destitute. Hundreds of volunteers stationed on busy streets invited pedestrians to drop money into a hand-held container; contributors were awarded a stringed tag to be worn for the day, identifying them as "givers."

My initial professional experience with the economics of aging came during the Great Depression, when workers by the million were unemployed, as the saying went, "through no fault of their own"; when thousands of businesses and banks were failing; and when farms were being foreclosed in similar numbers. President Hoover attempted to assure the country that the return to prosperity was "just around the corner" and that there would soon be "a chicken in every pot." He backed his optimism with firm resolve, sending General Douglas MacArthur on horseback to break up the March of the Unemployed on the Washington Capitol.

Hoover's obstinacy helped elect Franklin Roosevelt to the presidency. Taking office in March, 1933, Roosevelt forthwith launched a constellation of alphabet agencies—NRA, FERA, PNA, WPA, FCA, HOLC, AAA, FmHA, PHA, and CCC—to give depressed Americans a New Deal. Every agency addressed the economics of aging in one way or another.

Restless to have a part in the precedent-breaking government actions, I joined the research unit of the Federal Emergency Relief Administration (FERA) and shortly thereafter the Public Health Service's National Health Inventory, funded by the Works Progress Administration (WPA). The two experiences revealed that one-fourth of all workers and one-half of *older* workers were unemployed and that chronic illness and difficulty in obtaining medical care were especially prevalent among older people, particularly those with low incomes.

I therefore reacted with enthusiasm to President Roosevelt's appointment of the Committee on Economic Security under the chairmanship of Frances Perkins. The committee drew up specifications for an old age insurance program (OASI), modified before it became operative to include survivors; a program of old age assistance (OAA) to provide income to the needy while the OASI program was building an operating reserve; and an unemployment compensation program for short-term financial assistance. As Professor Schulz discusses in his book, the objectives of the OASI program were both to remove older workers from the work force and to assist the states in providing income to the elderly needy during a period of dire economic vulnerability. The means-tested OAA program served millions not covered by OASI and was replaced by the supplemental security income program (SSI) in 1974.

I agreed with the late Professor Fred W. Cottrell's appraisal that enactment of this social security legislation represented the most radical extension of government into the private lives of citizens ever taken by the American government. The supplemental security income program (SSI), which superseded OAA in 1974, was also a dramatic and far-reaching development. The coverage it provides closes gaps left by the other financial aid programs and attempts to assure that no older person today will be without at least a modicum of income. Responsibility for management of SSI was assigned to the Social Security Administration to help remove the stigma attached to receipt of noncontributory assistance.

Social security was designed originally to provide only a modest floor of income. The assumption was that additional support required to sustain an adequate level of living would be available from earnings, personal savings, pensions, and gifts from adult children.

As this book explains in detail, the assumption proved to be quite erroneous; social security has achieved a much larger role than originally anticipated. The older population was increasing rapidly, doubling between 1900 and 1930 and again between 1930 and 1950. The transformation to a mechanized, industrial economy led many employers to divest themselves of older workers in favor of the plentiful supply of youth eager for jobs. Private pensions were few, and many adults were unable to support both young families and older parents as well. I was gratified, therefore, to witness the amendments that liberalized social security by broadening coverage, expanding protection, and raising benefit levels.

I was equally pleased with the later emergence of private pension plans that raised many retirement incomes above the basic social security levels. The emerging pension movement was advanced significantly during World War II, when employers used the promise of pensions to recruit urgently needed workers. Growth continued when the Supreme Court sanctioned (1948–49) organized labor's effort to include pensions—rationalized as deferred wages—in collective bargaining. Private pension systems now cover about half of all private wage and salary workers.

Enactment of legislation in 1965 for establishment of the Medicare–Medicaid programs represented to me a third major development in the economics of aging during the period. The Committee on Economic Security in 1935 omitted health insurance from its recommendations on the assumption that it could be obtained easily after the basic social security program had been put in place. Instead, organized medicine, the life insurance industry, and others opposed to further government intervention into affairs of the private sector delayed health insurance legislation for 30 years.

As I have observed it, one of the most compelling issues in the economics of aging over the century has been that of achieving a harmonious relationship between chronological age, employability, and pension eligibility. As noted above, employers have responded to our transformation into an industrial economy by replacing older workers with what they presumed to be healthier, stronger, physically and mentally more agile youth. At the beginning of this century, Sir William Osler, a Canadian physician, rationalized management's position when he stated that men past 40 were comparatively useless and those past 60 were absolutely useless. Both Theodore and Franklin Roosevelt disparaged the physical and intellectual performances of those who had survived the middle years. The social security eligibility age of 65, reflecting a compromise between reality and affordability, was adopted by employers as the age for compulsory retirement, with additional inducements for even earlier withdrawal.

Most of us teaching, doing research, and thinking about aging policy rebelled at the prejudice, inequity, and costs of this negative view of older people. Supported by Department of Labor and other studies of older worker performance, gerontologists saw compulsory retirement at age 65 or earlier to be wasteful of experienced manpower—manpower demonstrated to be careful, conscientious, loyal, and reliable.

A succession of national conferences on aging held strongly to this view. By 1967 older worker advocates were able to persuade the Congress to pass the Age Discrimination in Employment Act prohibiting discrimination in employment after age 40.

As I look back over the years, I am pleased by the variety of actions that have been taken to protect the income and employment of older persons. Federal and state income taxes provide for liberal personal exemptions; most states offer partial property tax exemptions for the elderly. Federal–state community programs offer food stamps, group and home-delivered meals, reduced local transportation fares, special housing (often subsidized), assistance with legal problems, and long-term care options.

In *The Economics of Aging* Professor Schulz has shown that the United States has gone far toward assuring older people opportunity to continue to enjoy the amenities and security of living the country seeks for all of its citizens. Government programs have laid the foundation, and the private sector has played a key complementary role. But, as I have emphasized in my writings over the years, these efforts have not so much substituted for the traditional activities of individuals and families as they have enhanced them and made them more viable. To my mind, confronting the challenges of aging in America, including the *economics* of aging, is truly a cooperative endeavor among various groups and institutions. And that is the way it should be in today's enlightened society.

Editor's note: Clark Tibbitts retired in 1983, leaving the U.S. Administration on Aging after working 53 years in jobs related to aging. He was 80 years old at the time.

Chapter One

Changing Populations and Retirement Expectations

Not too many years ago it was relatively easy to write about the economic situation of the elderly population. All one needed to do was cite statistics that confirmed what everyone knew from either personal experience or observation. For years now everyone has known that most of the elderly have suffered from serious economic deprivation—that their incomes were inadequate, that inflation exacerbated the situation by reducing real incomes and eroding savings, and that the aged were one of the largest poverty groups in the country.

Today the situation is much more complex, due in large part to our nation's very positive response to the economic plight of the elderly. During the past few decades major breakthroughs have occurred in the development of private and public programs to deal with the economic problems of old age:

1. Over the past fifteen years, social security old age benefits have been increased by almost 200 percent, significantly faster than inflation over the same period.
2. Private pension programs have spread throughout industry and have grown rapidly—with dramatic increases in benefit levels.
3. Medicare and Medicaid were legislated—currently providing over $50 billion a year in benefits to older persons.
4. Property tax relief laws have been legislated in all our states.
5. Old age assistance has been abolished and a new Supplemental Security Income Program (SSI) has taken its place. This program roughly doubled the number of low income elderly eligible for income supplementation. And it raised benefit levels in 24 states above the previous levels of old age assistance—in some cases dramatically. In addition, a national food stamp program helps low income people of all ages.

Despite the economic problems that remain (which will be discussed later in this book), we must not lose sight of the important economic gains that have been made. Dramatic changes have occurred in the levels of income provided older persons, especially from public and private pensions. Consequently, there has been a significant improvement in the general economic status of this group—traditionally viewed as poverty stricken. In fact, a recent study by Timothy Smeeding (1982) finds that if both money and in-kind income (defined on p. 31) are counted, few elderly currently fall below the official government "poverty level." In 1979, counting only money income, the poverty rate was 14.7 percent. However, Smeeding estimates that only about 5 percent fell below the poverty level, if in-kind benefits related to food, housing, and medical care are taken into account.

The methodology used to make these estimates is controversial, and hence not everyone agrees with the results. The Smeeding findings serve to dramatize, however, the undisputed progress that has been made in raising many from the ranks of the "most poor" to the ranks of the "near poor."*

So rapid and so great has been this improvement in the welfare of the aged that assessments of their condition have not kept apace with progress. Not only the general public but also many professionals concerned with the problems of the elderly have a serious misconception regarding the current economic situation of the aged. A study by Erdman Palmore (1977) reports that about one-half of the graduate students and faculty in the field of human development and aging at two prominent universities did not recognize as an *incorrect* statement the true-false quiz question: "The majority of old people have incomes below the poverty level (as defined by the federal government)." In contrast, these same students and faculty answered correctly about 90 percent of the other questions in the aging quiz covering twenty-four other areas of knowledge about older persons.

There is no doubt that many people are unaware of the rapidly improving economic status of the aged in America. Still fewer have thought about its implications for policy on the aging. Given, for example, the projected shortfall of the social security system in meeting its projected obligations (see Chapter 6), this news of a greatly improved economic situation for the aged is a development to be welcomed. As various ways of raising additional revenues for the system are considered, it is certainly heartening to hear that older people today are economically much better off than they were little more than a decade ago.

The decline in the seriousness of the elderly's economic problems means that the task of helping the aged may not need to be as high on the social agenda as in prior years. In fact, given the rising costs of providing for the aged, some people have begun to argue that we have already gone too far.

Aged Programs, the Federal Budget, and the Elderly

The significant, semi-hidden story in the . . . federal budget is that America's public resources are increasingly being mortgaged for the use of a single group within our country: the elderly.

The above quote is similar to many statements made in recent years. But it was voiced over a decade ago by columnist David Broder (1973), writing in the

---

*Whether the progress is sufficient is a different question. In the next chapter we discuss, for example, the appropriateness of the official poverty index.

Washington Post. Broder's article was one of the first assessments to raise questions about growing federal expenditures for the elderly.

In 1978, Health, Education and Welfare Secretary Joseph A. Califano, Jr., became the first cabinet secretary to publicize the problem of rising federal expenditures for the elderly. He estimated that $112 billion was paid out that year by federal programs assisting the elderly. And he projected that these expenditures would rise from 24 percent of the federal budget in 1978 to 40 percent in the early part of the twenty-first century (Califano, 1979).

In 1980, a *Forbes* magazine article characterized the growing media attention given to the issue. A feature article titled "The Old Folks" was headlined: "The myth is that they're sunk in poverty. The reality is that they're living well. The trouble is there are too many of them—God bless 'em" (Flint, 1980).

More recently, Barbara Boyle Torrey (1982), an economist in the federal government's Office of Management and Budget, summarized the issue in this way:

> *The traditional tradeoff between guns and butter may in the future be better characterized as a tradeoff between guns and canes. The increase in the older population is likely to generate an increasingly powerful fiscal interest group, concentrating its attention on the federal government. The estimated outlay increases that could be expected in the future because of the increases in the older population are not insupportable. . . . It does, however, represent a clear shift in future priorities for the federal government that will need to be confronted.*

When the Reagan Administration took office in 1981, the aged felt the effects of the first broad action taken to cut back expenditures for the elderly. President Reagan's budget request for 1983 called for $6.5 billion less expenditures for aged programs than would have occurred under pre-Reagan policies. Ultimately $5.2 billion in cuts, over half in the Medicare programs, was legislated. In a review of both these spending decreases and the tax reductions occurring during this period, Storey (1983) concludes that the impacts varied greatly by level of income. The well-to-do aged received substantial tax cuts and escaped major benefit cuts; the middle-income aged were helped a little by tax cuts but were more affected by benefit cuts; and the low-income aged received no tax-cut benefits and bore the brunt of many of the largest spending cuts. "The net result of the policy changes made during the past 27 months [1981–83] has been to squeeze the resources available to the neediest among our Nation's elderly populations" (Storey, 1983).

According to political scientist Robert Binstock, the stereotypes that the aged are poor, frail, relatively impotent as a political force, and more deserving of help than some other groups in poverty have given way to a new set of axioms. The aged are increasingly perceived as relatively well-off and a potent political force that will soon pose an unsustainable burden on the economy. "These new axioms regarding older persons have provided the foundation for the emergence of the aged as scapegoat in American society. That is, the aged are bearing the blame for a variety of economic and political frustrations" (Binstock, 1983).

Have we collectively done enough for the elderly? Or have we, perhaps, done too much? To answer these questions we can no longer generalize about the economic situation of all the aged as one group. Instead we must look at the multitude of programs for the elderly and analyze their impact on various subgroups of the elderly population. We must distinguish, for example, between the very old aged (the "vulnerable aged") and those just retiring, between widowed and married women, and between those families with two or more pensions and those with only social security.

In the chapters to follow we will survey the major economic changes that have occurred among various groups of the aged. But before we do this, it is important to discuss the changes in retirement expectations that have occurred in American society and the important demographic shifts that are now occurring.

The Right to Retire

As observed by Donahue, Orbach, and Pollak (1960), "retirement is a phenomenon of modern industrial society. . . . The older people of previous societies were not retired persons; there was no retirement role." A number of developments, however, changed this.

Even *before* public and private pension systems were widely established, large numbers of older persons were not in the labor force. As early as 1900, for example, almost one-third of all men age 65 and over were "retired," in large part because of health problems. Prior to the institution of **pension*** systems, however, older persons not in the labor force had to rely on their own (often meager) resources, help from relatives, or public and private charity. Over the years recognition spread that complete reliance on these sources of old age support was unsatisfactory. *Public pensions were, in part, a reaction to the need of more rational support mechanisms for older persons unable to work.*

Industrialization created a new problem. In contrast to the farm, where people could almost always "work" (even if it was at reduced levels), industry was characterized by a large amount of job insecurity. Recurrent **recessions** and **depressions** and shifts in employment opportunities created competition for the available jobs. *Thus, another motivation for establishing pensions was to encourage older workers to leave the work force and create jobs for younger workers.*

But probably most important of all, industrial growth—fueled by rapid technological change—resulted in vast increases in economic output. As we discuss at length in Chapter 3, economic growth provides an expanding option for greater leisure with a simultaneous increase in living standards. That is, the rapid economic growth of the twentieth century made it possible to more easily support older people who could not (or did not wish to) work. Retirement became economically feasible.

---

*Many technical terms appearing in the text are defined or explained in a glossary at the back of the book. Terms in the glossary appear in boldface type the first time they appear in the text and, in the case of very important terms, at first appearance in subsequent chapters.

Thus, we see the institutionalization of retirement arising as a result of and reaction to (a) the needs of large numbers of elderly unable to work, (b) short-run fluctuations in employment opportunities for both the young and the old, and (c) expanding economic resources over the long run. Pension programs were developed that "provided compensation based upon years of service rather than upon need per se. They were to emerge as an 'earned right' and were to become instrumental in defining a retirement status as appropriate for the older worker" (Friedman and Orbach, 1974).

Changing Expectations

As just indicated, until recently retirement meant dependency—on relatives, friends, private charity, or government welfare. Indications are that many elderly tended to accept a subsistence lifestyle as the best that could be expected in old age. Attitudinal surveys have found, for example, that despite their relatively low economic status, very *high* proportions of the elderly viewed their economic situation as satisfactory and not below their expectations.*

In earlier periods, studies did find that many people *close to* retirement viewed the approaching period negatively. According to Friedman and Orbach (1974), "The widespread opposition to retirement reported in studies during the 1940s and the early 1950s reflected an overwhelming concern over the consequences of serious deprivation associated with retirement." More recent studies, however, have found attitudes toward retirement becoming more positive as the economics of retirement have improved. Studies by Shanas (1977) and Atchley and Robinson (1982), for example, found generally positive attitudes toward retirement both before and after retirement.

Thus, retirement expectations are changing. In part, this has resulted from increases in living standards at all ages. More importantly, the development of pension programs and the continuous improvement in their provisions have given the elderly increasing independence and for the first time placed a comfortable standard of living within the reach of many. Increasing pension benefits and pension coverage seem to stimulate demands for still higher retirement incomes.

Aging Populations

At the same time that retirement income expectations are changing, we are witnessing an aging of populations around the world. Demographers classify countries into "young," "mature," and "aged" populations according to the proportion of population age 65 and over. Cowgill and Holmes (1970) have suggested that countries with 4 to 6 percent aged should be classified as young, 7 to

*See, for example, the report of Louis Harris and Associates listed in the Suggested Readings at the end of this chapter. For a conceptual framework that incorporates the notion of relative deprivation to help explain the perceived financial adequacy among the elderly, see Liang and Fairchild (1979).

Table 1.   Population 65 Years and Over in Various Regions of the World, 1980

Region	Number (millions)	Percent
World	258	6
Developed	129	11
Developing	129	4
Africa	14	3
Latin America	15	4
Northern America	27	11
East Asia	67	6
South Asia	43	3
Europe	63	13
Oceania	2	8
USSR	27	10

Source: Based on data in George C. Myers, "The Aging of Populations." In Robert H. Binstock, Wing-Sun Chow, and J. H. Schulz, *International Perspectives on Aging: Population and Policy Challenges* (New York: United Nations Fund for Population Activities, 1982), Tables 2 and 4.

9 percent as mature, and 10 percent or more as aged. Using this classification scheme, Myers (1982) finds for 1980 that 89 countries of the world were young, 10 were mature, and 27 were aged. Table 1 shows the number and percentage of aged persons for various regions of the world in 1980.

In the United States, persons age 65 or older represent about 11–12 percent of the population. This age group has increased more rapidly than the whole population. Yet, as Siegel (1976) points out, the growth of this age group during the 1960s and early 1970s was below its growth during the 1950s and the preceding decades. Given relatively stable mortality and net immigration rates (see Figure 16, p. 120), fluctuations in population growth since the Second World War have largely been due to fluctuations in the **fertility rate** (births per 1,000 women 15 to 44 years old). Figure 1 shows the changing fertility rate over the 1930–1981 period.

Fertility is now at a historic low. If it remains near its present level, the U.S. Census Bureau projects a "graying" of the United States population with the following major characteristics:

1. The 65 and over population will rise to between 18 and 23 percent of the total population by the year 2035.
2. The "very old" in their late 70s and 80s will become an increasingly larger fraction of the elderly population—rising from 38 percent to 47 percent.
3. Since women's life expectancy exceeds that of men by a growing number of years, the proportion of widows will rise; and they will face an ever longer widowhood. The sex ratio of the 65 and over population showed 100 women for every 69 men in 1975; by the year 2000, the difference will grow to 6.5 million, or 100 women for every 65 men.
4. Given the "baby boom" of the 1940s and 1950s, the aged population will increase exceptionally rapidly around the year 2010.
5. The **median** age of the population will rise sharply—increasing from 29 in 1977 to about age 37 in the year 2020 (Figure 2).

Per 1,000
females 15–44

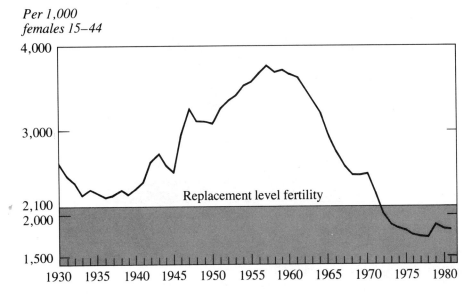

Figure 1. Total Fertility Rate, 1930–1981

Source: Based on U.S. Bureau of the Census, "Population Profile of the United States: 1981," *Current Population Reports*, Series P–20, No. 374 (Washington, D.C.: U.S. Government Printing Office, 1982), Table 5–1.

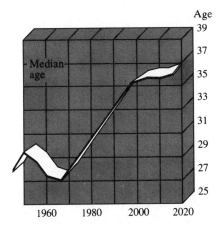

Figure 2. The Changing Median Age of the Population

Source: Reproduced from *National Journal, The Economics of Aging*, a National Journal Issues Book (Washington, D.C.: The Government Research Corporation, 1978). Used by permission.

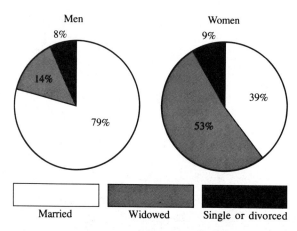

Figure 3. 1976 Marital Status of Older Persons

Source: National Clearing House on Aging, *Facts About Older Americans 1977* (Washington, D.C.: U.S. Department of HEW, 1977).

The progressive aging of the population and the longer life expectancy of women creates a new and growing problem. Older men are usually married (Figure 3) and relatively few live alone. In contrast, almost two-thirds of older women are widowed, divorced, or single, and almost half of them live alone or with nonrelatives. As Sheppard points out:

> Look at what's going to happen to a group of Older Americans that will *affect dramatically our individual lives and our government's commitments more than ever before: the population 80 and older, between 1977 and 2000. That age group will grow, not by 20 percent, but by 67 percent. . . . A smaller and smaller proportion of the very old who are in the greatest state of dependency will actually have any younger children who might otherwise be counted on to provide family based care"* [Sheppard, 1978].*

Dependency Ratios

An increase in the number of the aged causes concern among policy makers because this means an increase in the number of nonworkers who must be economically supported by the working population. Many people are now concerned about the increased competition that may arise among age groups as each strives for a larger share of the nation's output. For example, improving retirement income by increasing social security often heads the list of demands by the aged segment of the population; in contrast, this is a relatively unimportant priority for younger workers.

---

*This important point, along with other issues concerned with the impact of demographic changes on the family, is given expanded treatment in excellent articles by Shanas and Hauser (1974) and Tibbitts (1977). Demographic developments are much more complex than our brief comments in this section might suggest. For a good discussion of the various issues see Cutler and Harootyan (1975) and Myers (1984).

Given the various mechanisms for retirement income provision—social security, public assistance, private insurance, private charity, and/or personal savings—the fundamental economic fact remains that the part of national output consumed in any particular year by those *retired* is produced by the *working* population, regardless of the mix of mechanisms employed.* Figure 4 shows, for example, the proportion of total output estimated to be consumed by the aged in 1974. Some of this output was produced by persons over age 64 still in the labor force. But most of the aged, consuming about 10 percent of total output, did not participate in the production process.

To assess the changing relationship between consumption by the elderly, government expenditures for the elderly, and total economic output, it has been increasingly common to calculate what are called "dependency ratios." These ratios seek to measure the number of persons in the society not engaged in producing output relative to those in the labor force who are.

It is important to realize, however, that the recent interest in dependency ratios has arisen primarily as a result of concern about the growing social and economic costs and the "burdens" of the aged that arise with changes in the demographic structure and economic support mechanisms. Hence, the prejudicial term chosen was *dependency*—emphasizing the economically nonproductive potential of certain groups, such as children and retired persons.

The President's Commission on Pension Policy, a blue-ribbon panel appointed by President Carter, probably had the greatest impact in sounding an alarm:

> *After the turn of the century, an unprecedented shifting of older workers into retirement will begin to take place as the so-called "baby boom" generation grows older. Quite literally, this country's population will be coming of age.*
>
> *As the population of the country matures severe strains will be placed on our already overburdened retirement income system. The inequities and inadequacies of the present retirement income system will become critical as more people retire and the active work force to support their retirement shrinks. [President's Commission on Pension Policy, 1981]*

The Commission's focus on the retired population relative to the working population has also been the focus of policymakers, researchers, and the media who want to raise fears about the growing aged population. An article in the *New York Times*, for example, commented:

> *The "baby boom" generation, now 15 to 35 years old, will begin turning 65 in 2010, less than 30 years from now. At the same time, the productive working population of the country will be shrinking in relative size. In 2020 there will be only about three and a half working-age Americans for every person 65 or older, as against five today. [Emphasis added] [Weaver, 1981]*

As pointed out by Cowgill (1981), "from a demographic standpoint such fears are not warranted. The analysis on which they are based is one-sided and misleading." Cowgill shows that most modernized countries of the world, all with relatively aged populations, have quite low dependency loads, much lower than

---

*While working, individuals store up claims to output produced after they stop working by acquiring financial assets (saving) and by the accrual of pension credits.

*Figure 4. Consumption and
Investment of National Output in 1974*

Source: Estimated using data in *Economic Report of the President* (Washington, D.C.:
U.S. Government Printing Office, 1975).

[a]Includes government nontransfer expenditures apportioned on a per capita basis between aged and nonaged.

[b]Persons age 65 or more.

developing nations (Figure 5). Historically, *total* dependency ratios in the United States have been declining, and projections show that they are likely to continue to decline in the future.

The definition of dependency ratio used by the President's Commission and stated in the last sentence of the *New York Times* article quoted above focuses only on dependents arising as older people retire from the work force. As Cowgill (and others) have pointed out, this is a very biased measure of the non-working segment of the population. There are many other individuals who are not working: children, nonworking spouses, unemployed workers, and the severely disabled. Children have always constituted the major proportion of dependents in societies. While that burden has been sharply reduced in industrialized countries, children still represent a major dependency burden in developing countries (hence the results shown in Figure 5).

In a detailed analysis of dependency ratios, Adamchak and Friedman (1983) project "total dependency ratios" for the years 1900 through 2050. The ratio of all persons not in the labor force to those in the labor force *declines* from 127.0 in 1980 to 85.5 in 2050, if the social security eligibility age remains at 65. It declines to 76.8 in 2050 if the social security age for full benefits is increased to age 68.

Since projections of future labor force participation are difficult, all such projections of future ratios are subject to large errors. The Adamchak and Friedman estimates—and others by Cowgill (1981) and DeVita (1981)—do

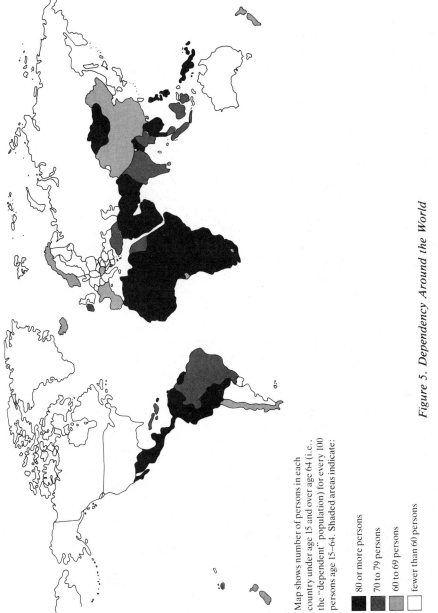

Map shows number of persons in each country under age 15 and over age 64 (i.e., the "dependent" population) for every 100 persons age 15–64. Shaded areas indicate:

■ 80 or more persons

■ 70 to 79 persons

■ 60 to 69 persons

□ fewer than 60 persons

Figure 5. Dependency Around the World

Source: Donald O. Cowgill, "Can We Afford Our Aging Populations?" Paper prepared for Conference on Economics of Aging, Kansas City, April 3–5, 1981. Mimeo. Used by permission.

serve to emphasize, however, that concerns about the economic burden of the aged based solely on *aged* dependency ratios may seriously overestimate the seriousness of the future problem.

The projected changes in the dependency ratio do indicate that we must continue to give attention to the changing numbers of *both* young and old. Thus, a related and perhaps more important question is the relative costs associated with young versus older dependents. Unfortunately, little information exists on the extent to which the reduced costs of fewer children might offset the rising costs of more retired persons. Robert Clark and Joseph Spengler (1978), using a broad measure of public support costs, find that government expenditures are three times greater for older dependents than for children. This is not surprising since, aside from education expenditures, most expenditures for children are made directly by parents—not, as in the case of the aged, through public expenditure or transfer programs. In contrast, Hilde Wander (1978) finds that in West Germany the total cost of rearing a child to 20 is one-fourth to one-third higher than that necessary to support someone 60 years old for the rest of his lifetime.

Even if the costs are less, the changing composition of the dependency ratio raises a number of major political questions as more must be paid out through the political tax–transfer process. Political scientist Robert Hudson argues that we can expect at least three political outcomes from these fiscal pressures: major new policy initiatives or appropriations for the aged beyond those provided for under existing legislation will meet with new and perhaps overwhelming resistance; agencies servicing the elderly will be subjected to more insistent demands for accountability; and, finally, the political influence of the aging and groups organized on their behalf will be put to a new and sterner test (Hudson, 1978).

The Need for Individual and National Retirement Planning

Today those who have not yet reached the retirement period of life can look forward to that period without many of the fears that worried so many in the past. A wide variety of institutional mechanisms are now available to help individuals provide for their economic needs. In fact, almost all individuals are *required* to make substantial provision for retirement by mandatory participation in social security and other pension programs.

With the emergence of retirement as a normative expectation and the development of a variety of institutional arrangements affecting the terms and conditions of retirement, the economics of aging takes on a different perspective. As we shall see in the chapters to follow, the level of retirement living has generally improved but is still subject to a large degree of variation and also to individual discretion. More importantly, however, the level and adequacy of retirement living are influenced by the many uncertainties and risks that are associated with the institutional mechanisms we have created. Savings opportunities completely secure from the risks of inflation are generally not available. Private pension coverage varies greatly among industries and occupations, and job change may mean the loss of some or all of these pension rights. The ultimate level of social security benefits can be severely reduced by the misfortunes of structural unemployment or illness and by the obligations of child care—all of which keep individuals out of the regular labor force for long periods.

People can and should begin to look forward to the challenges and opportunities of retirement. But there is still a major need for individuals to think about and plan for retirement. In this book we look at various economic aspects of that planning. The concurrent rise in (a) the level of benefits to the aged, (b) retirement expectations, and (c) the number of aged as a proportion of the population also generates a need for more *national* planning in the area of the economics of aging.

In the chapters to follow we will look at the retirement preparation problem, both from an individual and national standpoint. We begin with chapters concerned with the economic status of the current elderly and the special problems of older workers. We then discuss the nature and magnitude of the economic retirement preparation task. Finally, the concluding chapters of the book discuss pension and health programs and the major role they play in providing economic security in retirement.

Chapter One Highlights

What are the economic implications of "the graying of America"? Some of the important points made in this chapter are:

1. Dramatic improvements have occurred in the economic welfare of the aged.
2. At the same time, public officials have begun to voice fears regarding the "economic burden" of the growing elderly population.
3. The rapidly changing retirement patterns and expectations occurring in recent decades are, in part, a result of expanded opportunities for leisure resulting from significant economic growth over the long run. However, they are also a result of efforts to deal with recurrent unemployment in the American economy.
4. The American population is itself aging, primarily as a result of declining fertility.
5. Historically, total dependency ratios have been slowly declining and, contrary to often voiced concerns, are likely to decline even further in future years.

Suggested Readings

Binstock, Robert H., Wing-Sun Chow, and J. H. Schulz, eds. *International Perspectives on Aging: Population and Policy Challenges.* Policy Development Studies No. 7. New York: United Nations Fund for Population Activities, 1982.

One of the very few comprehensive overviews of aging in developing countries. See also the article by George Myers on "The Aging of Populations."

Espenshade, Thomas J., and William J. Serow, eds. *The Economic Consequences of Slowing Population Growth.* New York: Academic Press, 1978.

A discussion of all major aspects of the changing demographic profile and its economic implications.

Harris, Louis, and Associates. *The Myth and Reality of Aging in America.* Washington, D.C.: The National Council on the Aging, 1975.

A report on a representative national sample of 4,254 persons 18 years and over conducted in 1974. Topics covered are (a) public attitudes towards old age, (b) the public's image of "most" people over 65, (c) perceived social and economic contributions of the aged, (d) preparation for old age, (e) being old, (f) access to facilities, (g) the media's portrayal of the aged, and (h) the politics of old age.

Russell, Louis B. *The Baby Boom Generation and the Economy.* Washington, D.C.: The Brookings Institution, 1982.

This study examines economic developments, the housing market, and social security to determine whether the baby boom generation has been a major factor influencing the economy. One part of the study looks at projected expenditures for medical care and social security when the baby boom group reaches old age.

Sheppard, Harold L., and Sara E. Rix. *The Graying of Working America—The Coming Crisis of Retirement-Age Policy.* New York: The Free Press, 1977.

A book that attempts to push beyond the "conventional wisdom" in this area—emphasizing the potential problems and policy issues arising from demographic changes.

Storey, James R. *Older Americans in the Reagan Era—Impacts of Federal Policy Changes.* Washington, D.C.: The Urban Institute Press, 1983.

The publication analyzes the course and consequences for older Americans of federal policy changes since 1980 and discusses proposals in the 1984 budget of the president.

Chapter Two

The Economic Status of the Aged

> *The treatment of old people in America, many of whom have a hard life behind them, is remarkable. . . . [This is illustrated by] the terrifying extent to which old people are left in poverty and destitution. . . . It cannot possibly be the considered opinion of the majority of Americans that so many of those who in America are often called "senior citizens" should be left in misery, squalor, and often forbidding loneliness, unattended though they are in need of care. The situation is overripe for a radical reform of the old age security system.*

So wrote the well-known social commentator Gunnar Myrdal in his book *Challenge to Affluence* (1963). Myrdal was writing in the early 1960s. But as we noted in the preceding chapter, dramatic changes have occurred since then.

Contrast Myrdal's comment with a recent story that appeared in the *Washington Post* (19 August 1983):

> *A new Census Bureau study shows that the elderly in this country are much better off than previously believed and, in fact, are better off than the average American. . . .*
> *The new figures are likely to become factors in the inter-generational politics that have developed around Social Security and Medicare. Both these programs for the elderly have been in trouble lately, and Congress has had to choose between tax increases for the young or benefit cuts for the old.*

The article by Spencer Rich in the *Washington Post* goes on to describe how the per capita, after-tax income of the elderly was $6,300 in 1980 versus $5,964 for the population as a whole.

In this chapter we explain why the typical money income statistics usually reported do not give a full and accurate picture of the aged's economic status. We discuss a variety of factors, including family size and taxes, that should be taken into account.

Looking at the controversial Census Bureau findings reported by Rich and a number of other recent studies (discussed below), one can begin to see emerging a very important historical development. From a statistical point of view, *the elderly in this country are beginning to look a lot like the rest of the population*: some very rich, lots with adequate income, lots more with very modest incomes (often near poverty), and a significant minority still destitute. This is very different from the past when most were destitute.

Once we recognize that the similarities between the old and younger populations are increasing, we must also recognize the important and unique differences. While clearly most of those disadvantaged before old age remain disadvantaged, they are joined in old age by many for whom certain economic problems are unique:

The elderly widow who finds her income but a small fraction of the income enjoyed when her husband was alive

The retired couple whose retirement cushion is wiped out when the electric power consortium in the state of Washington defaults on bonds sold to build nuclear power plants that are no longer economically viable

The engineer who, despite years of private pension coverage, never gains a vested pension (see Chapter 8)

The retired executive who must sell off all his assets to pay for the institutional care needed for his wife with Alzheimer's disease

The retired teacher without social security whose state pension falls far behind needed purchasing power during the double-digit inflation of the late 1970s

The gas station mechanic who becomes unexpectedly disabled at the age of 50 and has nothing to supplement his meager social security disability pension

The appliance salesman living only on social security who was never covered by a private pension, and neglected ("could not afford") to contribute money into an IRA or some other investment account

The list could go on and on. But the point of the list is not to elicit sympathy for the aged or prove the need to do more. Rather, we seek to emphasize the heterogeneity of the aged and warn against those glib generalities: the aged are poor; or now, with greater frequency, the aged are well-off.

Prior to the 1960s there were relatively few data available to analyze the economic situation of the aged population in the United States. This situation changed dramatically in the early 1960s as a result of the Social Security Administration's very comprehensive survey of the aged in 1962 (Epstein and Murray, 1967). Since then, a wide range of statistics has been published by the Social Security Administration, the Census Bureau, the Administration on Aging, the Department of Labor, and various private organizations. These data provide a variety of information on various aspects of the elderly's financial status.

Two important notes of caution are immediately in order, however. First, because it takes time to collect, check, analyze, and publish statistics, there is often a considerable lag in the availability of information. Throughout the chapter we present illustrative statistics—the latest that were available at the time of writing. Many readers, however, will want to seek the newer data available. Second, all statistical information is subject to great abuse; unless users are very careful, they may misinterpret or misuse the available data. The discus-

Table 2.   1982 Total Money Income of the Aged[a]

Total Money Income	Families	Unrelated Individuals
Less than $5,000	5	32
$5,000–9,999	20	40
$10,000–14,999	21	13
$15,000–19,999	16	6
$20,000–29,999	20	6
$30,000–49,999	13	2
$50,000 and over	6	1
Median Income	$16,118	$6,424
Total Percent[b]	100	100

Source: U.S. Bureau of the Census, "Money Income and Poverty Status of Families and Persons in the United States: 1982," *Consumer Income*. Current Population Reports, Series P–60, No. 140 (Washington, D.C.: U.S. Government Printing Office, 1983).
[a]Head of unit age 65 or older.
[b]Totals may not add to 100 due to rounding.

sion below, therefore, also attempts to deal with two important questions: What are the most useful kinds of data for evaluating the economic status of the aged, and what are the major problems in interpreting the data available?

Aged Income

We begin our discussion of the elderly's economic status by looking at the income they receive. Income is not the only resource contributing to the economic welfare of the aged; later sections will look at a number of other important factors (for example, assets). But as Mollie Orshansky has observed, "while money might not be everything, it is way ahead of whatever is in second place" (Irelan and Bond, 1976).

Income Distribution   In 1982, one-quarter of families with head age 65 or older had money income of less than $10,000; a little less than half had money income of less than $15,000 (U.S. Bureau of the Census, 1983). Most of these families were older couples living alone.

The income situation of unrelated individuals age 65 or older—most of whom live alone—was much different. Nearly three-quarters had income below $10,000, and 85 percent had income below $15,000. Table 2 shows the distribution of income for both aged families and individuals.

Not all the aged are covered by the data presented in Table 2. Only units where an aged person is *head* of the unit are included. If an aged person lives with his children or if the children live with their aged parent(s), should the two units be reported separately, or should the income be lumped together into one big family? It often makes a significant difference in the final results that are reported. There is a tendency to combine all the incomes of people living together. The result has been that a lot of aged poverty in the past has been hidden be-

Table 3.   Rates of Increase in Median Income of
Aged Persons by Race and Sex, 1970–1981[a]

Subgroups	Median Income in 1981	Rates of Increase in Real [b] Income
Aged White Men	$ 8,586	14%
Aged White Women	4,934	34
Aged Black Men	4,875	10
Aged Black Females	3,528	28

Source: Based on data in Yung-Ping Chen, "Economic Status of the Aged." In Robert H. Binstock and Ethel Shanas, eds., *Handbook of Aging and the Social Sciences*, 2nd ed. (New York: Van Nostrand Reinhold, 1984).
[a]Calculations based on data from the Current Population Survey for various years.
[b]Real income was calculated using the annual average Consumer Price Index.

cause the poorest aged—those who are unable to live by themselves—were submerged into the bigger and usually more prosperous family unit.

One might argue that if the aged are living with a family unit and the family unit is not itself poor, then the aged standard of living is not likely to be poor. Using this perspective, one can argue further that there is no problem in such cases and that if you statistically separate the aged out (perhaps to try to justify higher pension benefits) you are basing the analysis on an artificial situation.

The opposing view, however, is that many of these people are not necessarily treated as members of the family. They are there by necessity, and often families do not permit them to share fully in the higher standard of living of the rest of the family. Or, even if the younger members of the family want them to share fully, many aged people are too independent to be willing to draw heavily upon the resources of the rest of the family. They would rather—even though they live within the family—live at a lower, perhaps subsistence, level.

Changes over Time   Historically we know that as social security benefit levels have increased many aged persons have moved out of these families at the first opportunity and set up independent households. Statistically, as a result of these family units breaking up, new units headed by an aged person show up in the data. Since these new aged units almost always have very low income, the process tends to increase the reported incidence of poverty among the aged. We find, for example, that during certain periods the number of persons in poverty has declined among nonaged groups but has risen among the aged (partly as a result of the separation of the aged out of other families).

Thus, when the statistics show aged poverty increasing, it is not necessarily true that the situation is actually getting worse. In part the statistics are a reflection of things getting better. As pension benefits go up, some of the poor aged who prefer independent living are able to break out of other family units and thus become identifiable statistical units. But, again, it can be argued that they were always poor, and all that has changed is their living arrangements.

Economist Yung-Ping Chen has measured the significant increase in income that occurred from 1970 to 1981. Table 3 shows by sex and race the per-

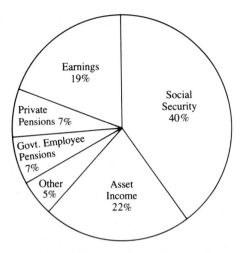

Figure 6. 1980 Sources of Aged Money Income

Source: Based on data in Melinda Upp, "Relative Importance of Various Income Sources of the Aged, 1980," *Social Security Bulletin* 46 (January 1983), Table 1.

centage increases in *real* income (that is, income increases after inflation has been accounted for). According to Chen's estimates, women experienced the largest increase and black men the smallest.

Sources of Income   Finally, Figure 6 shows the sources of income for the elderly. While social security is the major source (40 percent), asset income (22 percent) and earnings (19 percent) make large contributions. We must remember, however, that various income sources are distributed unevenly among the subgroups of the aged population. Earnings go mostly to the nonretired; asset income goes mostly to a few high-income elderly. In a subsequent section we examine more closely these differences.

An Important Statistical Warning   Almost all the statistics that have been presented in the prior sections were based on the government's Current Population Survey (CPS). The CPS is a household survey conducted by the U.S. Bureau of the Census. The survey is designed to gather monthly information on labor force participation and unemployment. At least once a year, however, information is obtained on the kinds and amounts of income individuals and families receive.

Income information from surveys like the CPS are subject to substantial reporting errors by those interviewed. Respondents do not know, remember incorrectly, refuse to answer, or give false information out of anger or fear of government retribution. Such errors can produce substantial underestimates of income and can distort the relative income positions of various socioeconomic groups.

The Social Security Administration's Office of Research and Statistics has been researching this reporting problem for many years. It has recently published startling findings with regard to the seriousness of the problem (Radner, 1982). Errors were found to be very large, especially for the elderly.

The study found that in 1977 the CPS underestimated the mean income of all family and single units by 11 percent. However, the incomes of family units headed by persons age 65 or older showed an increase, when adjusted for underreporting, of 41 percent! The extent of CPS underestimating was much larger for those with higher incomes and relatively small for those at the low-income levels. The major cause of error in the income estimates was underreporting of property income (interest, dividends, rent, royalties, and trust income) and to a lesser extent self-employment income (especially farm income).

The study also made less precise estimates for the year 1979. The adjusted mean income numbers for this later year are equally surprising:

Age of Head	Mean Income	
	CPS	CPS Adjusted
14–24	$10,511	$10,300
25–34	17,953	18,530
35–44	23,220	25,670
45–54	24,664	28,460
55–64	20,809	25,280
65 or older	**10,837**	**15,860**

The Social Security Administration's findings dramatically emphasize the need to be cautious in using and interpreting income statistics. Later in this chapter, when we look at asset statistics, the same caution applies—probably more so.

Oh, that the above were the only problems involved in measuring the economic status of the elderly. Unfortunately, once we understand the underreporting limitations of the CPS data, our problems are only beginning.

The Aged Are Not a Homogeneous Group

The statistics given in the first part of this chapter (pp. 17–19) unfortunately have other shortcomings: lumping all the aged population together seriously distorts the reality of the situation. It is common for writers and analysts to give only median incomes for all or large groups of the aged, but as we saw in Table 3, for example, there is a wide divergence in income among the aged.

Similar distortions result from grouping all the aged together and generalizing about their social problems. Most people who study old age and the process of aging (gerontology) are familiar with this aggregation problem in the social and psychological areas. There is no such thing as the collective aged; the aged are as diverse as the population itself, and this is just as true for economic status as it is for other areas.

If one views the aged as one homogeneous group, there is a tendency to try to develop for them one appropriate economic policy—just as in other areas we have tried to develop one appropriate housing policy and one appropriate health policy. We have learned over the years that such attempts almost always fail in diverse groups.

Unfortunately, much of the data published on a regular basis do not show the significant differences existing among the elderly. Probably the most frequently used economic data on the elderly are from the National Census and the Current Population Survey. But these published tabulations are generally for all (or large groups) of the aged. The most useful type of data for analysis and evaluation are those that break down the aged population into small subgroups. Unfortunately, in order to look more closely at the heterogeneous nature of the economics of aging, we must often use data that are less current.

The Retired Versus the Nonretired   The first step toward disaggregation of the data is very simple: separate the aged into at least two broad categories—the retired and the nonretired. Unfortunately, most of the data sources do not or cannot provide such a breakdown. They "do not" because often it simply does not occur to those presenting the data that this is an important distinction. They "cannot" because the questions asked in the survey providing the data do not always include the information necessary for judging whether a person is retired or not. Hence one sees data where the aged wage earners are grouped together with the non-wage earners. The earners, of course, tend to have much higher and more adequate incomes. When they are averaged together with the non-wage earners the total mean and median income for "the aged" is increased and makes the situation look much better than it actually is for retired people and much worse than it actually is for the employed.

If one wants to segregate the retired from the nonretired, one immediately runs into the problem of how to define retirement for statistical purposes. Many aged persons work to supplement their pension and other retirement income. Is a person who is working twenty hours a week counted as a retired person or is he or she partially retired? If the latter, what does that mean?

Thus, even if we divide the aged population on the basis of retirement, it is not clear whether there should be two categories or more than two. A three-category tabulation, for example, might be full-time workers, part-time and unemployed workers, and the fully retired. In general, most discussions of the economic status of the aged do not even attempt to deal with this problem when presenting data. This omission is unfortunate since (as we will show) this is such an important issue in evaluating the economic well-being of elderly people.

In recent years the U.S. Bureau of the Census has begun publishing some data giving income by employment experience. Table 4 shows income by employment status in 1981.

Different Age Groups   Another major problem in analyzing data on the aged is that it often is not appropriate to group people together who differ in age by as much as fifteen or twenty years. Most statistics on the economic status of

Table 4. 1981 Money Income of Aged[a] Families and Unrelated Individuals, by Work Experience of Householder[b]

Work Experience Last Year	Median Income	Less than $5,000	$5,000– 14,999	$15,000 or more	Total Percent
Families					
Householder Did Not Work	$11,632	16	47	37	100
Worked Part Time	14,729	12	40	48	100
26 Weeks or Less	12,825	19	40	41	100
Worked Full Time	26,671	2	17	81	100
26 Weeks or Less	12,722	16	43	41	100
Unrelated Individuals					
Householder Did Not Work	4,948	51	42	7	100
Worked Part Time	6,203	38	50	12	100
26 Weeks or Less	4,040	60	36	4	100
Worked Full Time	12,476	14	45	41	100
26 Weeks or Less	5,425	46	45	9	100

Source: Based on data in U.S. Bureau of the Census, "Money Income of Households, Families, and Persons in the United States: 1981," *Consumer Income.* Current Population Reports, Series P–60, No. 137 (Washington, D.C.: U.S. Government Printing Office, 1983), Table 36.
[a]Age 65 or older.
[b]Householder is a Census Bureau definition for the person (or one of the persons) in whose name the home is owned or rented. If the unit is jointly owned, either husband or wife may be listed first.

aged people group all persons age 65 and over together. Again, conclusions drawn from such data will be misleading. To begin with, it is important to realize that the needs of people at the two extremes of the retirement period are often quite different. Unfortunately, there is little specific information on the changing consumption patterns of the elderly. However, a recent study (McConnel and Deljavan, 1983) of *retired* persons' expenditures in comparison to those of older people still working provides some interesting findings. On the average, the retired spend a significantly larger proportion of their budgets on shelter, food for home meals, and medicine. However, as income increases, retired families commit a smaller proportion of additional income to necessities and a much larger proportion to gifts and contributions.

If one wants to develop a budget for the aged, then, it is probably better to develop different budgets for at least two age groups (even though the range of ages chosen must be somewhat arbitrary). Not that you cannot find persons 85 and 90 years old who are as active and vigorous as someone 65 (or maybe 25). But on the average there seem to be enough distinctions for analytical purposes to warrant taking a range of ages into account in the presentation and analysis of economic data.

Another reason for separating the aged into various age groups is that the accustomed standard of living for the *very* old is usually quite different from that of the *newly* old. Each group grew up and worked during dissimilar periods. Each group's final earnings and the resulting levels of living prior to retirement are different. Given the lengths of time involved, these differences can be quite substantial. Thus, in evaluating the adequacy of income for aged people, one should allow for the fact that the *very* old themselves may have lower expectations about their standard of living than aged persons who retire a decade or two later.

There is, however, another factor that works in the opposite direction. Among the very old the incidence of exceptionally high expenditures for chronic illness and institutionalization rises dramatically. For those elderly persons who experience these problems, economic need can rise catastrophically.

Furthermore, the incomes of those who have recently retired are often much better than those who have been retired a long time—mainly because the former group's earnings are typically higher and pensions based upon them are consequently better. Also, the newer retirees are more likely to reap gains from the recent establishment of private pensions or improvements in old plans.

There is a final reason why one should be sensitive to age differences in assessing the economic status of the elderly. In recent years it has become increasingly unsatisfactory to talk of only those people 65 and older as being aged—especially with the rise of early retirement in the United States. We know that to arbitrarily designate as old those who have reached a specific chronological age is a most inadequate way of approaching the problem of defining the aged. It takes no account of people's varying capacities for physical and mental activities and social involvement, among other things. We know that people age differently in terms of various characteristics.

The more serious economic problems of aging commonly arise from, or are aggravated by, the cessation of earnings following retirement. Thus it is important to study that part of the aged population having the most economic problems—those families where there are no regular workers. Increasingly this group includes people who are less than 65 years of age. If we look at persons younger than age 65, we can logically divide them into two groups: those younger than age 62 and those age 62 to 64. Age 62 seems to be an appropriate dividing point since at this age social security eligibility begins for everyone except widows (who can qualify at age 60).

Persons who retire before age 62 must rely on private pensions and/or their own assets and income from these assets. Data indicate that this group tends to be composed of both very high income people and very low income people—with very few in the middle (Kingson, 1979; Daymont and Andrisani, 1983). That is, we find among this very early retirement group those people who *have* to retire early even though they do not have enough money and those people who *can* retire very early because they have sufficient economic resources to live satisfactorily.

Those who retire reluctantly tend to be workers with health problems, difficulties obtaining and maintaining a job, and no pension to supplement social security. Those who retire voluntarily tend to be those with private pensions, those who worked for the government, those whose wives have pensions, and those who have good houses with no mortgage to pay (Morgan, 1980).

Thus, Karen Schwab's (1976) analysis of early labor force withdrawal found that most of the men leaving early reported health-imposed work limitations. Figure 7 shows the proportion of men age 58–63 no longer in the labor

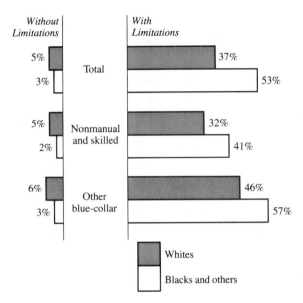

Figure 7. Percent of Men Aged 58–63 Out
of the Labor Force in 1969, by Type of Longest
Job, Health-Imposed Work Limitations, and Race

Source: Lola M. Irelan et al., *Almost 65: Baseline Data from the Retirement History
Study*. Research Report No. 49 (Washington, D.C.: Social Security Administration,
1976).

force in 1969. Of those with no work limitation, 63 percent had incomes over
$5,000—in contrast to only 30 percent for the health-limited group.

And a more recent study (Morgan, 1980) shows the importance of eligibility
for a second pension to supplement social security. Persons with a private pension or a civil service pension from the local, state, or federal government are
much more likely to retire very early. Of course ill health and a second pension
are not mutually exclusive. Morgan finds that workers with two pensions and
some illness experience are the most likely to retire.

Shifting from those who retire before age 62 to those age 62–64, we focus
on a group that is eligible for social security retirement benefits but at a reduced
level. Ever since the early retirement provisions under social security were first
introduced (in 1956 for women and 1961 for men), more than half of the men
and women starting to receive social security old age retirement benefits have
opted for reduced benefits before age 65. (Table 14, Chapter 5, shows the increasing proportion of beneficiaries electing early benefits.)

Income by Age   Again, published economic data on the income of various
age groupings of the elderly population are sparse. Table 5, however, presents
data for 1980 that illustrate the income differences between age groups by looking at younger versus older units.

Table 5.   1980 Money Income of Couples and Nonmarried Persons
Age 55 and Older

Age	Median Income	Less than $5,000	$5,000– 9,999	$10,000– 14,999	$15,000 or More	Total Percent
55–61	$20,370	10%	13	12	63	100[a]
62–64	15,510	13	18	17	51	100
65–67	12,400	17	23	18	43	100
68–72	9,660	21	30	19	30	100
73–79	8,450	27	32	16	26	100
80 and older	7,390	34	29	14	23	100

Source: Susan Grad, *Income of the Population 55 and Over, 1980* (Washington, D.C.: Social Security Administration, 1983).
[a]May not add to 100 percent due to rounding.

Black–White Differences   Differentiation of the aged population by various socioeconomic characteristics must also be made. One of the best studies of black–white differences is by Julian Abbott (1977), who analyzes data for persons aged 60 and older in March 1972. Abbott finds that only a small proportion of the elderly population depends on public assistance payments but that this proportion includes a much larger percentage of the black elderly (30 percent) than the white (7 percent). The reverse is true for the receipt of income from assets: 13 percent for blacks and 53 percent for whites. The two groups, however, are about equal in the proportion receiving income from earnings (44 percent).

Figure 8 illustrates the similarities and differences in the shape of the income distribution curves for each racial group. Despite aggregate differences in money income, a sizable majority of individual black and white elderly units had similar incomes. Using a technical measure of the extent to which income distributions overlap, Abbott calculates an "index of integration" (i.e., overlap) equal to 0.74 and an "index of differentiation" equal to 0.26. These indices indicate that incomes for about three-fourths of black and white units were *not* different. Even within the lowest income groups, however, black and white units differed substantially in their sources of income. Abbott concludes, therefore, "that efforts to improve the income adequacy of the elderly will have different effects on the two races. Benefit increases in any of the retirement pensions would provide relatively less for blacks because of their lower rate of coverage and their lower lifetime earnings. . . . Blacks would benefit more from the improved, but means-tested, assistance programs and from the continued availability of jobs for those still able to work."

The plight of the minority aged has been characterized by some writers as one of "double jeopardy" or "multiple hazards" (Jackson, 1970). Data from a fairly large sample of middle-aged and aged blacks, Mexican Americans, and whites living in Los Angeles County provide insight on this issue. Dowd and Bengtson (1978) investigated differences across and within ethnic categories.

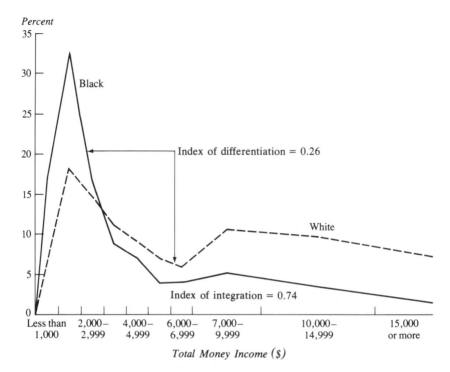

*Figure 8. Percentage Distribution of Black and
White Elderly Units, by Total Money Income in 1971*

Source: Julian Abbott, "Socioeconomic Characteristics of the Elderly: Some Black-
White Differences," *Social Security Bulletin* 40 (July 1977): 16–42.

Their analysis supported the double jeopardy characterization—especially with
regard to income and self-assessed health.

Similar findings are also reported by Shanas (1977). Almost twice as high a
proportion of the black aged as of white say they need medical and dental care
but have delayed treatment—primarily because of financial problems. And the
black elderly more often than the white report their financial situation at inter-
view time to be worse than it was when they were age 60.

There are some indications, however, that the situation is improving. In reviews of the studies and data on this topic, Markides (1981 and 1983) concludes
that while elderly members of ethnic minority groups continue to be socioeco-
nomically disadvantaged, data show a relative decline in the racial income gap
in old age over time.

Dual Pensioners   We discuss in later chapters the fact that a high proportion of wage and salary workers in private industry are *not* covered by private
pensions. The result is that many people reaching retirement age have to rely

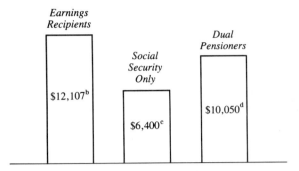

*Figure 9. 1976 Median Money Income of Aged
Families with Earnings, Social Security Only, or Two
Pensions* [a]

Source: U.S. Bureau of the Census, *Consumer Income*, Current Population Reports, No. 114 (Washington, D.C.: U.S. Government Printing Office, 1978).

[a]The second pensions are from either private or government employment.

[b]Total median income (i.e., earnings and all income other than earnings).

[c]Median shown is for families with social security and property income only.

[d]Median shown is for families with social security, another pension, and property income.

solely on social security pensions. Figure 9 illustrates the income disparity between aged families with dual pensions and those receiving only social security.

The median income of families with dual pensions was almost as high in 1976 as the income of the "most advantaged" aged—families with one or more members still working. However, those families with only pension income from social security typically had much lower income.

In later chapters we will discuss further this divergency of economic status among one- and two-pension families. One major policy issue currently being discussed is the extent to which government policy promotes a growing "pension elite" (i.e., dual pensioners with high pension income) while at the same time large numbers of aged have, essentially, only their social security income to rely on.

The Impact of Taxation, Assets, and In-Kind Income

Thus far we have looked only at the distribution of money income among the aged. Three other factors have an important impact on the economic status of elderly people. First, there is the extent to which the income is actually available to meet current needs (what economists call *disposable income*); some of the income goes to government in taxes. Second, we need to assess the size, type, and distribution of assets held by older persons. And, finally, not all income is *money* income; sizable amounts of *in-kind* income are received by the elderly, improving their economic status.

Taxation   Most income distribution statistics look at the pretax distribution of income. The aged, while they share in various advantageous tax provisions legislated for the general population, also have their own special provisions to reduce the amount of taxes they pay. The federal income tax (and many state) laws permit persons age 65 and over to double the amount of income deductible as "personal exemptions." More important, however, is the special taxation of social security. Until 1984 all such benefits were not subject to federal income tax. Starting in that year, half of benefits became taxable for individuals with very high income (in 1984 about 10 percent of beneficiaries).* Thus, nearly 40 percent of the elderly's income is currently not subject to income tax as a result of this special treatment.

Property tax reductions are now granted in all states for elderly persons (Fairholm, 1978). The most common type of reduction (25 states in 1974) is a "circuit breaker." Tax relief under this mechanism is tied to need, as defined by taxpayers' income levels in relation to their property tax liabilities. The amount of relief declines (or phases out) as taxpayer income rises, using a formula that avoids a sharp drop in relief at some arbitrary income level. For example, the Vermont circuit breaker comes into play when the property tax burden exceeds 7 percent of household income; for Minnesota it is 6 percent; for many states it is 3 to 5 percent. These and other provisions of the circuit breaker vary from state to state. Income ceilings or rebate limits are different; some laws do not cover renters.

Another common method of property tax relief is the "homestead exemption." Under this mechanism, a state excludes before the tax rate is applied a portion of the assessed value of a single-family home from total assessed value. A few states allow deferral of property taxes until after an elderly owner dies or sells his residence, and a few freeze the tax rate at the rate in force when the aged person reaches a certain age, usually 63 or 65.

Assets   In addition to current income, many of the aged own assets that provide housing, serve as a financial reserve for special or emergency needs, contribute directly to income through interest, dividends, and rents, and generally enhance the freedom with which they spend their available income. Most assets can be sold and thereby converted to money that can be used to buy goods and services. But one should distinguish between liquid assets and nonliquid assets. Fortunately, most published statistics on assets do make such a distinction.

Liquid assets are relatively easy to convert into goods and services or money (the most liquid of assets). These consist generally of cash, bank deposits, and corporate stocks and bonds. *Nonliquid assets* usually require more time to convert. The two major types of nonliquid assets are equity in housing and equity in a business.

Assets (or savings) are held by individuals because they perform a number of very useful economic functions. They are used as a precaution against unexpected happenings in the future. One puts money aside so that it can be drawn

*See p. 133 for a more detailed discussion of this provision.

upon should the need arise. This saving might be viewed as self-insurance. Assets are also accumulated in anticipation of known or planned large expenditures in the future: because of a worsening illness one might anticipate going into a nursing home; or one might save in order to take a round-the-world retirement cruise. Still another reason for saving is to leave a legacy to one's children or to other people.

One of the most important reasons for saving is to smooth out the irregularities in the flow of income coming to an individual over his lifetime. People are becoming increasingly aware of the fact that (given current life expectancies) there is often a ten- to thirty-year period of living in retirement after earnings from work have stopped. Thus, individuals must decide how to deal financially with this nonwork period of life and whether to provide through asset accumulation economic resources to supplement pension income.

However, assets put aside as a precautionary measure or for anticipated major expenditures in old age are not available for meeting immediate needs. If you are worried, for example, about having high medical expenses that Medicare will not completely cover, if you expect that you might have to go into a nursing home, or if you anticipate that property taxes will increase dramatically in your area, you must accumulate additional assets to provide for such events. Thus, studies (e.g., Danziger et al., 1982–84; Mirer, 1980) show that contrary to predictions by economists based on the life-cycle hypothesis, the elderly as a group tend to save, not dissave.

Similarly, if you have nonliquid assets such as housing, as long as you are determined to keep that housing and not sell the property, that asset is not convertible into income to be used for day-to-day living. In effect the asset is "locked in."

In fact, a high proportion of older people own a home or have an equity in it. About 80 percent of elderly couples live in an owned home, compared to about 40 percent of nonmarried elderly persons. The amount of mortgage debt on those homes is usually very low; in fact, about four-fifths of elderly homeowners own their homes free of any mortgage. Thus we find that many older persons have a sizable asset accumulation, but often most of it is not available for day-to-day living expenses. See Table 6.

Until recently in the United States there was no available financial mechanism that would permit people to sell the equity in their home, get back money over a period of time, and still be able to live in the house. In contrast, in France a home annuity plan called *viager* has been in existence for many years, and the *Boston Globe* (3 December 1978) reports that there are over 400,000 currently in existence. A *viager* arrangement is negotiated by the homeowner with a buyer and results in the buyer paying an agreed-upon down payment and a monthly payment to the owner for the rest of the owner's life (in return for the property at death). The amounts paid are mutually agreed upon—with the age and health status of the owner taken into account. The arrangement, to a certain extent, represents a gamble on the part of both parties. The buyer, however, can go to an insurance company and take out an actuarial insurance plan to help offset the payments promised in the resulting legal agreement.

Table 6. Home Equity of the Elderly in 1975

Equity	Percent
None	31
$1–7,350	8
7,351–14,999	12
15,000–21,999	17
22,000–29,999	9
30,000–49,999	18
50,000–74,999	3
75,000 or more	4
Total Percent[a]	100
Median for Units with Equity	$20,048

Source: Cynthia C. Dittmar and E. Meier, "Levels and Sources of Retirement Income." Chapter 7 in the Appendix of the Report of the President's Commission on Pension Policy (Washington, D.C.: mimeo, 1981).
[a]Does not add to 100 due to rounding.

Since January 1, 1979, the Federal Home Loan Bank Board (FHLBB) in the United States has allowed federally chartered savings and loan associations to offer *reverse annuity mortgages.* Under this mortgage, a homeowner may sell some equity in the house, receiving in return a fixed monthly sum based on a percentage of the current market value of the house. Reverse annuity mortgages are potentially available in all states, but each federal savings institution's program has to be approved by the FHLBB.

Because of unfamiliarity, the risks involved, and the small amount of income that often results, acceptance of this new type of financial arrangement in the United States has been slow—both on the part of consumers and financial institutions. For the interested reader, Scholen and Chen (1980) and Guttentag (n.d.) both give good introductions to the complex set of issues that must be satisfactorily resolved before "unlocking home equity" becomes commonplace.

Table 7 shows the total assets of the elderly in 1975. Analyzing these and other data, Juster (n.d.) estimates the amount of annual consumption that could be financed by liquidating net worth over the remaining lifetime of individuals.* He concludes that "elderly households who are not homeowners have very little likelihood of being able to add significantly to their consumption prospects by way of liquidating assets. . . ." However, again a note of caution is in order. As we discussed earlier in this chapter (p. 19), it is difficult to get accurate statistics on income and assets. Surveys to determine asset holdings of individuals have been undertaken very infrequently in the United States, and those attempted have been plagued by the problem that many people underreport their assets. Although surveys on the amounts and kinds of *income* also have underreporting problems, the amount of underreporting is greater when attempting to ascertain *assets*. In this regard, Juster, who is an expert on survey data, comments: "While my judgment is that we know remarkably little about

---

*Another study by Burkhauser and Wilkinson (1983) focuses on the effect of assets on the size of the poverty population.

Table 7. Total Assets of the Elderly in 1975

Amount	Total	Married Men	Nonmarried Women	Nonmarried Men
None	11	6	20	19
$1–2,999	12	7	20	20
3,000–14,999	19	18	23	20
15,000–29,999	19	20	17	14
30,000–49,999	17	21	11	13
50,000 or more	21	28	10	15
Total Percent[a]	100	100	100	100

Source: Cynthia C. Dittmar and E. Meier, "Levels and Sources of Retirement Income." Chapter 7 in the Appendix of the Report of the President's Commission on Pension Policy (Washington, D.C.: mimeo, 1981).
[a]Totals may not add to 100 due to rounding.

saving in the aggregate, except for a few components of saving that are well-measured and well-understood, what we know at the macrolevel represents a solid concrete-and-steel edifice compared to what we know at the microlevel" (Juster, n.d.).

In-Kind Income   In-kind income consists of goods and services available to the aged without expenditure of money or available at a price below its market value. According to the Congressional Research Service (U.S. House Select Committee on Aging, 1977) there are 47 major federal programs benefiting the elderly over and above those providing direct money income. Special housing programs for the elderly, for example, make apartments available at rates below the normal market price, a subsidy being paid by the government. The food stamp program issues coupons that can be used to purchase food in retail stores. And the largest in-kind programs, Medicare and Medicaid, provide various health care services to the elderly. Timothy Smeeding (1982) estimates that in 1980 the total market value of the major food, housing, and medical care benefits for both the aged *and nonaged* was $72.5 billion.

The major problem in estimating the impact of in-kind benefits on economic status is determining how best to value these benefits. As Schmundt, Smolensky, and Stiefel (1975) have noted, the value that the recipients themselves place on some in-kind goods may be substantially less than the market price.

Smeeding (1982) has estimated the value of major in-kind benefits using three alternative measures and finds that using different valuation techniques and different income definitions produces widely varying estimates. Table 8 shows that food and housing benefits for the aged reduce their poverty level slightly. If Medicare is taken into account, however, the poverty rate drops sharply.

Intrafamily Transfers   Another issue to be considered is the impact of transfers among various members of the family. While we know relatively little

Table 8.   Aged Poverty Rates Using Different
Valuation Techniques and Income Concepts, 1979

Valuation Technique	(A) Money Income Only	(B) A + Food and Housing Benefits	(C) B + Medical Care (excluding institutional care)	(D) B + Medical Care (including institutional care)
I[a]	14.7%	12.9	5.2	4.5
II[b]	14.7	13.1	9.3	7.0
III[c]	14.7	13.7	10.8	10.8

Source: Timothy M. Smeeding, "Alternative Methods for Valuing Selected In-Kind Transfer Benefits and Measuring Their Effect on Poverty." Technical Paper 50 (Washington, D.C.: U.S. Bureau of the Census, 1982).
[a]The "market value" approach: the value is equal to the private market purchasing power of benefits received by individuals.
[b]The "recipient or cash equivalent value" approach: recipient value reflects the program beneficiary's own valuation of the benefit; it is most often measured by the amount of cash that would make the recipient just as well off as the in-kind transfer.
[c]The "poverty budget share" approach: assumes that, for the purposes of measuring poverty, the value of an in-kind benefit can be no more than that implied by observed consumption levels for people near the poverty level.

about the magnitude and nature of these transfers, available data indicate that it is an important means of support for a significant number of the elderly.

Numerous studies have documented the fact that the elderly in this country prefer to live apart from their children. Moving into a household with relatives remains an act of financial or social necessity rather than preference (see, for example, Soldo, 1981). Often, in an effort to enable an elderly person who is otherwise functioning well to remain in his or her home or apartment, relatives may provide economic assistance to supplement public transfers. However, the greatest transfers go to unmarried older people who for one reason or another have been forced to move in with relatives (Morgan, 1978).

One recent study (Shuchman, 1983) found that in 1980 only 13 percent of those elderly (age 60 and over) living alone received family transfers. However, the amount they received was substantial—on average, about $2,000. In contrast, over one-third of those who lived with others received family transfers. Unlike those recipients living independently, they received a relatively small amount—with the majority receiving less than $100.

The Adequacy of Income in Old Age

In 1976 a task force of government experts reviewed ways of measuring poverty more accurately. In their final report they emphasize the fact that assessing income adequacy necessitates standards that are *relative*:

> Poor persons living in the United States in the 1970s are rich in contrast to their counterparts in other times and places. They are not poor if by poor is meant the subsistence levels of living common in some other countries. Nor are most poor like their counterparts in this country fifty or one hundred years ago. This country is

concerned about poverty, its causes and correlates. It is willing to relieve the poverty of some of the poor, and it wants to measure the effectiveness of its efforts to do so. None of this can be done without some idea of who is to be considered poor and who is not. [Poverty Studies Task Force, 1976]

In this section we look at various measures of adequacy in relation to the income of older persons. In early times, nations had little choice but to define basic needs in terms of survival. But for the more affluent nations of the world today, need becomes more relative and, hence, more difficult to measure.

The most popular measure of poverty in America today is the government's poverty index. Developed in the early 1960s by the Social Security Administration, it gained prominence in the Johnson Administration's declared War on Poverty. The index continues to be widely used today, despite the fact that the Nixon Administration—very early in its first term—discouraged government agencies from using the index, arguing that because of conceptual and measurement problems it was a misleading and unreliable measure.

A succinct description of the Social Security Administration's poverty index was presented in 1967 testimony by Wilbur Cohen before the U.S. House Committee on Ways and Means (1967a):

> *The starting point for the SSA poverty index is the amount of money needed to purchase the food for a minimum adequate diet as determined by the Department of Agriculture. The food budget is the lowest that could be devised to supply all essential nutrients using food readily purchasable in the U.S. market (with customary regional variations). The poverty line is then calculated at three times the food budget (slightly smaller proportions for one- and two-person families) on the assumption—derived from studies of consumers—that a family that has spent a larger proportion of its income on food will be living at a very inadequate level. The food budgets and the derivative poverty income cutoff points are estimated in detail for families of differing size and composition (62 separate family types) with a farm/ nonfarm differential for each type. This variation of the poverty measure in relation to family size and age of members is its most important distinguishing characteristic.*
>
> *Because the level of living implied by the poverty index is lower than we think most people would regard as an appropriate measure of adequacy of income for retired persons or disabled workers and their families or widows and children, we have also developed a slightly higher index. We call this the low income index, and it is definitely low income.*

It is an interesting fact that in actual practice the low income index has rarely been used for policy evaluation purposes. Instead the poverty index has almost exclusively dominated the discussions of how many nonaged and aged are in economic difficulty and what policies are needed to deal with these difficulties. It is important, therefore, to understand how the poverty index is calculated and its limitations.

Calculating the Poverty Index   Because of its wide use and importance, let us run through step by step the construction of this poverty measure. First, as was indicated in Cohen's statement above, an amount of adequate food for the family unit is determined, and then the cost of that food at prevailing prices is ascertained by pricing foods in retail stores.

For about thirty years the Department of Agriculture has produced "food plans" that meet the nutritional standards set out by an organization called the National Research Council. While these plans meet nutritional standards, they also try to make the quantities and types of food chosen compatible with the general preferences of American families, preferences determined by food-consumption studies. It is not simply a matter of giving poor people only beans. General eating habits are taken into account.

Thus, in constructing a food plan an attempt is made to respond to the fact that most people prefer meat to beans, although in terms of protein you can get more or at least as much protein from beans as you can from meat. The fact remains, however, that most of the protein in such plans is provided by nonmeat products.

It is also important to note that the food plans were originally devised for emergency periods only and that no one is expected to have to live over a long period of time on these very minimal food amounts. This implies that these food diets would be detrimental to your health over an extended period.

Finally, the Department of Agriculture makes no pretense of assuming that all families can skillfully budget, or are willing to eat, the foods specified in the plans. These assumptions need not be made, given the purpose of the plans. They were developed simply as a device to provide social welfare agencies with a needs standard that was not completely subjective in determining how much money poor people need to avoid serious malnutrition.

The next step in developing the poverty measure is to construct food budgets for different types of families. The poverty index is based on family units with different combinations of the following characteristics:

1. Age of head over or under age 65
2. Size of family (2 to 7 or more)
3. Farm and nonfarm
4. Male and female head of household
5. Number of related children under age 18
6. "Unrelated" family units

The final step is to multiply the cost of the various food plans by three. As explained by the Social Security Administration:

> The Agriculture Department evaluated family food consumption and dietary adequacy in a 1955 survey week and reported for all families of two or more—farm and nonfarm—an expenditure for food approximating one-third of money income after taxes. Two-person nonfarm families used about 27 percent of their income for food and families with three or more persons about 35 percent. A later study made in 1960-61 by the Bureau of Labor Statistics found for urban families that nearly a fourth of a family's income (after taxes) went for food. There is less variation by size of family than might have been anticipated, ranging between 22 percent and 28 percent. . . . The earlier relationship based upon the Department of Agriculture's study was adopted as the basis for defining poverty—that is, an income less than three times the cost of the economy food plan for families of three or more persons. [U.S. House Committee on Ways and Means, 1967]

Thus we see that the "three" used to calculate the poverty level is based upon a survey of the ratio of food consumption to other expenditures of *all* families in the United States. Averaging all families, the Agriculture Department came out with an estimate of three. The Bureau of Labor Statistics' estimate of four was ignored by the Social Security Administration for unstated reasons.

How Good a Measure?   The ratio of food to other expenditures is a key factor in constructing the poverty index. As we indicated above, a higher ratio based on Bureau of Labor Statistics data was not used when the index was first constructed. However, other data that have become available since 1955 also suggest that a higher ratio is appropriate. Tabulation of the 1965 Food Consumption Survey produced a 3.4:1 ratio. "More significantly, the Consumer Expenditure Surveys of 1960–61 and 1972–73 seem to indicate that the ratio exceeds 5:1" (Poverty Studies Task Force, 1976).

A related issue is the measurement of the minimum food requirements used to estimate food costs in the ratio. The current index uses a measure of adequate diet based on the Department of Agriculture's 1963 Economy Food Plan. In 1975 the Department of Agriculture replaced this food plan with a new Thrifty Food Plan. The Thrifty Food Plan reflects revised allowances for essential nutrients and newer data on family food selections.

Mollie Orshansky (1978) points out that the new food plan implies poverty income thresholds that are about 40 percent higher than current levels. "Shifting to the more realistic update . . . would just about double the number of aged poor to include nearly a third of all persons 65 or older, and the number either poor or near poor would embrace approximately two in every five" (Orshansky, 1978).

Another problem involves not counting low income persons as poor if they are institutionalized or living with relatives. In 1976 there were over a million "hidden poor" (mostly unmarried women) who were living with relatives because their low incomes did not permit independent living (Orshansky, 1978).

Poverty Index Statistics   In 1981 the poverty index level for a nonfarm, two-person family with head age 65 or more was approximately $5,500; the one-person level was about $4,400.

In 1981 (the latest year for which data were available) there were 3.9 million aged (or 15.3 percent of all the aged) with *money* income below the poverty level. Figure 10 shows the sharp decline that has occurred in the rate of poverty over the 1959–1981 period. But Table 9 shows that there are wide differences in poverty rates among ethnic subgroups of the elderly. For example, while the poverty rate for the white aged was 13 percent in 1981, it was 39 percent for the black aged.

As we discussed previously, it is important to remember that the statistics discussed above are based on *money* income before paying taxes. If in-kind income is included, taxes are taken out, and other adjustments are made, a very different picture emerges. Earlier (p. 31) we reported the estimates by Smeeding (1982) based on adjustments for in-kind income showing that official poverty rate figures are too high. Another study by the Institute on Poverty at the Uni-

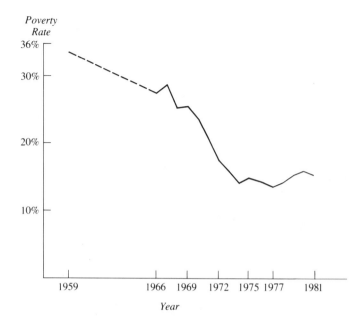

Poverty Rate

Figure 10. Percent of Aged with Money Incomes Below the Poverty Level, 1959–1981

Source: Based on data in U.S. Bureau of the Census, *Consumer Income*, Current Population Reports, Series P–60, No. 134 (Washington, D.C.: U.S. Government Printing Office, 1982).

Table 9.   Poverty Rates: 1959, 1968, 1977, and 1981

	1959	*1968*	*1977*	*1981*
All Persons in U.S.	22%	13	12	14
All Persons Age 65 and Over	35	25	14	15
White Aged	33	23	12	13
Nonwhite Aged	61	47	35	37
Black				39
Spanish Origin				26

Source: Based on data in U.S. Bureau of the Census, *Consumer Income*, Current Population Reports, Series P–60 (Washington, D.C.: U.S. Government Printing Office, various years).

versity of Wisconsin-Madison takes the money income of the elderly and makes three different adjustments, focusing on the economic status of the elderly relative to the nonelderly (Danziger et al., 1982). The aged are more likely than their younger counterparts to own their own homes and other consumer durables (except cars). The study estimates the value of the contribution these durables made to family income (for example, the amount not spent for rent by owning a home). Since the aged have special tax advantages, they also adjust incomes for federal and state income tax and local property taxes. Finally, household size varies with age; households in the prime age groups (35–54) on average contain twice as many persons as those headed by someone age 65 or older. Since a four-person household, for example, requires more income than a two-person one to achieve the same living standard, some adjustment is needed.

Danziger et al. apply these adjustments to a national sample of families in 1973. In 1973 the average money income of the aged was only 49 percent of all other families. Their estimates indicate, however, that the adjustments listed above raise the relative income of the aged to 90 percent of the rest of the population. If in-kind income were added in, the situation would be even better—significantly better. Reporting on the Danziger et al. findings, the Institute on Poverty at the University of Wisconsin-Madison (1983) concludes, "Thus it can be safely said that today the aged are *at least* as well off economically as the rest of us."

But remember: there are quite a few people at all ages who are economically disadvantaged. The University of Wisconsin study does not refute that fact. Rather the study shows that the aged as a group are not—as in years past—an exceptionally nor uniquely disadvantaged group. The study also warns us about using the poverty index. We can use poverty index statistics as an indicator of changes in the economic status of the low-income population. But they should be used with great caution and sensitivity to their many limitations.

Thus far we have talked only about *how the poverty index understates the economic status of the elderly*. Many people argue, however, that other measures are more appropriate for assessing the economic status of the *general* elderly population. As one major critic of the index has observed, "To tout a 'poverty line' based on a starvation diet and an outdated concept of a family's budget as an adequate measure of what is necessary to humanely survive is indefensible" (U.S. House Select Committee on Aging, 1978).

The Retired Couple's Budget   The second major way of measuring the adequacy of aged income is the Bureau of Labor Statistics' Retired Couple's Budget (1966): "The retired couple is defined as a husband age 65 or over and his wife. They are self-supporting, living independently in their own home, in reasonably good health, able to take care of themselves."

Actually there are three budgets—indicative of three different levels of living. The illustrative family is assumed to have, for each budget level, *average inventories* of clothing, house furnishings, major durables, and other equipment. The budgets pertain only to *urban* families with the specified characteristics. No budgets are available for rural families. The budgets are not intended to represent a minimum or subsistence level of living but rather a level described by the Bureau of Labor Statistics as "modest but adequate."

The history of this budget is interesting. Originally the Bureau of Labor Statistics had only one budget for a *nonaged* family of four persons, first developed in 1946–47. It was recognized quite early, however, that it was inappropriate to measure an older couple's needs in terms of the needs of a family of four.

The younger family, for example, has extra expenses for the clothing and education of children.

Reacting to the different living situations of different families, the Social Security Administration developed concurrently with the Bureau of Labor Statistics' budget effort a separate budget for retired couples. In 1959 the Bureau of Labor Statistics revised the older couples' budget. This budget was then updated every three or four years to take account of price changes. But more importantly, the budget was periodically adjusted in an attempt to account for general increases in the standard of living. Thus, for example, in the 1959 budget *five out of six* aged families were assumed to have home telephones (which were used for local calls only). By 1966 the budgets assumed that *all* older couples needed to have phones and that provision for some long-distance calls was appropriate.

How are the budget changes in living standards determined? Most are based on "consumer expenditure surveys" of families with different incomes. As average income increases, average expenditures for different goods change. As described by the Bureau of Labor Statistics, the amount chosen for the budget is "the point on the income scale where families stop buying 'more and more' and start buying either 'better and better' or something else less essential to them."

By means of this technique a majority of changes in the budget level reflect changes in the real standard of living of individuals (rather than just price changes). Thus the Bureau of Labor Statistics' budget standard is not locked into a mechanism similar to the Social Security Administration's three-times-the-food-budget assumption. Once again, however, the assumptions made are somewhat arbitrary. In the words of the Bureau of Labor Statistics: "In general, the representative list of goods and services comprising the standard of budget reflects the collective judgment of families as to what is necessary and desirable to meet the conventional and social as well as the physical needs of families in the present decade."

In the autumn of 1971 the Bureau of Labor Statistics issued for the first time not one but three budget levels for an aged couple: a "lower," an "intermediate," and a "higher" budget. The development of alternative budgets was in part stimulated by the fact that some people were saying the Bureau of Labor Statistics' budget was too high for their purposes, while others were saying it was too low:

> It has been evident that no single budget at one specified level would meet all of the important needs. Throughout the decade of the 1940s, for example, state public assistance agencies appealed to BLS [Bureau of Labor Statistics] to develop a budget for a lower living standard or to suggest ways in which the moderate budget could be scaled down. . . . On the other hand, representatives of voluntary social and welfare agencies providing services to families with a special problem . . . frequently requested budget estimates for a standard higher than moderate to consider in determining eligibility or establishing a scale of fees paid for the services provided. [U.S. Bureau of Labor Statistics, 1967]

A major revision in the Retired Couple's Budget was made in 1969. The budget has been updated annually in succeeding years by adjusting various components of the budget by changes in the Consumer Price Index. For the fall of 1981 the Bureau of Labor Statistics (1982) set the Retired Couple's Budget at $7,226 (low level), $10,226 (intermediate level), and $15,078 (high level).* Unfortunately, one result of the multiple budget levels is that there is even more tendency toward arbitrary interpretations; we do not have one budget but three to choose from—with no very explicit explanation as to why one should be used over another.

Chen (1984) has calculated the proportion of retired couples with money incomes that fall below the low and intermediate budgets:

Year	Below Low	Below Intermediate
1970	29%	49%
1975	21%	42%
1980	18%	35%

His estimates show a steady improvement over the 1970–1980 period. However, by 1980 there were still 2.3 million couples (35 percent) with incomes below the intermediate level.

Maintaining Living Standards   Today older workers are retiring at increasingly early ages (see Chapter 3). Following their departure from the labor force they are faced with the prospect of expenditure needs that do not decrease as much as many would like to believe. In the retirement period there are usually rising health expenditures, increased leisure activities, and increased need for supportive services. There is also a continuing need for the basic essentials of food and housing. Moreover, the retired quickly become aware of any rise in the living standards of nonretired families as these younger families share in the general, long-run economic growth of the country. Such increases no doubt generate a desire among many of the aged to "keep up."

It is this ability to keep up that we will focus on. In addition to the aged who find their income near or below the poverty level, there are other aged whose earnings during the working period allowed them to maintain a comfortable living standard but whose retirement incomes have dropped far below their preretirement levels.

This decline in living standards in retirement has become increasingly unacceptable in the United States. It is a generally accepted goal of retirement planning to provide enough income in retirement to prevent living standards from dropping significantly. Thus, the President's Commission on Pension Policy (1981) expressed the goals this way:

> *Individuals should be able to maintain their preretirement standard of living during retirement years. Retirees should not have to experience a sudden drop in their standard of living. These goals should be accomplished by using income from all sources, including benefits from retirement programs as well as from income derived from individual efforts.*

---

*This is the last year for which the index is available. BLS has discontinued estimating the budget as a result of budgetary cutbacks.

In later chapters we discuss in great detail the extent to which pensions replace preretirement earnings and the use of replacement rates to assess pension income adequacy. In anticipation of that discussion, a few statistics from a study by the Social Security Administration (Fox, 1982) are given to show the magnitude of the problem. Of those couples who began receiving social security benefits in 1968–1976, about 90 percent received social security benefits below the amount necessary to maintain their preretirement living standard. For about 30–40 percent, social security benefits alone were so low that in the absence of other income, living standards would have dropped dramatically. Some families, however, also received public employee or private pension income. About 40–50 percent of these dual pension families or individuals had total pension incomes high enough to enjoy a living standard close to their preretirement situation.

Thus, many of the aged have incomes above the poverty level but fail to achieve the adequacy levels specified by the older couple's budget. But even among the better-off elderly who meet the BLS standard, there are many who find themselves faced with a sharp decline in income over their preretirement levels and a consequent decline in their living standards. (We will have much more to say about this problem in chapters to come.)

The Impact of Inflation

Economic instability, causing unemployment and inflation, creates insecurity for families and individuals of all ages because of the uncertainty of when and how it will strike. For those actually affected, inflation or unemployment can have a major impact on their economic situation by changing the real value of their wealth or affecting their earning power.

The phenomenon of inflation is without doubt one of the least understood of economic occurrences.* Almost everyone feels *harmed* by inflation; yet the truth is that some people and institutions *gain* from inflation. One person's loss is typically somebody else's gain. The result is a redistribution of wealth and income that can be both quite drastic and quite haphazard.

Inflation is a general and widely diffused increase in the level of prices. In any period the prices of some goods are declining; for example, calculator and computer prices have fallen dramatically over the past twenty years. When there is inflation, however, the quantity of goods and services with rising prices far outnumbers those with declining prices.

The most commonly employed measure of inflation is the Consumer Price Index (CPI). Until January 1978, the CPI measured changes in the prices of goods and services purchased by urban wage earners and clerical workers. In 1978, however, the Bureau of Labor Statistics began publication of a new version of the CPI for all urban consumers. This new **index** takes into account the expenditures not only of wage earners and clerical workers but also salaried

---

*We can go only briefly into the economics of inflation in this book. Readers interested in a relatively nontechnical but more extensive discussion of the issue should read Solow (1975).

professionals, technical and managerial workers, the self-employed, retirees, and the unemployed. This new index covers approximately 80 percent of the total noninstitutional civilian population—about twice the coverage of the old index.

The CPI is a weighted aggregative index with fixed weights; it seeks to represent the annual consumption patterns of various individuals. Consumption patterns are measured by the Survey of Consumer Expenditures. Based on this survey, a "market basket" of about 400 goods and services is randomly selected and weighted. Prices for the CPI market basket are then obtained monthly, mostly by personal visits to a representative sample of nearly 18,000 stores and service establishments.

The CPI has a major effect on most Americans. Through its widespread use as an escalator of wages, pensions, and welfare benefits, about 57 percent of the organized workers under contract have some of their earnings pegged to the CPI (Minarik, 1981). Moreover, virtually everyone is affected by its direct impact on aggregate economic policies instituted by the president, Congress, and the **Federal Reserve**.

While inflation affects people of all ages, we will restrict the discussion that follows to the older population. There are five principal ways older people can be affected adversely by inflation:

1. If net creditors, assets that do not adjust in value for inflation will depreciate in value, reducing the **net worth** of the individual or family.
2. If recipients of transfer (pensions, unemployment benefits, etc.) or other income, adjustments in these various income sources may lag behind inflation, reducing real income.
3. If employed, adjustments in earnings levels may lag behind inflation, reducing real wages.
4. If taxpayers, the real burden of federal and state income taxes may increase because the tax brackets in the laws have been defined in *money* rather than *real* terms.
5. If inflation is concentrated among items such as food, which comprise a larger proportion of elderly persons' budgets, the older age group may be differentially affected—especially if indexes used to measure and adjust various sources of income do not correctly reflect aged buying patterns.

Wealth   With regard to the first item, the impact of inflation on the wealth position of the elderly, the evidence is most clear. As we indicated earlier in this chapter, substantial financial assets are held by the elderly, but these assets are highly concentrated in the possession of a relatively small number of the aged. On the other hand, tangible assets—such as homes, automobiles, and the like—are held by a large proportion of the aged population.

In general, the money value of tangible assets tends to increase with inflation, leaving the real value of this portion of the aged's wealth unaffected. But, apart from common stock and mutual funds, most *financial* assets do not adjust when the general level of prices changes. Persons holding bonds, checking accounts, savings accounts, and insurance policies often find the real value of these assets falling with inflation; in contrast, persons with debts—such as an outstanding mortgage on a home—find the real value of these debts also falling (which is to their advantage).

A number of studies have investigated the effect of unanticipated inflation on the distribution of wealth among households. They have found that when households are grouped according to age of head, the largest decline in wealth occurs among families headed by elderly persons. In contrast, the largest *increase* in wealth occurs among those age 25 to 34 who tend to be net debtors. It is the minority of the aged with substantial nonadjusting financial assets who are most severely affected. That is, for those aged fortunate enough to have substantial savings, inflation is often a serious problem.

Transfer Income   With regard to the second item, lagging **transfer income**, again the impact is relatively clear, but in a way that will surprise some readers. Since persons living primarily on relatively fixed incomes are clearly hurt by rising prices and since the aged are so heavily dependent on pensions, the aged traditionally have been cited as the major group harmed by inflation. While this was a major problem for the aged in years past, recent developments have substantially moderated it. *The major source of retirement income, the social security program, now adjusts benefits automatically for inflation.* Over the 1978–1984 period, for example, the following cost of living increases were given to all beneficiaries:

Year	Increase
1978	6.5%
1979	9.9%
1980	14.3%
1981	11.2%
1982	7.4%
1984	3.5%

As we discuss in later chapters, concern about rising pension costs caused Congress in 1983 to delay for six months the inflation adjustment due that year. Congress also passed legislation that, starting in 1985, the automatic benefit adjustment would be based on the increase in the CPI *or average earnings*, whichever is less. However, this latter provision is to go into effect *only* if the combined social security pension reserves fall to a specified low level, and "catch-up" benefit payments are to be made when the reserve situation improves.

Thus, we see that social security benefits are generally well protected against inflation. Unfortunately, many people do not realize this, including some older people currently receiving benefits. A survey by Peter D. Hart Research Associates (1979) for the National Commission on Social Security found that there was a significant lack of understanding about this aspect of social security. Over half of those interviewed did not think (or were not sure) that "social security benefits go up automatically to match the rise in the cost of living." Quite surprising was the fact that 24 percent of retirees receiving benefits thought the statement was not true.

The social security pension programs are not the only programs indexed for inflation. The federal Supplemental Security Income (SSI) program, food stamps, and civil service and military pensions adjust fully for inflation. Many state and local pension plans are adjusted automatically, but these automatic increases are typically limited to 2 to 4 percent per year.

The three major income sources that do *not* adjust automatically are veterans' pensions, private pension benefits, and most supplemental state payments under SSI. Also, the levels of allowable income determining eligibility for SSI, food stamps, and some Medicaid programs are not changed automatically.

Overall, then, we see that the bulk of aged income is currently adjusted for inflation with a relatively short lag. Those elderly who depend heavily on income from assets and/or private pension income are more vulnerable.

Earnings and Tax Brackets   Both of these items share the common characteristic of being very difficult to predict with regard to inflationary impact. While earnings generally increase over time, partly in response to inflation, earnings in particular firms or industries may lag behind inflation. Some of the aged still working will find this to be a problem, but in general few are affected because not many of the elderly continue to work full time and because not all that do are employed in firms where earnings lag behind inflation.

Similarly, many aged do not pay income taxes because their incomes are low and social security income is exempt from federal taxes for all but those with very high incomes. Those who do, however, face two problems: some of the added income to compensate for inflation will be taxed away and, moreover, will be taxed away under **progressive tax** structures at progressively larger marginal rates.

Regarding the latter matter of tax brackets, Congress has passed legislation to index the brackets for inflation, thereby eliminating the problem. This provision is scheduled to go into effect in 1985.

Expenditure Patterns and Cost-of-Living Indexes   During inflationary periods, the prices of various goods change by different amounts. Since the expenditure patterns of individuals and families differ, any particular pattern of inflationary price increases will have a varying impact, depending on the particular expenditure patterns of the individuals. For example, if food and housing prices go up faster than other goods and services and if the aged spend a larger share of their income on food and housing, the result is a larger increase in prices paid by the aged than the nonaged.

Thus there is concern that the CPI used to measure inflation and adjust social security benefits does not reflect the aged's buying patterns. Certain organizations and individuals have advocated, for example, that a separate price index for the elderly be established. Numerous studies over the years have investigated this question.* Rarely has there been such agreement among economists on

*Hollister and Palmer (1972), Torda (1972), Mirer (1974), King (1976), Borzilleri (1978), Michael (1979), DRI (1980), Minarik (1981), Barnes and Zedlewski (1981), Bridges and Packard (1981), and Boskin and Hurd (1982).

research findings. *All studies have found that the differences between the CPI and a special aged index are likely to be very small.* Thus, Minarik (1981) concludes that "given the absence of solid evidence that . . . [a multiple price index system] would yield different indexing outcomes over the long haul, we should probably leave special group indices alone."

Instead of a special index for the aged, a better approach would be to improve the existing CPI. Measuring general price changes accurately is a very difficult task. The most serious problem is a general upward bias in the CPI. This is due primarily to a lag that occurs in the introduction of new products and quality improvements in old products into the index (see Gordon, 1981). With regard to quality change, for example, the CPI usually does not take into account improvements in product performance when prices of a product go up. Thus, the prices of motor oil, tires, light bulbs, appliances, and so forth, have increased, but the service life of many such products has also increased. And, thus, in an important sense not all the price increases are inflationary.

The Bureau of Labor Statistics does occasionally improve the index. Recently, for example, the bureau changed the way owner-occupied housing is handled. This item in the index had become particularly troublesome when interest rates, including mortgage rates for housing loans, rose to unprecedented levels over the 1969–1972 period. The old way of handling the item in the index did not distinguish between homeowners who took out mortgages some years ago at much lower rates and those who had purchased housing recently.

Many problems with the CPI remain. Given the amount of indexing that now occurs based on this index, it would seem appropriate for the government to undertake a major program for improving the index.

Chapter Two Highlights

We have tried to show in this chapter that attempts to assess the economic status of the elderly as one group are not very meaningful. Mindful of this danger of overgeneralizing about the aged, let us now summarize some of the major observations presented in preceding sections:

1. The economic status of the elderly has changed dramatically in recent years, primarily as a result of rising social security, private pension, and government employees' pension income.
2. Great caution is in order in generalizing from available statistics on income and assets. Both underreporting and the lack of disaggregation cause serious problems.
3. The major source of elderly income is social security, but earnings still represent a large proportion of the total—going to the minority of aged still working.
4. Money incomes of the aged tend to be lower than those of younger persons. The 1979 median income (adjusted for underreporting) was $28,460 for families headed by persons aged 45–54. For heads 65 or older, it was $15,860.
5. However, expanding the analysis to include such factors as in-kind income, special tax provisions, and household size narrows the differences considerably.

6. Poverty among the aged, as measured by the government's poverty index, has practically disappeared. Large numbers of the elderly, however, still suffer a large drop in living standard when they retire.
7. Economic deprivation still exists on a large scale among the elderly, especially if we take into account rising expectations.
8. Contrary to popular belief, the aged have a large measure of protection from inflation. Those heavily dependent on financial assets and private pensions are most vulnerable.

Suggested Readings

Blinder, Alan S., Irving Kristol, and Wilbur J. Cohen. Three views on "The Level and Distribution of Economic Well-Being." In Martin Feldstein, ed., *The American Economy in Transition*. Chicago: The University of Chicago Press, 1980.
Blinder's paper and the reaction comments by Kristol and Cohen provide an excellent overview to this chapter.

Clark, Robert L., and Joseph J. Spengler. *The Economics of Individual and Population Aging*. Cambridge, England: Cambridge University Press, 1980.
A good review of the literature on most of the topics covered in this book. Chapter 4 is on the "economic status of the elderly."

Epstein, Lenore A., and Janet H. Murray. *The Aged Population of the United States*. Office of Research and Statistics, Research Report No. 19. Washington, D.C.: U.S. Government Printing Office, 1967.
The "1963 Survey of the Aged." This was the first comprehensive survey of the United States aged in 1962. It includes information not gathered in the census or other sample surveys and analysis of these data by the staff of the Social Security Administration.

Federal Council on the Aging. *The Impact of the Tax Structure on the Elderly*. Washington, D.C.: U.S. Government Printing Office, 1975.
A review of various taxes as they apply to various subgroups of the elderly population.

Grad, Susan. *Income of the Population 55 and Older, 1980*. Washington, D.C.: Social Security Administration, 1983.
Informative data on the economic status of the elderly—data not published elsewhere on a regular basis.

Lamale, Helen H. "Measuring Retirees' Living Costs." *Aging and Work* (Fall 1978): 251–258.
An explanation of the new revised Consumer Price Index and the Retired Couple's Budget. The author assesses the relative merits of different indices in measuring the impact of inflation on the elderly.

Moon, Marilyn. *The Measurement of Economic Welfare—Its Application to the Aged Poor*. New York: Academic Press, 1977.
A good theoretical discussion of nonmoney factors affecting economic welfare. The book also presents empirical measures for the aged.

Poverty Studies Task Force. *The Measure of Poverty*. A Report to Congress as Mandated by the Education Amendments of 1974. Washington, D.C.: U.S. Department of Health, Education, and Welfare, 1976.
"Must reading" for those who want a sophisticated understanding of issues involved in measuring poverty and collecting needed data.

Rogers, Gayle Thompson. "Aged Widows and OASDI: Age at and Economic Status Before and After Receipt of Benefits," *Social Security Bulletin* 44 (March 1981): 3–19.
Many aged widows are poor. This article looks at widows before and after they begin receiving social security, comparing their living standards.

Social Security Bulletin. Washington, D.C.: U.S. Government Printing Office
(monthly).

This journal reports changes in social security and other similar legislation
and also publishes the results of research studies by the SSA (and SSA sponsored research projects), various survey findings, and international social security developments.

U.S. Senate Special Committee on Aging. *Developments in Aging.* Washington, D.C.:
U.S. Government Printing Office (annual).

This yearly report by the committee reviews a wide range of developments
in aging, including economic aspects. An appendix contains reports from federal departments and agencies with specific activities affecting the elderly.

Chapter Three
To Work or Not to Work

Every individual during his or her lifetime makes important choices regarding the type and amount of work to be undertaken. The individual chooses some combination of work in the labor force (paid and volunteer), unpaid work in the nonmarket sector, and leisure. Economists emphasize the trade-off between work—which produces goods and services or results in income to buy the goods and services of others—and leisure—which in itself is something that people also find useful or valuable. Thus, more leisure is bought at the expense of fewer goods and services for the whole economy.

Paid employment results in the economic output—**gross national product**—measured by **national income accounting** techniques and reported regularly by government statistics. *Nonmarket work*, for example homemaking, is not included in the national income accounts but adds significantly to total output; Nordhaus and Tobin (1973) estimate that in 1965, for example, nonmarket work equaled 48 percent of gross national product. *Not working* translates into a given amount of leisure over the lifetime.*

The Work–Leisure Trade-off

Measuring work in terms of hours per week, we begin at a zero level in early childhood. At some point the individual might start a paper route, do some baby-sitting, or engage in some other part-time work. In the teenage years, part-time work may increase, and some begin full-time work. Others go to college and "stop work." Through the middle years most men and about one-third of all women work in the labor force full time; most women also work in the nonmarket sector, and some work part time in the labor force. At age 65 (or, increasingly, earlier) work stops abruptly for many. This brief summary approximates the work pattern of the typical American worker today. Granted, of course, there are lots of variations to this pattern.

---

*The work–leisure dichotomy is not as simple as we make it seem. See Robinson et al. (1984) for a good discussion of the difficulty in defining leisure.

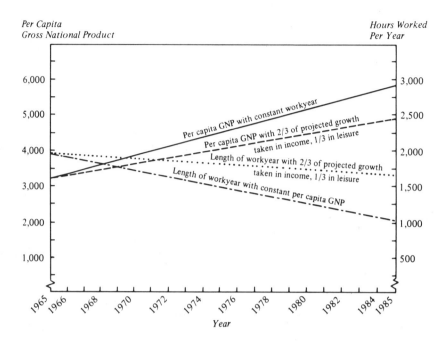

Figure 11. Alternative Uses
of Economic Growth Per Capita Gross
National Product and Hours Worked, 1965–1985

Source: Juanita Kreps and Joseph Spengler, "The Leisure Component of Economic Growth," in National Commission on Technology, Automation and Economic Progress, *The Employment Impact of Technological Change*, Appendix Vol. II (Washington, D.C.: U.S. Government Printing Office, 1966), pp. 353–389.

Back in 1966, Kreps and Spengler developed estimates of the growth–leisure trade-off confronting the United States in the 1960s. Although the projections are out of date, they illustrate well some of the options a nation (and its workers) faces as it looks to the future. Figure 11 presents their projections of the various possibilities of additional gross national product (GNP) and/or leisure available over a 20-year period (1965–1985). As the various factors influencing economic growth (technological change, **investment**, rising quality of labor, and so forth) increase productivity, new opportunities for increased leisure and/or increased consumption arise:

> *With regard to the possible future growth in leisure and its probable distribution . . . at one extreme, assuming no change in working time, per capita gross national product could rise from $3,181 in 1965 to $5,802 in 1985, or by about 80 percent. At the other extreme, if one supposes that all growth is taken in leisure time except the amount necessary to keep per capita GNP constant at $3,181, the possible changes in working time would be as follows: the workweek could fall to 22 hours, or the workyear could be limited to 27 weeks per year, or retirement age could be lowered to 38 years, or almost half the labor force could be kept in retraining programs, or additional time available for education might well exceed our capacity to absorb such education. [Kreps and Spengler, 1966]*

If we took all the increased growth potential in the form of greater per capita output, Kreps and Spengler estimate that by the year 1985 we could almost double the level of per capita output achieved in 1965. This projection assumes that there are no "costs to growth," an assumption increasingly questioned by economists. Some of the growth, for example, will have to go into pollution control devices, sewage treatment plants, and defense (tanks and bombs); to say that this growth in output represents an increase in our standard of living is stretching a point.

Also the projections assume that the government encourages the potential growth by use of appropriate **monetary** and **fiscal policy** and that the assumptions about future changes in technology and the growth of capital based on past occurrences are correct. Accepting these qualifications, we can nevertheless see from Figure 11 that one major option available to the nation is a sizable increase in the future real standard of living of individuals in the society. Alternatively we can choose fewer goods and services but more leisure.

The Pattern of Leisure   In addition to the choice between work (more output) and leisure, there is the question of when leisure is taken. The increases in leisure experienced early in this century came primarily in the form of shortened workweeks and longer vacations. In contrast, much of the new leisure in recent decades has been allocated to the end of the lifespan.

Suppose that a country wants to hold constant the total amount of work and leisure over the lifespan but wishes to alter the way in which they are currently distributed. One procedure would be to determine at what point in the life cycle it might be appropriate to taper off weekly hours of work, if the option were available. Providing more leisure by reducing hours of work means, however, that some people *must work more* at some other time—later or earlier in their lives. Realistically, providing increased leisure without a significant drop in lifetime income probably means working longer when older.

Why do many professionals advocate changes in our present mix of work and leisure? Why do some urge, for example, that we stop the trend toward earlier retirement? Some people are concerned about the rising trend toward "no work"; they claim that some people die earlier, partly as a result of the change from an active to a more sedentary lifestyle (Bradford, 1979). Some social gerontologists argue that termination of work results in psychological problems connected with the loss of social role and adjustment to retirement realities.* Economists worry about the problems of financially supporting a growing retired population with its accompanying rise in public and private pension costs.

While gerontologists and advocates on behalf of the elderly have been almost unanimous in calling for more flexibility in retirement age policies, much of the movement has been in the opposite direction. For example, as we will show in later chapters, public and private pensions have been designed to encourage retirement to help deal with America's chronic unemployment

---

*In a later section of this chapter we discuss mounting evidence that disputes this pessimistic view.

problems. Economist Juanita Kreps has succinctly summarized the current situation:

> *Retirement, a relatively new lifestage, has quickly become a . . . device for balancing the number of job seekers with the demand for workers at going rates of pay. Insofar as retirement practice is used to drain workers from the labor force, a reversal of the downward pressure on retirement age would seem to be possible only if labor markets tighten. Extensions beyond the usual retirement age are granted when there is a demand for specific talents. Given current levels of unemployment, however, there is no incentive to prolong worklife in general; quite the contrary. As a result of worsening job prospects for youth, lower retirement age or reductions in working time through . . . . union negotiations seem likely. Except for current concern for the solvency of the public and private pension funds, labor market conditions would probably signal moves to encourage retirement as early as sixty. [Kreps, 1977]*

Legislation passed in 1978 to prohibit mandatory retirement before age 70 is a step in the opposite direction. But, as we argue later in this chapter, the impact of this new law has been minimal (see pp. 58–62).

Changing Labor Force Participation   There is general agreement that one of the most important labor force developments of recent decades has been the dramatic rise in labor force withdrawals by older men. Figure 12 shows labor force participation in the United States by age for various groups of men and women over age 54 in 1980. The participation rate is highest for couples, where participation is defined as one or both partners working. In recent years there has been a very sharp drop in participation during the later years. Withdrawals cluster around the eligibility ages for initial (age 62) and regular (age 65) social security pension benefits. As a consequence, the labor force participation rate for males over 64 has dropped from 57 percent in 1955 to only 18 percent in 1981. But perhaps even more striking is the relatively recent decline in participation at earlier ages. The labor force participation rate for men age 60 to 64 continues to fall (Rones, 1978):

Year	Age 60 to 64
1957	82.5%
1962	80.2%
1967	77.6%
1972	72.5%
1977	62.9%
1982*	57.2%

In contrast, the proportion of females in the labor force has risen sharply in almost all age groups, with an overall increase from 26 percent in 1940 to over 52 percent in 1981. Regarding older women, the labor force participation rate

*Unpublished estimate by the U.S. Bureau of Labor Statistics.

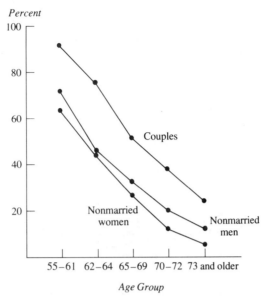

*Figure 12. 1980 Labor Force
Participation Rates of Persons Age 55 and Over*

Source: Based on data in Susan Grad, *Income of the Population 55 and Older, 1980*
(Washington, D.C.: Social Security Administration, 1983).

of women age 55–64 rose from 27 percent in 1950 to 41 percent in the mid-1960s and has been relatively stable ever since. For those women over age 65 participation has remained relatively constant over the past three decades with a slight drop in recent years to slightly below 10 percent.

For both men and women, part-time work is most common among the very young and the very old. About half of employed persons over age 64 work part time (in 1981, 52 percent of men and 60 percent of women). Much of this part-time work is concentrated in the service and trade occupations where wages tend to be low.

Almost all the older persons working part time do so by preference. Some seek to supplement other income sources—primarily pension income. Others are forced by health limitations to cut back on the hours they work. Some prefer a gradual withdrawal to an abrupt stop. And finally, there are no doubt many who want more leisure but still value highly the various social and monetary benefits arising from some amount of labor force attachment.

Table 10 shows variation among nine nations in the proportion of people working after age 65. Compared with other industrialized countries, United States labor force participation by the aged falls in the upper range. Only Japan (where pensions are very low and many workers continue in lower paid work out of financial necessity) has higher participation rates.

Table 10. Labor Force Participation Rates of Older Workers,[a]
Nine Countries in the Early 1960s and 1980

Country	Men		Women	
	Early 1960	*1980*	*Early 1960*	*1980*
United States	33	19	11	8
Australia	23	11	4	3
Canada	30	15	6	4
France	24	9[b]	9	4[b]
Germany	25	8	8	3
Great Britain	23	9	6	3
Italy	25	8	7	2
Japan	57	41	24	15
Sweden	35	12	9	3

Source: Constance Sorrentino, "International Comparisons of Labor Force Participation, 1960–1981," *Monthly Labor Review* (February 1983), Table 4.
[a]Age 65 or older.
[b]Data are for March 1979.

Economic Problems of Older Workers

In recent years there has been increasing recognition that a variety of special economic problems confront middle-aged and older workers: (a) age discrimination in hiring, (b) job obsolescence, (c) changing job-performance capabilities, necessitating job change (or job redesign), and (d) adverse institutional structures (such as mandatory retirement). In addition, older workers, while often protected by seniority against job loss, generally find themselves almost as vulnerable as younger workers to plant shutdowns and many of the dislocations arising from mergers and government spending cutbacks. Not only do these problems create immediate difficulties for workers and their families, but they often have an economic impact on their situation during the retirement years. Long-term unemployment, for example, makes saving difficult if not impossible. Moreover, periods of unemployment often result in lower pension benefits in retirement.

These special employment problems associated with aging are part of a larger set of factors influencing individuals in their decisions to work or not to work. In this regard, economists talk about labor force participation and seek to understand the choices made in the relative amounts of time allocated between work and leisure, the latter including home work and volunteer work as well as leisure. We emphasize in this section the institutional pressures and constraints placed on individuals in their determination of *when* to retire. We begin with a discussion of some of the economic problems confronting older workers and end with a discussion of the retirement decision.

An important distinction in terminology must be kept in mind here. Throughout most of the book when we talk about the aged or older persons, we are usually referring to those over age 65. In this chapter we talk about older workers but are not focusing exclusively, or even primarily, on persons over age

Table 11.   Unemployment Rates for Men, by Age Groups,
Selected Years, 1968–1981

Year	25–54		Age 55–64		65 +	
	U^a	$U + D^b$	U^a	$U + D^b$	U^a	$U + D^b$
1968	1.7	1.8	1.9	2.3	2.8	6.6
1970	2.8	2.9	2.8	3.1	3.3	5.5
1972	3.1	3.2	3.2	3.6	3.6	6.2
1974	3.1	3.2	2.6	2.9	3.3	6.0
1976	4.9	5.2	4.2	4.7	5.1	8.9
1978	3.5	3.7	2.8	3.3	4.2	7.2
1980	5.1	5.4	3.4	3.9	3.1	6.5
1981	5.5	5.8	3.6	4.2	2.9	6.3

Source: Philip L. Rones, "The Labor Market Problems of Older Workers," *Monthly Labor Review* 106 (May 1983), Table 1.
[a]The official unemployment rate, calculated by dividing total unemployment by the civilian labor force.
[b]An unemployment rate that includes all "discouraged" workers.

65. Rather, the major focus of this chapter is on workers who have reached middle age and those approaching retirement age (generally, the 45–65 age group).

Work Problems   As shown in Table 11, unemployment rates vary little with age but tend to be slightly higher in the later years than in the middle ones. Insulated from unemployment by job-dismissal customs and formal seniority rules, older workers are not as likely to lose their jobs. With changing consumer expenditure patterns, however, many established industries have experienced a stagnation or gradual decline in employment opportunities. In contracting or closing businesses even senior jobholders are adversely affected. Declines, for example, in the cotton and woolen textile, agriculture, railroad, and shoe industries have encouraged or forced millions of workers to seek alternative jobs. Older workers confronted by a job change often find themselves faced with a variety of problems.

Table 11 shows that prior to the late 1960s the official unemployment rates for those 55 and over tended to be slightly *higher* than for those men age 25–54. This relationship began to change in the 1970s, with the rates for men 65 and older falling well below those 25–54 by the 1980 recession. But Rones (1983) shows that these statistics may be deceptive. Using data from the Current Population Survey, Rones estimates the number of workers who report that they want a job but are not looking because they believe they cannot find one—that is, "discouraged workers."

Table 11 shows that when discouraged workers are added to the official unemployment rate, the rates for men over age 64 rise dramatically—doubling and surpassing the other age groups. In part this results from the fact that since most persons in this age group are outside the labor force, there is a huge pool of potentially discouraged workers. It takes only a relatively small number from this pool to be identified as "discouraged" to shift the percentages in the table. While interpretation of the data is not easy, the statistics do suggest the probability that many older persons who want to work perceive that there is a lack of acceptable job opportunities.

There has been a clear bias in private and public employment policy against older workers. They have been discriminated against in job hiring. Work and job structures have been made relatively inflexible, making midcareer adjustments very difficult. Various policies have encouraged or forced workers to retire and then have discouraged or prevented them from returning to the work force.

In 1965 the nation was made aware of the extent and nature of discrimination toward older workers through a report issued by the Department of Labor. This report documented that at that time more than 50 percent of all available job openings were closed to applicants over age 55 because of employers' policies *not* to hire any person over that age. Moreover, about 25 percent of the job openings were closed to applicants over age 45.

Since its passage in 1967, the federal **Age Discrimination in Employment Act** has attempted to protect individuals from age discrimination in hiring, discharge, compensation, and other terms of employment. This law originally covered (with some exceptions) persons between the ages of 40 and 65 but was amended in 1978 to include workers up to age 69. As a result, the more blatant signs of discrimination—such as newspaper ads restricting jobs to younger persons—have declined significantly.

It is difficult to determine, though, the extent to which actual discrimination has in fact lessened, for little comprehensive evidence exists on the matter. Data on the duration of unemployment, however, may be one important indicator that serious problems still exist. While unemployment is relatively low among men age 45–65, men in this age group who become unemployed typically remain unemployed much longer than younger workers.

This longer average duration of unemployment is not all caused by age discrimination, however. Often older workers lack the necessary skills to qualify for available jobs or are not living in areas where job opportunities exist. Competing for jobs in the growing electronics and computer industries, for example, is difficult for many older workers. Many skills developed in the old established industries cannot be readily used in the new high-technology industries. And no large-scale programs exist in the United States to provide these older workers with the required newer skills.

Moreover, the problems arising from this incompatibility of skills have been aggravated by shifts in industries from their locations in the Northeast, Middle Atlantic, and North Central states to the Southeast, Southwest, and West. Many older workers with usable skills have been left behind with little hope for suitable new employment.

With the growth of social security and **private pensions** has come the recognition that fringe benefits in the pay package represent another possible factor contributing to the reemployment problems of older workers. Management may be reluctant to hire older workers because it is usually more costly to provide such workers with a specified private pension benefit. This higher cost results primarily from two factors: (a) a shorter work history over which employer pension contributions must be made and thus lower investment income arising from the pension contributions, and (b) a declining probability with age of employee withdrawal (job turnover) between hiring and retirement. That is, the later the age of job entry, the shorter the period over which contributions can be made, the shorter the period over which interest is earned on pension funds, and the less likely the worker will die or leave the plan before qualifying for any benefit. "Very definitely, then, most employers with pension plans have added costs if they hire older workers. If anything the differential has increased in the last decade, making it relatively even more costly to employ the experienced jobseeker" (Taggart, 1973).

Finally, evidence indicates that older workers have difficulty finding new jobs because of their "job seeking" behavior and the lower priority given to them by various manpower agencies. Sobel and Wilcock (1963) in a study of 4,000 job seekers found that older workers displayed less willingness (a) to change types of work methods or methods of looking for work, (b) to engage in job retraining, (c) to adjust salary expectations, and (d) to move to areas of higher employment opportunity. Sheppard and Belitsky (1966) in a study of 500 workers in one locality found that older workers were also "more restrictive" in their job search techniques and less persistent in their activities. Rones (1983) reports that in 1981 only about one-half of discouraged workers age 65 years and older indicated plans to look for work during the subsequent 12-month period. This compared to two-thirds of persons age 55–64 and six out of seven age 25–54.

Older workers often get lower priority from government agencies set up to aid the unemployed. A 1973–1974 study by the National Institute of Industrial Gerontology reaffirms earlier findings of the Sheppard and Belitsky study: there are no age differences in the proportion of unemployed persons seeking job assistance from the employment service but there is differential treatment by age (Heidbreder and Batten, 1974). Figure 13 shows by age group the proportion of various employment service applicants receiving employment services, referral to a job, and placement in a job. Significantly fewer older workers were (a) tested, counseled, or enrolled in training,* (b) referred to employers for job interviews, or (c) actually placed in a job. Likewise, while older workers constitute a large proportion of the long-term unemployed, they have always been an almost insignificant proportion of the persons trained under the various manpower training programs operated or financed by federal and state governments. In general, most government officials and employers do not consider it worthwhile or cost effective to train older persons (compared to younger persons) because of the expectation of shorter work lives, lower levels of education, and a belief that learning abilities decline with age. (But see our discussion on pp. 62–63.)

---

*Similar but more recent findings on counseling and testing are reported by Pursell and Torrence (1979).

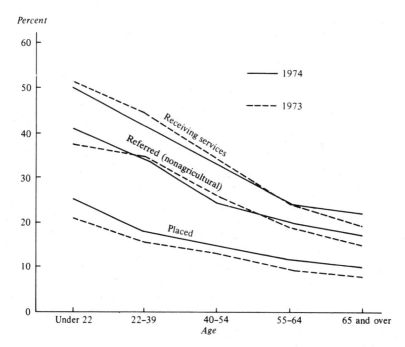

Figure 13. Action Taken:
Employment Service Applicants by Age

Source: Elizabeth M. Heidbreder and M. D. Batten, "ESAR II—A Comparative View of Services to Age Groups," *Facts and Trends* No. 4 (Washington, D.C.: National Council on Aging, 1974). Used by permission.

There is one major employment program for older workers: the Senior Community Service Employment Program. Administered by the Department of Labor, this program provided about 54,000 part-time jobs in 1982 for workers age 55 and over. To be eligible, workers have to have been chronically unemployed and have an income below 125 percent of the official poverty level.

There are also a number of private agencies specializing in job services for older persons seeking employment. Studies by Rosenblum and Sheppard (1977) and Doctors et al. (1980) indicate that older workers can be placed in jobs by these agencies. However, older workers tend not to be hired in jobs that utilize their skills and abilities to any high degree. Instead, they are most likely to be placed in part-time positions, usually with small employers in various service occupations.

The Retirement Decision   In view of traditional work-oriented values in the United States and the importance of income derived from work, retirement is one of the most important decisions made by persons in our society. Aging in general and the retirement decision in particular involve more complex choices than just deciding between more or less income. The amount of income and assets available is certainly one of the major considerations in deciding when to retire, but there are other *personal considerations*. For example, the individual must consider his health and evaluate the physical and emotional difficulties of continued employment on a specific job vis-à-vis the benefits and problems of alternative employment or of leaving the work force.

Various *institutional realities* also affect the individual's retirement decision—factors that, in part, are beyond the person's own control. Included among these factors are such things as (a) the provisions of public and private pension plans, (b) changing pension levels and eligibility ages, (c) prospects for earnings levels, (d) job security and available employment opportunities, and (e) the institutional setting prescribed by work rules and government legislation.

Prior to 1962, men could not get social security benefits before age 65. In that year, the law was changed to allow men the same option granted to women in a 1956 amendment—early retirement at ages 62 through 64 with actuarially reduced benefits. The result was an immediate and major increase in the number of men opting for early retirement.

Some workers apparently retire before age 65 because they can afford to, often supplementing their reduced social security benefits with a private pension or other income. There is another group of workers who have already stopped working before the initial social security age of 62. The Social Security Administration's Survey of New Entitled Beneficiaries provides information on this group of workers. "Forty-one percent of the nonworking men entitled [becoming beneficiaries] at age 62 had been out of work for six months or more; 33 percent had not worked for at least a year; and 17 percent had been out of work three or more years" (Reno, 1971).

Deterioration of health is one of the most important factors encouraging early retirement. Some persons are unable to continue working because of disabling illness. Even those persons who, despite health problems, could continue to work in their current job, or perhaps in a less demanding one, may decide to retire at age 62—given the alternative income from a pension now available.

Many studies have documented the importance of health in the retirement decision. A recent one is a 1966–1981 national longitudinal study of men initially age 45–59. The survey found, for example, that, other things being equal, men with health problems in 1966 were twice as likely to have retired between 1966 and 1971 as those who were free of health limitations (Andrisani, 1977).

This survey is of particular interest because it measured the influence of health problems *before* retirement on *subsequent* withdrawal from the work force. Most other studies have asked people *after* they retire why they retired, and consequently it has not been entirely clear whether the high proportion who cite health reasons are, in fact, giving what they consider to be a more socially acceptable reason for retirement. Joseph Quinn (1975), for example, reports that in the Social Security Longitudinal Retirement History Survey, 11 percent of the men and 18 percent of the women reporting good health and "no health limitations" gave (in another part of the survey) health as a prime motivation for their *early* retirement.

Later years of the National Longitudinal Survey also included a series of questions inquiring about the extent of particular physical or mental impairments, such as difficulty in standing, walking, and dealing with people. From these questions an index of impairment was constructed. When this index was related to labor force participation or hours worked (controlling statistically for other factors), a strong relationship was found between health and participation. "For instance, an average blue-collar worker with even a moderate degree of impairment is 9% less likely to be in the labor force and works 9% fewer hours per year than a comparable individual with no impairments" (Parnes, 1981).

Thus, the availability of pension income and/or poor health are powerful influences in the retirement decision. Many researchers have pointed to the growing role of institutional factors that interact with these two factors. The labor impact of various social security provisions is currently being hotly debated in the pension literature: the earnings test, payroll taxes, early and delayed retirement benefit adjustment provisions, disability regulations, and the asset value (or wealth effect) of future benefits (see the survey in Mitchell and Fields, 1982).

As we discuss in Chapter 8, regular private pensions are often designed to encourage early retirement. During the severe recession of the early 1980s, increasingly large numbers of corporations also began offering their employees special enticements to leave called "special early retirement plans" (or "open window" plans). For most companies the window period runs from 60 to 90 days, though for some it may be as short as a month or as long as a year. Financial benefits provided under these plans vary greatly. Typically companies offer a special benefit payment for one or two years or a special lump sum payout (Leavitt, 1983). This is in addition to the regular pension plan benefits that the worker may receive (sometimes unreduced for early retirement under provisions of the special company offer).

Finally, regarding the factors influencing retirement, Foner and Schwab (1983) point out the increased availability of organizational supports to facilitate and reduce the stress of retirement. Over the years there has been a significant expansion of activity clubs and centers, retirement counseling, senior citizen organizations, special housing, and volunteer organizations to provide community service opportunities.

Mandatory Versus Flexible Retirement Options

There used to be a stigma to going out. He was over the hill. But now it's a looked-for status. Those retirement parties, they used to be sad affairs. They are darn happy affairs now. The peer pressure is for early retirement.

The above observation (Flint, 1977) is by Victor M. Zink, Director of Employee Benefits at General Motors Corporation. Early retirement is increasing, and workers' attitudes toward retirement seem to be changing dramatically. The statistics show the average age of retirement dropping rapidly in many companies—down at General Motors from age 70 in 1950 to the current age of

58. Barfield and Morgan (1978a) report that twice as many workers today want to retire early as did fifteen years ago.

At the same time, many recent gerontological studies show retirement to be less traumatic than was initially perceived.* Atchley (1976) observes, for example, that "the general trends very definitely contradict the myth that retirement causes illness. . . . It appears that retirement is a welcome change for couples in good health who enjoy middle or upper socioeconomic status." Barfield and Morgan (1978b) reach a similar conclusion but state it in a different way. Analyzing data from two surveys taken at the beginning and end of the last decade, they derive "a view of the dissatisfied retiree as one whose health problems contribute significantly to leaving the labor force and whose retirement income is low, but not extremely so."

Paradoxically, as retirement ages decline and retirement living is becoming increasingly popular, public policy has taken a big step toward allowing workers to continue longer on their jobs. Bills amending the Age Discrimination in Employment Act swept through Congress in 1977. The House passed legislation abolishing mandatory retirement with only four dissenting votes. The Senate quickly followed with only seven dissenting votes.

The resulting new law extends protection against age discrimination to non-federal employees up to age 69 and eliminates the upper age limit entirely for most federal workers. Mandatory retirement rules (including those associated with pension plans) are now banned before age 70 except for executives with large pensions. Executives or persons in high policymaking positions are exempted if entitled to employer-financed private retirement benefits of at least $27,000 annually.

What was the impact of the now illegal mandatory retirement provisions? How many older persons want to work? Will the continued employment of older workers interfere with the employment opportunities of younger workers? It is to these issues that we now turn.

Mandatory Retirement Practices   During the past few decades, mandatory retirement rules were introduced by a large number of organizations in both the private and public sectors. A comprehensive study of the prevalence and nature of retirement-age rules was carried out in 1961. The study was based on a sample survey of industrial firms in the United States with 50 or more employees (Slavik, 1966). Perhaps the study's most important finding was that industrial establishments without pension or **profit sharing plans** overwhelmingly had flexible retirement policies (over 95 percent of establishments without pension plans, about two-thirds of those with only profit-sharing plans). Among all establishments with formal pension plans, the majority (60 percent) had a flexible age policy with no upper age limit. The remainder (40 percent) had either (a) compulsory retirement at the "normal retirement age" or at an age later than

---

*Shanas et al., 1968; Cottrell and Atchley, 1969; Atchley, 1971; Streib and Schneider, 1971; Atchley, 1976; Atchley and Robinson, 1982; Foner and Schwab, 1983; and Palmore et al., 1984.

the "normal retirement age," or (b) some combination of retirement age flexibility and compulsion.

But this surprisingly high incidence of *flexible* retirement rules was strongly related to establishment size. For example, 68 percent of the establishments with 50 to 99 employees had flexible rules as compared to only 30 percent of establishments with 500 or more. In fact, of 6 independent variables investigated, the study found that only "size of [entire] company" and the "retirement benefit" showed any significant association with the existence of flexible retirement age policy.

If mandatory retirement was more prevalent in large firms, what proportion of workers in the labor force were subject to such rules? Two different studies found that in 1971 less than one-half of workers age 60–65 were subject to such rules (Parnes and Nestel, 1979; Clark, Barker and Cantrell, 1979). How many workers, however, were *actually terminated* as a result of mandatory retirement regulations?

A partial answer to the question is provided by data found in the Social Security Administration's Survey of New Beneficiaries. In an analysis of the questionnaires completed by *men* age 62–65 who were not working at the time of the survey, the Social Security Administration reports that 12 percent indicated that compulsory retirement was "the most important reason for leaving their last job." And among social security beneficiaries entitled at age 66 or older, it was found that only 10 percent of the nonworking men and women surveyed said they left their last jobs because of a "compulsory retirement age" (4 percent) or because they had "reached retirement age" (6 percent). These findings indicate that the overwhelming number of retired workers were not directly affected by mandatory retirement rules.

To understand more clearly why so few workers' jobs were actually terminated by mandatory retirement rules, it is useful to break down the retirement population into categories. First of all, many workers were not subject to mandatory retirement rules because they worked for establishments without such provisions. And, of course, all self-employed persons were unaffected by such provisions.

Next, it is important to realize that many workers potentially subject to such rules left establishments *before* reaching the age maximum. Early retirement has become a normal occurrence in recent years, while retirement at or after the normal retirement age has become less common. Furthermore, as Streib and Schneider (1971) have documented, "not *all* persons subject to retirement at a certain chronological age are reluctant to retire; some welcome the step." And, of those who do *not* want to retire, a certain proportion are encouraged by health or physical condition to "accept" mandatory retirement and do not try to reenter the work force. Finally, some of those able and willing to work do, in fact, seek and find new jobs on a part-time or full-time basis. Figure 14 illustrates these various alternatives.

The percentage estimates shown in Figure 14 are based on a 1968–1970 survey of social security beneficiaries and exclude those not covered by social security (e.g., federal and certain state and local government workers). The data

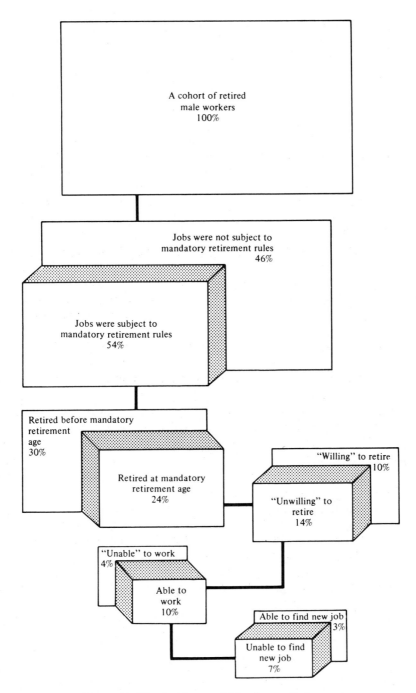

Figure 14. The Incidence of Mandatory Retirement

Source: James H. Schulz, "The Economics of Mandatory Retirement," *Industrial Gerontology*, Vol. 1, New Series (Winter 1974): 1–10. Used by permission.

show that about two out of five males (age 65 or less) *who reach a compulsory retirement age* are able and willing to work but are not working. As the figure shows, however, these workers represent less than 10 percent of the total cohort of retired males.

The Economics of Encouraging or Forcing Retirement

Each year, then, before 1977, there was a small but significant number of workers forced to retire who would have preferred to continue working. With age 70 the age at which mandatory retirement can now be imposed, some workers are still forced to leave. But more importantly, employers have liberalized pension benefits and developed enticements to encourage workers to leave their jobs many years before age 70 (see p. 157). What are the economic implications of these developments?

The Firm and Worker Productivity   Whether the firm gains economically from arbitrarily terminating older workers at some specified age depends in large part on the **productivity** and earning levels of those terminated versus (a) those of workers hired as replacements (in the case of constant or expanding output) or (b) those of other employees of the firm who would be otherwise terminated (in the case of contracting output). The question is not easy to answer because of the great difficulty in measuring the productivity of particular workers.

It is often asserted that, for example, mandatory retirement provisions increase the productivity of a business. Professor Dan McGill, for example, states in his pension book that one of the most important reasons why private pensions with mandatory retirement provisions were introduced was the desire of management to increase levels of work force productivity. He argues that private pensions permit "the employer to remove overage employees from the payroll in an orderly fashion, without fear of adverse employee and public reaction, and to replace them with younger, presumably more efficient workers" (McGill, 1975).

The evidence on the question of whether retiring older workers raises productivity indicates that one should be cautious about generalizing. The results of a relatively large number of research studies bearing on this issue are available, but the findings are far from conclusive:

> *Collectively, leading studies on various aspects of the effects of aging document the conclusion that chronological age alone is a poor indication of working ability. Health, mental and physical capacities, work attitudes and job performance are in-dividual traits at any age. Indeed, measures of traits in different age groups usually show many of the older workers to be superior to the average for the younger group and many of the younger inferior to the average for the older group. [U.S. Depart-ment of Labor, 1965]*

> *Studies under actual working conditions show older workers performing as well as the younger if not better on most, but not all, measures. . . . Age patterns of ac-tual performance do not necessarily reflect the comparative capacities of all older*

persons versus younger people, but are traceable in part to labor market conditions and to selective processes that may, for example, retain in their jobs the competent older workers, promote the superior . . . or recruit [the] younger . . . of entirely different types. [Riley and Foner, 1968]

(1) While some declines with age in productivity have been observed in certain industries (e.g., clerical, manufacturing, sales), older workers are more productive than younger workers. (2) There are wide differences in productivity within age groups. (3) There are some declines with age in physical capacity, but environmental conditions are important in mitigating the effects of decline. . . . (4) Older employees score well or better than younger employees on creativity, flexibility, facility of information processing, absenteeism, accident rates, and turnover. [Robinson, Coberly, and Paul, 1984]

Factors working against older workers are (a) their on-average *formal* education deficit compared to younger workers (which may or may not be offset by their greater on-the-job experience), (b) their greater risk of chronic illness and the possibility of declining physical and mental capacity, and (c) some degree of work assignment inflexibility due to the interaction of work rules, seniority systems, and pay scales. Although it is probably reasonable to assert that most employers recognize that the productivity of some of their older employees is as high or higher than that of younger workers, these employers also argue that it is difficult (and costly) to identify such workers. Thus, they argue, retirement rules and pensions provide a practical administrative procedure that is objective, impersonal, and impartial and avoids charges of discrimination, favoritism, or bias in the termination process.

A 1974 national opinion survey conducted by Louis Harris and Associates for the National Council on the Aging collected interesting information on the public's mixed reaction to this issue:

The public 18–64 and the public 65 and over were somewhat ambivalent about their attitudes toward mandatory retirement. Eighty-six percent (both groups) felt: "Nobody should be forced to retire because of age, if he wants to continue working and is still able to do a good job." About three-fifths agreed that "most people can continue to perform as well on the job as they did when they were younger." On the other hand, almost half (48 percent) of the 18–64 group and more than half (54 percent) of those 65 and over agreed that "since many people are ready to retire at 65 years of age, and it's hard to make exceptions for those who are not ready, it makes sense to have a fixed retirement age for everyone." [Meier, 1975]

There has been an important initial effort to develop techniques for providing management with relatively objective ways of assessing workers' capabilities. In Canada, Dr. Leon Koyl has developed functional criteria to measure mental and physical fitness for various jobs. Koyl's system has been applied successfully for almost two decades by deHavilland Aircraft, Ltd., in Toronto, Canada. More recently, a demonstration project based on the Koyl system was carried out in Portland, Maine, by the National Council on the Aging. This project reported favorable results for the system as a job placement instrument for workers over 40 (Batten, 1973).

Without operational measures of fitness, employers are faced with choosing among three options: (a) terminating workers arbitrarily at a specific age,

(b) allowing workers to decide when to retire, or (c) undertaking potentially expensive activities for "sorting out" the insufficiently productive older workers. More importantly, the employer must justify these termination decisions so that general worker morale will not be adversely affected. Historically, employers have been reluctant to terminate workers solely on the basis of age—especially given past levels of social security old age pensions. But with the establishment of supplementary private pension plans, management (especially in larger firms) apparently felt such practices were much less inequitable. With the passage of legislation delaying the age at which private management can impose mandatory retirement, there has been renewed interest in techniques of measuring performance (see, for example, Walker and Lupton, 1978).

Do the Aged Want to Work?

A Louis Harris poll in 1974 was devoted to "the myth and reality of aging in America." One of the most widely publicized findings from that survey relates to the number of older persons wanting employment. For example, *Newsweek*, in a cover story on "The Graying of America," reported the Harris poll finding that "nearly a third of the nation's over-65 retirees said if they could they still would be working" (28 February 1977, p. 52).* When this finding is cited it is almost invariably (as in the *Newsweek* story) a part of a discussion examining the importance of work to the aged and the problems caused by mandatory retirement. Yet earlier in this chapter we presented data for the late 1960s that indicated less than 10 percent of those approaching retirement were forced to retire because of mandatory retirement provisions. Are the two findings compatible?

What most discussions of the Harris survey fail to report are the answers to a related question asked in the survey. Those older persons not working who said they would like to work were asked, "What's keeping you from working?" The answers broke down as follows (National Council on the Aging, 1975):

Poor health	57%
Too old	28
No work available; lack of job opportunities	15
Lack of transportation	10
Other interests	8
Would lose pension benefits or pay too much in taxes if worked	4

As we discussed previously, the high number of people giving health as a reason for not working is difficult to interpret; some people may use this answer as an excuse in place of less socially accepted reasons. What is clear, however, is that

*Another Harris poll in 1979 reporting on the high proportion of people desiring to work in old age also received national publicity. The same qualifications discussed in the text apply to this newer survey.

there is not one but a wide range of reasons why people who "would like to work" do not work. Thus, when those aged who were retired or unemployed were asked if they would come back to work or take on a new job that "suited them well," only 11 percent responded that they would definitely consider it. Moreover, only 12 percent of the retirees reported in the survey that they had some skills they would like to use but that no one would give them a chance to use the skills.

Another relevant and interesting set of findings is reported by Dena K. Motley (1978) from the Social Security Administration's Retirement History Study. Motley investigated men and women age 62–67 in 1973 who had retired since 1969. She measured their availability for work through survey questions on attitudes about work and their need for income. Again, the study found that very few retirees were available:

> It appears that no more than 12 percent of such retirees would be very likely or even able to return to work. . . . Twenty-four percent of the respondents constitute an ambivalent group whose members might return to work if the drawing power of their need for more income were strong enough to override a disinclination for work or if a preference for employment were strong enough to prevail over the comfort of an adequate retirement income.

A recent study by Goudy (1981) found that work expectations change dramatically during the years associated with retirement (see also Morgan, 1980). A 1979 Lou Harris poll (Johnson and Higgins, 1979) reported that nearly half (48 percent) of workers age 50–64 said they intended to continue working instead of retiring at the usual time. From such findings, it was concluded that in the future more people will want to defer retirement.

Using data from the Longitudinal Retirement History Survey, Goudy discovered, however, that such survey findings are unreliable predictors of actual practices. His study indicates that retirement "attitudes are relatively volatile; many change within 2 or 4 years, and *large numbers retire shortly after they've stated that they never expect to stop working for a living*." [Emphasis added]

Once retired, most older persons adapt quickly to their new life situation and indicate a high degree of satisfaction with their life. As we previously noted, a variety of studies over the past two decades have documented that a high proportion of the elderly are relatively satisfied with their lives after retirement. Those who express dissatisfaction often perceive themselves in poor health and/or without adequate income. But these persons are a small minority, with most elderly expressing general satisfaction with their health and income (National Council on the Aging, 1975; Liang and Fairchild, 1979).

The evidence is now very clear that most older workers want to retire as soon as financially possible, and that once retired, they adjust well to their new situation in society and enjoy their increased leisure. In their review article on work and retirement, Foner and Schwab (1983) provide an interesting answer to the question, "to work or not to work?":

> Many if not most newly retired persons welcome the opportunity to slow down. . . . It is well to remember that many jobs are not intrinsically satisfying;

they do not enhance feelings of self-worth, encourage autonomy, or permit the exercise of independent judgment. Many jobs—in factories, mines, and some types of institutions—are actually harmful. . . . Retirement can be a rewarding experience for what it does not entail. Failure to appreciate this factor may be a result of the relatively privileged positions of those who write about retirement—reporters, professors, and physicians, for example, all of whom have some degree of control over the pace and direction of their work. Indeed generalizations about work and retirement on the basis of such work experiences may have contributed to myths about retirement.

Thus, increasing numbers of workers are looking forward to the retirement period—retiring at increasingly early ages and raising their expectations about retirement living standards. The issue of planning financially for the retirement years, therefore, moves right to the top of the decision-making agenda of most *older* workers.

Planning for Retirement

President John F. Kennedy once remarked that "it is not enough for a great nation merely to have added new years to life—our objective must also be to add new life to years." For those approaching retirement, the challenge is to take advantage of those years in a creative and fulfilling manner. And there is little doubt that preretirement planning by individuals can help many achieve this end.

As we will see in the succeeding chapters of this book, however, the problems involved in preretirement planning are very complex. Hence, most people, having a natural inclination to live for today and avoid thinking about old age and death, give very little systematic thought to the problems until they come face to face with them—which is usually too late. The flood of criticism about the adequacy, financial viability, and equity of social security and private pensions (regardless of their merits) creates confusion and distrust among workers—further discouraging early thinking about retirement preparation.

In recent years, the major efforts to deal with this problem have shifted from the individual to private and public collective efforts. Businessmen, labor leaders, and gerontologists all bring different perspectives to their efforts to deal with and improve preretirement planning. Their goal, however, is similar: to generate a greater awareness among workers and their spouses of the problems and potentials of approaching old age and to assist where appropriate in the preparation for successful retirement.

Studies by Reich (1977) show a significant growth in group preretirement education and the range of institutions offering programs: community colleges, adult education schools, social service agencies, chambers of commerce, religious institutions, universities, unions, private companies, government, senior citizen organizations, and profit-making organizations.

The development of preretirement programs is still in a very early stage. Significant numbers of workers do not have access to a program. Moreover, there is still disagreement over the need for such programs and whose responsibility it is to provide them (NCOA, 1980). A number of studies have argued that many programs are neither suitably designed nor well implemented (see, e.g., Kasschau, 1974). Many employers, for example, offer little more than fringe benefit information, and many are skeptical about the worth of preretirement programs.

One major effort in retirement planning was developed by the National Council on Aging in cooperation with a consortium of nine major corporations and four large unions (Fitzpatrick, 1979; NCOA, 1980). The program is designed to reach employees early—in their forties and fifties. Another large program is Action for Independent Maturity conducted in association with the American Association of Retired Persons. This program trains industry officials to be discussion leaders and provides materials for the retirement-planning seminars.

The challenge is (a) to increase the availability of preretirement education to persons seeking such information, (b) to improve the quality of available programs, and (c) to encourage people to begin preparing for retirement at a relatively early age.

As we shall see in the chapters that follow, financial planning for retirement is a difficult and complex matter. Planning shortly before retirement (even ten or fifteen years before) is usually too late. In the chapters that follow, we look at the options for dealing with this dilemma.

Chapter Three Highlights

Given the increasing numbers of people no longer working in the later years, much attention has been given to understanding the various factors influencing older workers' choices between work and retirement. Some of the important points made in this chapter are:

1. When an economy is growing and is at a full-employment level, a choice must be made between more leisure or more income (i.e., more goods and services). But when there is high unemployment, nations often encourage and facilitate more leisure through retirement mechanisms—attempting to deal with the unemployment problems by encouraging older workers to retire.
2. Few Americans are still working after age 65, and one-half of those still employed work only part-time.
3. Even though their productivity does not necessarily fall as they grow older, most older workers face a variety of barriers to reemployment when they become unemployed and receive relatively little help from private and government organizations in dealing with the problem.
4. Health and potential retirement income are the two most important factors influencing the decision by workers to retire.
5. Few workers are "forced" to retire; most retire as soon as they think it is financially feasible and, once retired, usually adjust well to their new situation.

Suggested Readings

Aging and Work (quarterly).

Formerly called *Industrial Gerontology*, this journal focuses on the inter-relationships of work and age for middle-aged and older workers, as well as the problems and prospects of retirement. Some of the nation's leading authorities on aging from government, industry, and academia contribute to this, the only journal concerned exclusively with the problems of middle-aged and older workers.

Daymont, Thomas N., and P. J. Andrisani. "The Health and Economic Status of Very Early Retirees." *Aging and Work* 6 (1983): 117–135.

This article, and others by Morrison, Parnes, Myers, and Kingson in the same volume, provide an excellent overview of issues related to health and retirement. Special attention is given to workers who retire before age 62.

Foner, Anne, and Karen Schwab. "Work and Retirement in a Changing Society." In Matilda White Riley, B. B. Hess, and K. Bond, eds., *Aging in Society: Selected Reviews of Recent Research*. Hillsdale, N.J.: Lawrence Erlbaum Associates, 1983.

An excellent overview article, with up-to-date references to the literature.

Graebner, William. *A History of Retirement*. New Haven, Conn.: Yale University Press, 1980.

The best book available that gives in-depth consideration to the relationship between pensions and the employment policies of management, unions, and the government.

Kreps, Juanita. *Lifetime Allocation of Work and Income*. Durham, N.C.: Duke University Press, 1971.

A series of essays that discuss various aspects of work and leisure over the lifespan.

Migliaccio, John N., and P. C. Cairo. "Preparation for Retirement: A Selective Bibliography, 1974–1980." *Aging and Work* (Winter 1981): 31–41.

A useful guide to the retirement planning literature.

Parnes, Herbert S. *Work and Retirement—A Longitudinal Study of Men*. Cambridge, Mass.: The MIT Press, 1981.

A collection of articles presenting findings from the National Longitudinal Survey of Older Men. This book is the fifth publication in a series of reports (some of which are difficult to obtain) and covers the survey cohort from 1966 through 1976.

Parnes, Herbert S., ed. *Policy and Issues in Work and Retirement*. Kalamazoo, Mich.: W. E. Upjohn Institute for Employment Research, 1983.

A collection of papers presented at a conference on work and retirement sponsored by Rutgers University.

Robinson, Pauline, Sally Coberly, and C. E. Paul. "Work and Retirement." In Robert H. Binstock and Ethel Shanas, eds., *Handbook of Aging and the Social Sciences*, 2nd ed. New York: Van Nostrand Reinhold, 1984.

A comprehensive review of the work and retirement literature.

Tracy, Martin B. "Older Men's Earnings Tests and Work Activity: A Six Nation Study." *Research on Aging* 5 (June 1983): 155–172.

The study examines the impact on older worker labor force activity of changes in the social security retirement test in six countries. The basic finding is that labor force participation rates have not increased when the test has been eliminated or liberalized.

U.S. House Select Committee on Aging. *Abolishing Mandatory Retirement*. Washington, D.C.: U.S. Government Printing Office, 1981.

A report initially withheld by the U.S. Department of Labor because of its controversial findings. The report examines the impact of the 1978 Age Discrimination in Employment Act amendments on older worker employment.

U.S. House Select Committee on Aging. *Mandatory Retirement: The Social and Human Cost of Enforced Idleness*. Washington, D.C.: U.S. Government Printing Office, 1977.

The report was written to justify the need for the 1977 legislation liberalizing mandatory retirement rules.

Winter, Dorothy. *Help Yourself to a Job—A Guide for Retirees*. Boston: Beacon Press, 1976.

Practical suggestions on where to look for jobs, how to apply, and how to get assistance.

Chapter Four

Retirement Income Planning

We now turn from employment problems and the retirement decision to the issues of financial provision for retirement. There are various ways in which individuals can provide income in the retirement years, when normal income received from work declines or stops. Figure 15 lists the major mechanisms and institutions available in the United States today for providing economic assistance in retirement. These are divided into two broad groups—private and public. The private mechanisms are either individual preparation or preparation undertaken by the individual as a part of group action. For the public mechanisms it is important to distinguish two major categories: those mechanisms for which there is a **means test** and those for which there is no such test.

Private		*Public*	
Individual	*Groups*	*Means Test*	*No Means Test*
Physical assets	Private pension	Supplemental security	Social Security
Insurance claims	funds	income	Medicare
Other financial	Family gifts	Medicaid	Veterans' benefits
intermediaries	Charity organi-	Veterans' benefits	(service-connected
claims	zations	(nonservice-	disability)
Direct financial	Friends' and	connected disability)	Government-financed
investment	neighbors'	Housing programs	services to the aged
claims	gifts	Federal old age	
		tax benefits	
		(means test in	
		reverse)[a]	
		State property tax	
		reductions	
		Food stamps	

Figure 15. Options for Retirement Income

Source: Adapted from James H. Schulz et al., *Providing Adequate Retirement Income—Pension Reform in the United States and Abroad* (Hanover, N.H.: New England Press for Brandeis University Press, 1974), Figure 1. Used by permission.

[a]Federal tax benefits can be utilized only by people with taxable income high enough to require that they pay taxes and hence take advantage of special tax provisions.

In this chapter the focus is primarily on private mechanisms, especially the task that faces an individual who wants to prepare for retirement. In the absence of group mechanisms, both public and private, what must the individual do to have adequate retirement income?

We begin with this focus or emphasis not because this is the most common way that preparation for retirement is currently being carried out, nor because it is the most important way that we would expect it to be carried out in the future. Rather, beginning with individual preparation is a useful way of developing a good understanding of many of the concepts and issues involved in income-maintenance problems of old age. By starting at this level, it is easier to show some of the personal options, the major problems, and the magnitude of the task the individual faces. Thus, we can obtain some needed perspective on the whole problem.

Retirement Provision by Individuals

First, let us list some of the problems faced by an individual in preparing systematically for retirement:*

1. He doesn't know with certainty when he will die.
2. He doesn't know exactly what his future income flow will be.
3. He doesn't know what his basic retirement needs will be nor what lifestyle he will ultimately prefer for that period.
4. He doesn't know when he will retire.
5. He cannot easily predict the future rate of inflation, which, if it occurs, will depreciate the value of those retirement assets that do not adjust fully and reduce the buying power of income from those assets.
6. He cannot easily predict the rate of economic growth—which is likely to affect his economic position *relative* to the working population.

The number and magnitude of problems listed indicate that individual retirement planning is a very difficult job; the personal decision-making process involved in preparation for retirement is very complex. First, as listed above, not knowing when one is going to die is a major complicating factor in ascertaining the amount of money needed for retirement. To plan for adequate income the individual needs to know the number of years for which income is required. Thus arises a major justification for not providing for retirement entirely by individual mechanisms; one can simplify the decision-making process and reduce uncertainty by entering into an insurance arrangement, either public or private, that provides collective protection by grouping those who live short, medium, and long lives (discussed later in the chapter).

The second problem is the uncertainty of the income flow the individual will receive over his working life. The problem here arises from such possibilities as ill health or disability (either short term or long term). More importantly, problems are created by unemployment in the labor market, job obsolescence, and unequal economic opportunity for various groups. For example, the

*The pronoun "he" is used generically in this list.

recurrent periods of recession and inflation are outside the control of the individual and are very difficult to predict, yet these factors have a significant, if not dominating, impact on the flow of income and the total amount of income individuals receive over their lifetimes.

A third problem arises from not knowing what retirement needs will be. A major factor here is the great uncertainty that exists with regard to the state of one's health when one gets old. Will chronic or serious illness develop? Will nursing care be required? Will institutionalization be necessary? Not only does health status directly influence medical costs, it also affects retirement mobility—influencing recreation and transportation expenditures.

Yet another difficulty arises if one is married. There is uncertainty as to whether the family unit will break up (divorce) and about how long each spouse will live. Pension benefits paid out often change if the eligible worker dies. Thus, the amount of money each spouse will need or will have in retirement is essentially unpredictable as far as the individual is concerned.

A fifth problem occurs because of the variability in the age at which people retire. Although the individual has a large measure of control over when he retires, increasingly the decision is based on factors he doesn't control. Such things as deteriorating health, mandatory retirement rules, the growth of early retirement options (sometimes accompanied by management and/or union pressures to retire), and discriminatory practices in hiring older workers often dominate.

Perhaps one of the most difficult retirement preparation problems is that of predicting the rate of **inflation** that will occur before and *during* retirement. This problem is so very important because to the extent that the individual accumulates assets (or pension rights) for the retirement period that do not automatically adjust in value for inflation, he is faced with the prospect of these assets shrinking in value—being of little worth in the retirement period.

Finally, the individual preparing for retirement might be concerned about changes in his relative economic status in retirement. After he retires the real incomes of the working population will continue to rise over the years. If the retiree wants to keep up with the general rise in living standards, he will have to make some estimate of the growth that will occur while he is in retirement and provide additional retirement funds that can be drawn upon to keep his economic status rising along with that of everybody else. Some people will decide that they do not want to bother dealing with the growth of income problem; they will be content just to keep their standard of living constant. Some may even prefer to allow it to decline. Nevertheless, this is an important point that should not be overlooked. There is a choice to be made, and it should not be made passively because individuals are unaware of the nature of that choice.

Required Rate of Saving for Retirement

To see the retirement preparation issues clearly, let us assume certain answers to most of the questions listed above in order to answer the following question: Suppose an individual (on his own) wants to save a sufficient amount for his retirement; how much should he save? To put the question another way, suppose you were a preretirement counselor and someone came to you and said, "I'm twenty-five. I don't have much confidence in the present pension mechanisms available to prepare for retirement; I just don't trust them. Instead, I want to sit down and work out a savings plan for myself that will provide me with adequate income in retirement. How much should I save?"

The answer to this question depends on a great many factors. Most important are the following:

1. The standard of adequacy chosen
2. The number of years one plans to be in retirement
3. The number of years one plans to work and earnings and other income over that period
4. The yield (if any) one can anticipate on one's savings
5. The expected inflation that will occur over the period

Let us look first at the standard of adequacy. The two standards described extensively in Chapter 2—the Social Security Administration's poverty index and the Bureau of Labor Statistics' Retired Couple's Budget—are possibilities. But a retirement counselor would probably argue that these are not very good standards for most people to use. Instead, it is common to propose that individuals with near- or above-average incomes choose a standard of adequacy based upon the concept of "income replacement." An income replacement standard seeks to provide the individual with income in retirement that is a certain specified percentage of his average income prior to retirement. Immediately, a key question arises. What should that replacement goal be; what rate should be chosen—100, 80, or 50 percent?

What Must I Save for Adequate Retirement Income?

The amount of financial resources needed in retirement depends upon the standard of adequacy used. If the retired person's living standard is to be related in some way to a standard of living experienced before he retired, sources of retirement funds must enable him to replace a certain proportion of the income lost when work stops.

It is generally agreed that expenses in retirement will be somewhat lower than before retirement and, hence, that a 100 percent income replacement is not necessary. Various estimates of the differences in pre- and postretirement expenditures have been made by different researchers. For example, the Bureau of Labor Statistics (BLS) has developed an "equivalency income scale" for families of different size and age (on the basis of the relation between food expenditures and income). BLS estimates that an elderly couple generally requires 51 percent as much income for goods and services as a younger four-person husband–wife family living on the same standard. While the BLS equivalence scale shows a difference of 51 percent in expenditures needs when comparing a *middle-aged four-person family* with an *aged couple,* the difference between couples age 55–64 and couples aged 65 or more is much less. The scales show only a 13.5 percent difference in goods and services needs.

We can use these findings to help establish a retirement living standard: maintaining the same living standard in retirement as existed just prior to retirement. In addition to the 13.5 percent expenditure difference, one also must take into account the reduced income tax burden in retirement due to special federal and state income tax provisions for persons age 65 and over. Also, presumably the individual upon reaching retirement can discontinue saving for retirement, a requirement that reduces his disposable income in the working years. Taking these three factors into account, the appropriate replacement is about 65–70 percent of *gross* income for a middle-income worker.

In 1980 Preston Bassett calculated a whole set of target replacement rates for a presidential commission considering pension policy. Using a slightly different methodology from that discussed above, Bassett estimated target replacement rates for single and married persons. Table 12 shows his estimates for a wide range of preretirement income levels. Target replacement rates vary from 86 percent for a couple with gross preretirement income of $6,500 to 51 percent for a single individual with an income of $50,000.

Using the appropriate target, one can calculate the saving rate necessary to achieve a specified living standard in retirement. That is, one can determine what amount must be saved every year out of income up to the point of retirement. The year one begins saving is arbitrary. One could decide to start saving at, say, age 25, or one could decide to postpone the task till age 45 and then save more over a shorter period.

Let us assume, for example, that one begins to save a certain percent of annual income starting the first year of work and that one saves the same proportion of income throughout one's whole lifetime. Assume a life expectancy equal to the current average life expectancy and retirement at age 65. Assume an investment return on savings of 4 percent.

Suppose one's goal is to provide retirement income equal to 60–65 percent replacement of average earnings during the last five years prior to retirement. *To do this, one would have to save about 20 percent of one's earnings each and every year!**

An individual might desire, however, to save at a lower rate in the earlier years when earnings are relatively low compared to anticipated earnings later in his career. In this case, later savings rates would have to be much higher, and disposable income in the years prior to retirement would be lower.

In addition, the question of child-rearing expenses arises. A family with children has a lower standard of living than a family without children but with a similar income. Once a couple's children are self-supporting, the couple's standard of living may rise as a result of the reduced expenditures of this sort. This depends in part on whether the family has incurred previous debts—arising, for

*A full description of how this estimate was made can be found in Schulz and Carrin (1972). Alternate estimates are found in Morgan (1977) and Diamond (1977).

Table 12.   Target Replacement Rates Needed to Maintain Preretirement Living
Standards in 1980

			Single Person			
Gross Pre- retirement Income	Federal and State Taxes [a]	Work Related Expenses [b]	Savings [c]	Net Pre- retirement Income	Post- retirement Income Tax [d]	Target Rate
$ 6,500	$ 1,003	$ 330	$ 0	$ 5,167	$ 0	79%
10,000	2,008	480	240	7,272	0	73
15,000	3,703	678	678	9,941	0	66
20,000	5,783	853	1,280	12,084	198	61
30,000	10,355	1,179	2,357	16,109	1,282	58
50,000	22,249	1,665	4,163	21,923	3,752	51
			Married Couple			
$ 6,500	$ 578	$ 355	$ 0	$ 5,567	$ 0	86%
10,000	1,444	513	260	7,786	0	78
15,000	2,860	728	734	10,684	0	71
20,000	4,488	922	1,405	13,185	0	66
30,000	8,047	1,317	2,646	17,999	63	60
50,000	17,824	1,931	4,841	25,419	1,965	55

Source: Adapted from Tables 19 and 20 in President's Commission on Pension Policy, *Coming of
Age: Toward a National Retirement Income Policy*, Report of the Commission (Washington, D.C.:
The Commission, 1981), pp. 42–43.
[a]Includes federal income and OASDHI taxes. State and local tax estimate based on state and local
income tax receipts, which were 19 percent of federal income tax receipts. Property taxes are not
included.
[b]Estimated as 6 percent of income after taxes.
[c]Savings rates vary with income after taxes and are based on survey data.
[d]Postretirement taxes are on income in excess of social security benefits, which were not taxable in
1980.

example, from educational or unusual medical expenses. Paying off these debts
might prevent any significant increase in living standard in the preretirement
years.

The Role of Pensions

Our estimated required savings rate of about 20 percent assumed that one
saved for retirement without the help of either public or private pension plans.
In reality pensions in the United States play a major role—we will argue a domi-
nant role—in providing retirement income. Before looking at the operation of
the social security program and other pensions in the United States, we first
need to understand the basic rationale behind their development.

The Great Depression of the 1930s went a long way toward exposing the
great political lie of American welfare debates: that poverty was generally the
result of the laziness or personal unworthiness of particular individuals. In the
thirties it became painfully obvious to everyone that this was not the case. Millions of jobless workers and their families suffered severe financial problems

because of an economic catastrophe caused by factors unrelated to their own personal activities. Moreover, the cures for their problems lay almost entirely outside the range of their individual reactions.

Up until this depression there had been a great deal of controversy in the United States with regard to the role of (and need for) some sort of public **pension** system. Many other countries had quickly followed the example of Germany, which established the first comprehensive social insurance program in the 1880s. But in the United States there was no widespread public support for public pensions until the economic upheavals of the Great Depression. And although there was a scattered handful of employee pensions provided by government and private firms in existence during the first half of the twentieth century, the significant growth of these pension programs has occurred in the relatively recent years of the 1950s and 1960s.

Thus, the social institution of pensions has had a relatively short history in the United States. And there has been continuing discussion and debate over just what are the appropriate roles to be played by both public and private pensions. We now look at this question and discuss some of the important goals for a good pension program; in later chapters we look at social security and private pensions as they currently operate in the United States.

Why Pensions?

Some of the debate over pensions has revolved around the advantages and disadvantages of public versus private pensions, but there are two even more basic questions that should be discussed: Why is there a need for *any kind* of pension program, and should individuals be compelled (either by the government or an employer) to join a particular pension program?

You will recall that earlier in this chapter we listed and discussed a number of problems confronting an individual making economic preparations for retirement on his own. The first problem is that the individual does not know exactly when he or she will die—that is, how long a period to provide for. This means that any person, or family, preparing for retirement must assume the "worst"—a long life—and put aside enough money to take care of that eventuality; or one must be prepared to rely on private or public charity if one lives "too long" and one's own economic support is exhausted.

A pension program provides an attractive option by utilizing a basic insurance principle. If the number of individuals in a pension program is sufficiently large, mortality tables of life expectancy can be constructed that estimate average **life expectancy** at particular ages. Retirement preparation costs can then be geared to *average* life expectancy, with the "excess" payments of individuals who die before the average age going to those who live beyond it. The result is that no one has to pay more than he or she would need to put aside personally if it was known with certainty that he or she would live for a period of years equal to the average life expectancy.

The second problem discussed earlier in this chapter in connection with individual retirement preparation is the lack of predictability of future income.

For example, chronic low earnings, ill health, or periods of unemployment as a result of a variety of factors may make sufficient saving for retirement very difficult or even impossible. Also, health or employment problems may force an individual to leave the labor force unexpectedly and much earlier than was originally planned.

Collective arrangements to deal with this problem are not new. Since earliest times people have attempted to mitigate or eliminate economic insecurity by banding together in groups—families, tribes, associations, guilds. Especially important has been the family. Throughout history individuals have relied heavily on family ties to protect themselves from economic insecurity in old age. Even today in the United States, the family remains an important source of economic and social support for many older persons. And in some other countries—particularly those less industrialized—the family still remains the major source of economic protection and security in old age.

The major problem with the family (and many other group associations) for sharing risk is that the number of people involved is relatively small. As Kenneth Boulding (1958) has observed, "It is when the 'sharing group' becomes too small to ensure that there will always be enough producers in it to support the unproductive that devices for insurance become necessary. When the 'sharing group' is small there is always a danger that sheer accident will bring the proportion of earners to nonearners to a level at which the group cannot function."

The commonly held view that in earlier America most of the aged lived in rural communities together with, or in close proximity to, adult children who provided financial support in the later years is not supported by the facts (Tibbitts, 1977). Nuclear parent-child families have always been the more common family type in the United States, and the three-generation family has been relatively rare.

Thus, the need for better collective arrangements to deal with the economic problems of old age has probably always been with us. The earliest available statistics on the economic status of the elderly prior to the establishment of pensions indicate that most of the aged were poor and that, in fact, many were completely destitute. The reasons why pension programs were not developed sooner are not entirely clear, but various writers have pointed to the *relative* economic prosperity throughout America's history, the country's decentralized governmental structure, and (most importantly) the individualistic ethic of much of the population.

Why Compulsory Pensions?

Although individual self-reliance and voluntary preparation for retirement—together with family interdependence—dominated the early discussions of old age security provision, it is now generally accepted that this is not the appropriate cornerstone of an income maintenance policy for the aged. Instead, there is widespread support for relying on compulsory pensions. A number of prominent American economists have written about the rationale for compulsory pensions. In a chapter in his book on the *Principles of Economic Policy,* Kenneth Boulding (1958) concisely states the principal argument:

> [*If an individual*] *were rationally motivated,* [*he*] *would be aware of the evils that might beset him, and would insure against them. It is argued, however, that many people are not so motivated, and that hardly anyone is completely motivated by these rational considerations, and that therefore under a purely voluntary system some will insure and some will not. This means, however, that those who do not insure will have to be supported anyway—perhaps at lower levels and in humiliating and respect-destroying ways—when they are in the nonproductive phase of life, but that they will escape the burden of paying premiums when they are in the productive phase. In fairness to those who insure voluntarily, and in order to maintain the self-respect of those who would not otherwise insure, insurance should be compulsory.*

Richard Musgrave (1968), writing on the role of social insurance, makes a similar point:

> *Insurance could be purchased privately, but becomes a matter of public concern only because* [*some*] *will not do so, while* [*others*] *will. Given their humanitarian premise, Calvin and Homer must bail out Jack should the contingency arise. They will require therefore that Jack should insure. Social insurance is not insurance in the technical sense, but its basic function (and especially the rationale for making it mandatory) is again to avoid burdening the prudent.*

Pechman, Aaron, and Taussig (1968) in their book on social security, after an extensive discussion of the rationale for pensions, conclude:

> *There is widespread myopia with respect to retirement needs. Empirical evidence shows that most people fail to save enough to prevent catastrophic drops in post-retirement income. . . . Not only do people fail to plan ahead carefully for retirement; even in the later years of their working life, many remain unaware of impending retirement needs. . . . In an urban, industrial society, government intervention in the saving-consumption decision is needed to implement personal preferences over the life cycle.* There is nothing inconsistent in the decision to undertake through the political process a course of action which would not be undertaken individually through the marketplace. [*Emphasis added*]

The first systematic studies of this issue have been carried out by Peter Diamond (1977) and Kotlikoff et al. (1982). Both studies conclude that without social security (or its equivalent) a substantial fraction of the population would be inadequately prepared for retirement. The data analyzed in both studies indicated that a large proportion of the population is likely to undersave for old age.

Social Security Decision Making

J. Douglas Brown, who helped draft the original social security program, writes in his book on the history of social security that the drafting group never seriously considered anything other than a compulsory program. The drafting group did worry, however, about whether a national compulsory program would be constitutional.

Hoping that it might be possible to avoid a court test of the constitutionality of social security, the drafting group did consider briefly a plan that would have permitted elective social security coverage by states and various industrial groups, but rejected it. According to Brown, the plan was "so cumbersome, ineffective, and actuarially unsound that no further attempt was made to avoid a head-on constitutional test of a truly workable system" (Brown, 1972).

As it turned out, during the debates that followed, the principal argument for compulsion was a financial one. It was argued that an optional coverage program would make it **actuarially** impossible to project both benefits (costs) and revenue. It was feared that this problem would create financial instability and make it difficult to guarantee adequate, equitable, and improved benefits as social security developed.

The original Social Security Act required participation by all workers in commerce and industry except those working for railroads.* A number of groups, however, were specifically excluded from coverage—the major ones being farm workers, the self-employed, and government employees (including military personnel). Over the years, as coverage was extended to these groups, optional coverage was introduced for certain specific groups: employees of nonprofit institutions, state and local governments, and most clergymen. But in each case, coverage was not optional for the individual, depending instead on the collective decision of the organizational unit.

The decision of the United States to have a compulsory pension program is in no way unique. There is no country in the world with a social security old age pension program that has designed a large amount of voluntary coverage into the program. Like the United States, many countries have special public pension programs for certain groups of workers (especially government employees), and many exclude from coverage certain groups (such as farm workers, the self-employed, or employees of very small firms). Some countries—for example, Ghana, the Federal Republic of Germany, Kuwait, Liberia, Peru, Uganda, and Zambia—have voluntary coverage, but these noncompulsory provisions are all limited to certain (usually small) groups in the country.

If we shift our attention from public pensions to private pensions in the United States, we find that the situation is not very different. The vast majority of workers who are covered or not covered by private pension plans have not achieved that status by personal election. Not all firms have established private pension plans for their employees, but almost all private pension schemes that have been set up are compulsory. Typically, once a worker joins a firm he automatically becomes a member of the pension plan—sometimes after a short waiting period. There are a few private plans, however, that provide for an employee contribution out of salary; such plans sometimes make coverage optional.

In summary, we see that the usefulness of pensions in helping to provide for economic security in old age is generally accepted and that compulsory coverage remains a feature of both public and private programs.

---

*Railroad workers were exempted because similar legislation on their behalf had already been enacted in 1934. Although this original legislation was later declared unconstitutional, new (and still separate) railroad pension legislation was enacted in 1935 and 1937.

What Makes a "Good" Pension Program?

If one wants to evaluate a pension program or a pension proposal, what characteristics or features of the plan should be examined? With an institutional arrangement as complex as pensions, one can generate a long list of plan features that might be studied. Opinions differ widely as to which of these are most important. Moreover, there is little agreement on the relative weights that should be assigned to each feature when making an overall judgment about a particular pension plan. Some important characteristics of pension plans, however, that would probably appear on almost everyone's list, are discussed in the pages that follow.

The Adequacy of Pension Benefits   Any discussion of a particular pension plan's adequacy must explicitly recognize the variety of means available to the individual (or society) in achieving a particular level of income in old age. A pension plan is rarely designed to be the sole source of such income. Thus, in evaluating the adequacy of any particular pension benefit, it is necessary to relate such analysis to a general framework for evaluating individuals' general economic status and the variety of means available to achieve or change that status. Are individuals *expected* to accumulate personal savings for their old age? Are all individuals *able* to save for old age? What noncash programs (such as health insurance) are available to provide economic support? How large are both public and private pension benefits; who is currently covered by each; who should be covered?

There will never be complete agreement about the appropriate roles for the various means of providing income in old age—collective pension schemes are only one major way (see Figure 15, p. 70). Rather, it is almost certain that there will be continuing political debate and private discussion among bargaining groups over these matters. Out of such discussions come decisions on legislation, employment contracts, and employer policies in the area of pensions. As these decisions are made, it is possible to evaluate their economic implications for retirement income adequacy, estimating the contribution the resulting pensions will make to a particular individual's or group's goal.

The Certainty of Benefits   In addition to estimating or projecting the size of pension benefits, one can examine particular pension plans and estimate the degree of uncertainty associated with the *promised* benefits. Three major contingencies can be evaluated:

1. Plan termination: what provisions are made to ensure that the plan will survive economic or political adversity, such as a change in government (public pensions) or bankruptcy of the firm (private pensions)?
2. Inflation: how well are the workers' future benefits and the pension recipients' actual benefits protected from general increases in the level of prices?
3. Job termination: what happens to pension rights if a worker involuntarily or by choice stops working or changes jobs?

Flexibility and Discretion for Varying Conditions or Preferences The larger the pension program in terms of people covered, the greater the differences in the circumstances and preferences of these participants. It is generally desirable for pension plan provisions and rules not to be too rigid. The introduction of greater flexibility, however, usually results in greater administrative costs (see Low Administrative Costs, below). And by complicating the program, flexibility often makes it more difficult for participants to become knowledgeable and to understand their pension program.

Adequate and Nondiscriminatory Coverage The determination of eligibility for pension coverage is a very complex but important factor in assessing pension plans. Most people would agree that individuals in similar circumstances (e.g., working for the same employer) should not be arbitrarily excluded from coverage under a pension plan or excluded because of age, sex, race, and so forth. But the actual determination of who should and who should not be included is often difficult because of a variety of administrative, technical, political, and economic considerations.

Equity Whether a pension program is perceived as fair depends in large measure on how the program treats different individuals and how these individuals think they *should* be treated. The major issue around which equity questions usually cluster is financing—how much do the benefits received cost the individual in contrast to other benefit recipients and, possibly, nonrecipients?

Low Administrative Costs Apart from the benefits paid out by a pension program, there are a variety of expenditures connected with keeping records, determining benefit eligibility, collecting and managing the funds used to pay benefits, and informing individuals of their rights under the plan.

Boulding (1958) has argued that one valid criterion for choosing between private and public programs is whether there can be significant economies of scale in their operation:

> If there are these economies—that is, if the cost of administering the insurance declines with every increase in the amount of insurance written—then a state monopoly will almost inevitably be cheaper than a number of competing private companies. . . . We may venture a hypothesis that where the operations of insurance are fairly routine, the case for state or national monopoly is stronger than where the operations involve great difficulties of definition of rights.

Simplicity and Ease of Understanding It is important that individuals know whether they are covered by a pension plan, what the conditions of entitlement are, what benefits they (or their family) can or will receive, what the risks of losing benefits are, and various other facts about the plan. Over the years a large amount of evidence has accumulated that indicates a great lack of knowledge and much misinformation exists among workers in the United States with regard to their own expected pensions, both public and private. As the number and variety of pension programs grow and many of these programs become more complicated, this problem will also grow. Therefore, in reviewing existing programs or proposals for pension changes, the complexity of the program should be considered. An assessment should be made of the resultant impact on the employees' ability to understand the pension program and to incorporate it realistically into their preretirement planning.

Integration   A particular pension plan is almost always only one of a number of collective programs operating to provide economic assistance. It is not sufficient to view a particular pension program in isolation from these other programs. For example, eligibility or benefit determination under one program is sometimes related to benefits received from another program (see Schulz and Leavitt, 1983).

This is an especially important issue with regard to public programs. The value of social security pension benefits to the elderly depends, for example, on (a) the tax treatment of these benefits and (b) whether the benefits are counted as income in determining eligibility for Supplemental Security Income, food stamps, Medicare and Medicaid, housing subsidies, and so forth (see, for example, Federal Council on Aging, 1975).

What Mix of Public and Private Pensions?

Despite the fact that the first pension plans were established about a century ago, there is still little agreement about the relative virtues of public versus private pensions and what the ideal combination of the two types should be. There is great diversity in the mix of pensions existing in various countries—but there are fewer countries where private programs assume a major role than there are countries that rely primarily on public pensions.

Relatively little has been written that attempts objectively to approach the question of the most desirable pension mix and present data for evaluation purposes. In the United States, the well-known economist Milton Friedman has been a consistent critic of social security and one of the few academics actually to advocate complete abolition of public pensions: "Social Security combines a highly regressive tax with largely indiscriminate benefits and, in overall effect, probably redistributes income from lower to higher income persons. I believe that it serves no essential social function. Existing commitments make it impossible to eliminate it overnight, but it should be unwound and terminated as soon as possible" (Cohen and Friedman, 1972).

There has been very little support for Friedman's rather extreme position. Instead, the more common negative view toward social security advocates a relatively minor role for it and, consequently, seeks to limit any future growth of the program—either by expansion of real benefits or by adding additional functions.

Robert J. Myers, chief actuary for the social security program between 1947 and 1971, labels advocates of a greater role for social security in aged income maintenance as "expansionists" and designates as "moderates" those persons who believe the program should not be expanded. Myers summarizes the moderate viewpoint as one that seeks a governmental program that would provide benefits "sufficient so that, with assets and real estate normally accumulated, the vast majority of beneficiaries will be able to have at least a *reasonable subsistence.*" [Emphasis added] (Myers, 1970)

Over the years concern about further expansion of the role for social security and raising social security benefits has not been the major issue raised by critics. Rather, most of the concern and criticism has centered on the way benefits have been financed. In Chapter 6 we discuss many of the issues connected with social security financing. In general, the program is criticized because of the heavy tax burden it places on the poor and near-poor and because of the very great differences in contributions paid in versus benefits received among different socioeconomic groups and between current and future generations.

Criticism of social security, however, has been relatively limited in comparison to support voiced for it. On the positive side, three major arguments have been advanced in its favor:

1. That the nonbenefit costs of social insurance are much lower than the costs for *private pension* administration, fund investment, mobility, disclosure to recipients, supervision and regulation, and reinsurance.
2. That it is easier to make social security pensions both inflation proof—adjusting for inflation at and during retirement—and adjustable for economic growth.
3. That it is relatively easy to cover all workers and provide complete portability of credits under social security, whereas private pensions present formidable problems in this regard (unless coverage is mandated by the government).

Costs   Although the structure of social security in the United States is far from being uncomplicated, there are many aspects of its operation that are relatively simple. Consequently, the collection and benefit payout process permits the extensive use of computers. This in turn permits the handling of large numbers of claims in a way that allows significant economies of large-scale operation to be realized. In fiscal year 1981, for example, administrative expenses were only 1.1 percent of payroll contributions for the old age and survivors program (OASI). These low expenses are in sharp contrast to public perceptions. A recent Roper opinion poll found that only 2 percent of those interviewed thought that social security administrative costs were less than 10 percent of contributions collected (Social Security Administration, 1981). The median estimate was 52 percent!

Comparing costs between social security and private pensions is complicated by the fact that social security financing in the United States is essentially on a pay-as-you-go basis, whereas private pensions are funded (see Chapter 8). Private pension funding costs generated as a result of financial investment on behalf of employers (and, in part, indirectly benefiting the economy) have no analogous counterpart in the United States social security program. Also, another difference between the two types of pensions is the fact that employers and the Internal Revenue Service give lots of "free" administrative services to the social security system.

Insurance companies, unions, corporations, and banks administer private pension plans. Although there has been no study of the costs of private pension plans compared to social security, it is hard to imagine that the current conglomeration of thousands of private plans, many covering fewer than a hundred workers, can have lower administrative costs. A study by Mitchell and Andrews (1981) analyzes expenses in multiemployer plans. Annual plan expenses were estimated to range from about $13 per participant for large plans (20,000 participants) to $138 per participant for small plans (100 participants).

Pension Adjustments for Inflation   Another important argument made in favor of public pensions is their ability, in contrast to private plans, to deal with the need to respond to inflation and economic growth. The problem of inflation has plagued pension programs since their inception. All countries have had to struggle with this problem, continually adjusting pension programs and benefits to offset increases in price levels. Inflation has varied, for example, from the catastrophic rate in post-World War I Germany (which completely wiped out the monetary value of that country's social security reserves and benefits) to the relatively mild price increases averaging less than 2 percent in the United States during the 1958–1968 period to the much higher rates thereafter (including double-digit inflation).

Gradually most industrialized countries (including the United States in 1972) have introduced some sort of automatic benefit adjustment mechanisms into the social security program to deal more effectively with the inflation problem. In contrast, private pension plans, with few exceptions, virtually ignore the need for regularized adjustment mechanisms. This results, in large part, because of employers' unwillingness to make financial commitments based on guesses about future price levels and the fear that the cost of these adjustments may be too high. In addition, most private pension analysts feel that it is virtually impossible to devise an acceptable inflation-proofing mechanism (see Munnell, 1979).

It is much easier for governments to deal with the inflation problem, given their inherent taxing powers and their ability to minimize the size of the monetary fund necessary to guarantee the financial soundness of the pension program. A pay-as-you-go system, for example, makes it easier to increase revenues to pay for inflation-adjusted wages because the earnings base is also rising with inflation. In contrast, many securities in a reserve fund will not adjust upward in value with the inflation.

The actual history of social security programs in various countries dealing with inflation supports that conclusion; even after runaway inflations, countries have been able to adjust pensions to the new price level. In addition, public pension programs have shown an ability to devise equitable ways of permitting retired persons to share systematically in the real economic growth of the country. Social security programs in some countries—such as Belgium, Canada, Norway, and West Germany—provide for automatic or semiautomatic adjustments in *real* benefit levels. Still others adjust benefits systematically by various ad hoc processes.

Coverage   It has proven to be a relatively easy matter in all countries to extend social security coverage to large segments of the labor force. Coverage of agricultural workers and the self-employed has presented problems—especially in developing countries—but, in general, extension of coverage all over the world has been quite comprehensive. In the United States, for example, coverage of the gainfully employed is now complete.

In contrast, as we discuss in Chapter 8, extension of private pension coverage presents serious problems. It has been especially difficult to extend coverage to workers in small firms. As a result, a sizable proportion of the work force in countries with private pensions may not be covered by such pensions.

One possible solution to the coverage problem is for the government to require that all employers provide private pension benefits. Some countries have done this. Great Britain, for example, is in the process of implementing such a requirement as a supplement to social security. British employers must provide pension protection equal to government minimums or contribute to a quasi-public funded pension scheme.

In 1981 the President's Commission on Pension Policy recommended mandatory private coverage for the United States, but thus far the recommendation has received little support in Congress.

Arguments in Support of Private Pensions

There are two major arguments supporting the existence and expansion of private pensions:

1. That social security—because of its broad coverage—must remain very uniform in its benefit provisions, while private pensions are flexible and can be tailored to meet differing situations and conditions (e.g., hazardous conditions) of various industries, particular firms, or different occupational groups
2. That private pensions are vital to assure the saving necessary to provide sufficient investment in a growing economy

Flexibility   On the one hand, a private pension can be a flexible management tool. As Charles A. Siegfried (1970) of the Metropolitan Life Insurance Company has observed, "a pension plan can be devised to attract and hold employees or it can be devised to facilitate the separation of employees from employment." On the other hand, pension objectives may vary to accommodate different employee wishes and aspirations, these being determined by decisions of the employers (unilaterally or in consultation with workers) or by collective bargaining.

The late Edwin S. Hewitt, a well-known pension consultant, arguing the case for private pensions before the U.S. Senate Special Committee on Aging, emphasized the flexibility factor:

> It is extraordinary how flexible an instrument for providing adequate security the private plan has proved to be. There are two kinds of flexibility and perhaps this fact is underrated when we oppose what private plans are doing.

First is their flexibility in terms of adapting to different needs. Very real differences in security problems exist among different companies, different industries, different age groups. . . .

The second dimension is the flexibility between periods of time. Private plans have exhibited amazing flexibility to make their provisions meet the different needs that a group may have at different times.

The initial job of most pension plans when first established is to concentrate on retirement income for the older worker, hence the importance of past service benefits.* As plans become better funded, they tend to branch into other areas. Variety increases as plans are able to spend more money and give attention to tailormade benefits to meet specific needs. [Hewitt, 1970]

Pension Saving and Capital Formation   A much more controversial argument made in favor of private pensions is their role in the mobilization of national saving for economic **investment**. Charles Moeller, an economist for the Metropolitan Life Insurance Company, has argued the positive aspects this way:

The key to any nation's economic growth is its ability to direct substantial portions of its output into real investment, i.e., to defer current consumption of output through saving and to permit investment in productive facilities for use in future production processes. . . . In effect, what pension funding operations and other forms of contractual saving do is to improve the efficiency and stability of the capital markets. . . .

The importance of the saving function for private pension plans cannot be too strongly emphasized. The need for encouraging the accumulation of individual saving flows and for recirculating these funds back into the economy through the investment process has been spotlighted by the dramatic events of recent years including the "crunch" of 1966 and the "liquidity crisis" of 1970. [Moeller, 1972]

It is a common misconception that there is a direct relationship between the personal saving of individuals (for retirement and other reasons) and economic growth. While there is a need for saving to facilitate investment in the economy, there is general agreement that there are a variety of ways such saving can be accumulated. Hence, there is no agreement on the need or importance of any one accumulation process—such as through personal saving or private pensions.

In the key growth sector of *corporate* production, the overwhelming majority of funds needed to finance new investment comes from the *internal* funds saved by the corporations themselves. "If you subtract housing investment from total capital investment funds, more than 99 percent of real capital investment funds took the form of corporate *retained earnings* or *depreciation allowance* in 1973" (Thurow, 1976). Other possible sources of savings are unincorporated business, individuals, and government budget surpluses.

Moreover, there is disagreement over the extent to which there is any insufficiency of saving in the United States relative to investment opportunities and the willingness of business to undertake investment. Economist Arthur Okun (1975) observed that "the specter of depressed saving is not only empirically implausible but logically fake. . . . The nation can have the level of saving and in-

---

*Past service benefits are credits for years of work in the firm prior to the establishment of the pension plan. Most benefit formulas pay benefits that rise with years of service with the company.

vestment it wants with more or less income redistribution, so long as it is willing to twist some other dials." A *New York Times* article reviewing this issue reiterates the caution of many economists that even if the savings rate were to rise, this would not necessarily increase investment, productivity, and growth. Quoting well-known economist Robert M. Solow:

> *Increasing savings only matters when what is limiting investment is capacity, and that is not the case now. The problem affecting investment now is one of profitability. How will more saving make the automobile or steel industry more profitable?* [*Arenson, 1981*]

Currently there is also disagreement among economists about the impact of social security on personal savings. In 1974 economist Martin Feldstein was the first to present statistical evidence indicating that growing social security benefits may have reduced total personal savings in the United States. A great deal of additional research and debate followed Feldstein's original article. For example, Barro (1978) argued that evolving social security has changed the pattern of voluntary intergenerational transfers (from parents to children and vice versa). Barro presented statistical evidence (disputed by Feldstein) indicating that this changing pattern of family transfers offsets the savings impact of social security. Lesnoy and Leimer (1981) then demonstrated a serious error in Feldstein's original study and reached the opposite conclusion from the same data. Reviewing these and other studies to date, both Munnell (1982a) and Aaron (1982) find that *there is little evidence to conclude that the pay-as-you-go social security system has depressed personal saving in the United States.*

Finally, it should be noted that the generation of savings through pensions is not limited to private pensions. Public social security reserve funds can also be generated. For example, the financing rates for the social security program in Sweden have been deliberately set high enough to help generate savings in the Swedish economy. In fact, public pension reserves may be a particularly attractive means of mobilizing savings in developing countries where private pensions are virtually nonexistent.

The Pension Mix in Various Countries

If we look at the pension programs currently existing in various industrialized countries, we find that there is a tendency to rely heavily either on public pensions or on some sort of private/public combination *with extensive regulation of the private sector.* In countries that rely heavily on private pensions, the tendency is for the private and public pension programs to be closely coordinated by a large number of complex legislative and administrative mechanisms and regulations. In France, for example, it is difficult to make a distinction between social security and the widespread private pension programs—given the elaborate coordinating mechanisms that have been established.

In the United States, both public and private pension plans have assumed a growing share of responsibility for providing retirement income needs. The indications are that this collective share will continue to grow. But it is not yet clear how that responsibility ultimately will be divided.

Chapter Four Highlights

What are the mechanisms available for providing economic support in retirement? How should choices be made among the alternatives? In this chapter we emphasized the following points:

1. While there are many ways of providing for retirement, a major choice is between personal saving and collective pension programs (both public and private).
2. Planning for retirement by individuals is complicated by (a) a variety of uncertainties, such as future health and employment possibilities, and (b) the need to take action far in advance of the actual event.
3. A reasonable planning goal for a middle-income worker is retirement income equal to 65–70 percent of preretirement income.
4. Assessments of pension alternatives should be based on differences in adequacy, the certainty of receipt, flexibility, coverage, equity, costs, simplicity, and integration mechanisms.
5. A more controversial criterion for assessing pension alternatives is the impact of particular types of pensions on national saving.

Suggested Readings

Boulding, Kenneth. "Income Maintenance Policy." In *Principles of Economic Policy.* Englewood Cliffs, N.J.: Prentice-Hall, 1958, pp. 233–257.
  One of the best discussions of the rationale for pension insurance and one of the few discussions available on the relative merits of public versus private pensions.

Cagan, Phillip, ed. *Saving for Retirement.* Washington, D.C.: American Council of Life Insurance, n.d.
  A report on a mini-conference on saving held for the 1981 White House Conference on Aging. The report contains an excellent collection of papers on saving, the aged, and pensions.

Esposito, Louis. "Effect of Social Security on Saving." *Social Security Bulletin* 41 (May 1978): 9–17.
  An explanation for noneconomists of the relationship of social security to saving and capital formation. A variety of relevant data and research findings are summarized.

Heidenheimer, Arnold J., Hugh Heclo, and Carolyn Teich Adams. *Comparative Public Policy—The Politics of Social Choice in Europe and America.* New York: St. Martin's Press, 1975.
  Chapter 7 of this book is an excellent comparative discussion of various social welfare programs. Included in the discussion is consideration of issues influencing how and when social insurance was introduced in each country.

Meier, Elizabeth, C. C. Dittmar, and B. B. Torrey. "Retirement Income Goals." Chapter 5 in the Appendix of the President's Commission on Pension Policy, *Coming of Age: Toward a National Retirement Income Policy.* Washington, D.C.: The Commission, 1981.
  A discussion of adequacy goals and estimates of amounts required to achieve them.

Scholen, Ken, and Yung-Ping Chen, eds. *Unlocking Home Equity for the Elderly.* Cambridge, Mass.: Ballinger, 1980.
  Proceedings of a conference on issues related to converting nonliquid assets locked up in home equity into retirement income.

Schulz, James H., and Thomas D. Leavitt. *Pension Integration: Concepts, Issues and Proposals.* Washington, D.C.: Employee Benefit Research Institute, 1983.

A comprehensive discussion of the historical development of social security integration provisions in private pension plans and the controversial issues arising from them.

Schulz, James H., et al. *Providing Adequate Retirement Income—Pension Reform in the United States and Abroad.* Hanover, N.H.: New England Press for Brandeis University Press, 1974.

This book presents a more extensive treatment of the topics in this chapter. It emphasizes the replacement of average preretirement earnings by pensions as a measure of adequacy. Innovative pension systems in five countries are analyzed.

Chapter Five

Social Security Old Age and Survivor Benefits

The first American social security benefit ever paid was $22 a month and was received by Miss Ida Fuller, a retired law firm secretary, in early 1940. Ida Fuller's experience with social security dramatically illustrates one of the major benefits of public pensions discussed in the prior chapter. Miss Fuller (who died in 1975) lived to be over 100, paid into the program less than $100, and over the years received about $21,000 in social security benefits.*

In response to the needs of Ida Fuller and millions of other persons approaching retirement, the United States social security system was created in 1935 and has grown over the years to be one of the major expenditure programs of the federal government.

The Social Security Act of 1935 established the basic federal old age pension program (OAI) and a federal-state system of unemployment insurance. Various key events occurred in succeeding years: in 1939 survivors' and dependents' benefits were added (OASI). In 1956 social security was expanded to include disability insurance to protect severely disabled workers (OASDI). In 1965 Medicare was added, establishing a comprehensive health program for the elderly (OASDHI). Over the years, successive groups of workers have been brought into the system: certain farm and domestic workers (1950), most of the self-employed (1954), members of the uniformed services (1956), Americans employed by foreign governments or international organizations (1960), physicians (1965), ministers (1967), and new federal employees (1984). Automatic adjustment of benefits for inflation was legislated in 1972 and begun in 1975. The railroad retirement program was integrated with the social security system

*As we discuss in Chapter 6, one of the reasons why many people like Ida Fuller receive significantly more benefits than the contributions they paid into the program is because Congress decided to reduce the eligibility requirements (i.e., the work/payment period) for older workers approaching retirement when the program was first established (and later when new groups were brought into the program). Of course, Ida Fuller lived far beyond the average life expectancy, and this also raised her benefits relative to her contributions.

in 1974.* **Indexing** of earnings was legislated in 1977 (see p. 95). Finally, beginning in 1984, beneficiaries are required to pay income tax on up to 50 percent of their social security benefits if adjusted gross income plus 50 percent of their benefits exceeds $25,000 (individual) or $32,000 (married couple filing jointly).

Total annual OASDHI expenditures have grown from less than $1 billion in 1950 to $175 billion in 1982. This chapter focuses primarily on the social security old age pension program (OASI). The pension discussion is mainly on benefits, however, since Chapter 6 is devoted to a discussion of financing issues. Chapter 7 discusses the medical, disability, and Supplemental Security Income programs.

The Changing Social Security System

Paradoxically, the major motivating force behind the passage of the Social Security Act in 1935 was not the provision of adequate retirement income but the creation of jobs. Passed in a period that at one point witnessed more than a quarter of the labor force without jobs, the social security legislation was one of many New Deal laws aimed at job creation and relief for those out of work. The 1935 legislation encouraged the creation of state-administered unemployment programs to help unemployed workers find work and to provide them with financial support while they looked. Old age pensions were provided to help the elderly financially but also *to encourage them to leave or remain out of the work force.* Old age benefits to otherwise eligible persons age 65 or over were made conditional on meeting a "retirement test." In the original 1935 act, benefits were *not* to be paid to persons receiving any "covered wages from regular employment."

Regular employment, however, was not specifically defined in the 1935 act. In the 1939 social security amendments, the retirement test was made less ambiguous; it specified that no benefits would be paid to anyone earning more than $14.99 a month in covered employment.

Over the years the earnings exemption was increased periodically by specific increments. In 1984, the exemption amount, or retirement test, was $6,960. Legislation passed in 1983 schedules further liberalization (see p. 101).

Over the past three and a half decades there have been a great many adjustments in the social security system, but except for the introduction of disability insurance in 1956, medical insurance (Medicare) in 1965, and price indexing in 1972, there have been few, if any, major changes. Two historical developments are of particular interest, however. First, as a result of a series of legislated liberalizations, there was an expansion of persons covered by the system. Currently the only major groups of gainfully employed workers not covered are (a) certain state and local government employees with other pension coverage, (b) farm and domestic workers who do not earn or work "enough," and (c) self-employed persons with very low net earnings. Second, legislation over the years

---

*We do not discuss the railroad retirement system in this book. Those interested in developments should read Skolnik (1975).

has gradually moved the system further away from financing procedures that would result in the creation of a large monetary reserve fund.

Although we discuss financing in Chapter 6, some initial remarks are appropriate here. Currently the social security system is almost completely "unfunded" (i.e., few reserves are accumulated and obligations are met essentially on a pay-as-you-go basis). From the very beginning social security was never completely funded. It was recognized from the start that this was not necessary since (a) mandatory participation resulted in the involvement of a large part of the employed population, (b) the pension system could be assumed to operate indefinitely, and (c) the taxing power of the government ultimately stood behind the system.

Initially, legislated contribution rates were expected to provide the money for a fairly large trust fund as payments came in over the years. But as this reserve fund began to accumulate and **actuarial** projections predicted that it would grow much bigger, congressional leaders began to argue that there was no reason for the fund to grow so big. Instead, the decision was made to liberalize the system and to use the scheduled increases in contributions to pay for these liberalizations.

Historically, the gradual adoption of an almost completely pay-as-you-go funding policy facilitated the liberalization and improvement of the system. New groups were added to the system with retroactive benefits provided. Cost-of-living increases in benefits were legislated periodically. And, in 1972, a major increase in real benefits was provided for everyone in the system.

The historical evolution of social security financing is important to keep in mind. Some argue that the current and projected financial problems of the system are, in part, a result of overly liberal expansion decisions made in earlier years. In response, others argue that Congress *deliberately* legislated benefits considerably in excess of contributions, to keep millions of elderly out of almost certain poverty. This was accomplished through a program that avoided the stigma of needs-tested public assistance programs. In their opinion, the costs of this approach to the system and future retirees are to be expected and should not be viewed with alarm. In fact, the original designers of social security in the 1930s called for later government contribution out of general revenues to meet the costs of providing benefits to the several initial generations who had not contributed very much into the system.

The Principles of Social Security

The social security legislation that was accepted by President Roosevelt and the Congress was based on a number of principles.

First, participation was compulsory for the designated groups. Workers could not opt out of the system. Nor were high-income or high-earnings members of the covered groups entirely excluded.

Second, it was set up as an earnings-related system. When this decision was made in the 1930s, it was not at all obvious that social security should be based upon an earnings-related principle. Many countries in Europe had flat-rate pensions. And Dr. Francis E. Townsend, a California physician, had proposed in 1933 a flat pension of $200 per month for all persons aged 60 and over—resulting in the Townsend movement of 4,550 clubs within two years.

The decision against the flat rate is explained by J. Douglas Brown (1972), one of the architects of the system: "It was early recognized that a single flat rate of benefits for a country as diversified as the United States would fail to meet the needs of those living in the high-cost urban areas of the Northeast while being unduly favorable to those in the rural South."

Third, social adequacy was to be taken into account in the determination of benefits for various recipients. A set of weighted benefits that favored workers with lower earnings was established. Also, a contribution cutoff point (the maximum contribution ceiling) was established; the earnings above the ceiling of very highly paid earners were excluded. The intent was to restrict the focus of the program to those people who would have the greatest problems and the greatest need for a public benefit (while allowing all eligible earners to participate).

Fourth, it was decided that social security should be only one of many sources of economic protection and that further supplementation, either through group or individual means, would be needed to maintain an adequate living standard in retirement. Social security was often referred to as providing "a floor of protection."

Fifth, funds for operating the program were to come from earmarked taxes, called contributions. Social insurance was to be "a cooperative institution taken over by the state, but still a reflection of the responses of workers who are willing to contribute from their earnings today to protect themselves and their families from the hazards of tomorrow" (Brown, 1972).

Sixth, social security benefits were to be a matter of right; there was to be no **means test.** Workers were to earn their benefits through participation in and contributions to the program. The system was to be self-supporting through these worker contributions, together with so-called employer contributions.*

Seventh, as indicated above, a retirement test was established; pension benefits were to be withheld, initially, if an age-eligible person worked and eventually if a person earned above a specified amount.

Retirement Benefit Provisions**

To be eligible for retirement benefits under the old age and survivors' insurance program, a worker must have worked in covered employment for the required number of calendar quarters. Prior to 1978 a quarter of coverage was defined as a calendar quarter in which the worker earned at least $50 in covered employment. In 1978 the reporting of social security wages was changed from a

---

*We discuss in Chapter 6 the question of who actually pays the employer contribution—the employee through reduced wages, consumers through higher prices, or the firm itself.

**The disability program is not discussed until Chapter 7. Some students of social security, however, see it as an important part of a *retirement* program, providing transitional protection for many of those unable to continue working up to the OASI eligibility ages.

quarterly basis to an annual basis (to reduce administrative costs). Currently, therefore, the number of quarters credited depends on annual earnings, one quarter (up to four) credited for each $390 of wages paid in 1984.*

The number of quarters required for eligibility varies by age—this, to make it easier for older workers to achieve eligibility during the early history of the program (see p. 118). A worker age 62 in 1984 needed 33 quarters. The total number of quarters required increases by one quarter in each succeeding year. Ultimately the maximum number of quarters required will be 40, or about 10 years of covered employment.

Benefits paid under the old age and survivors' insurance program to eligible workers and their spouses can be broken down into the following components:

1. The *basic benefit*, currently paid at age 65, is based on the worker's average indexed monthly earnings below the "earnings ceiling" in covered employment and is derived from a legislated benefit formula that is weighted to provide workers with lower "average earnings" a relatively greater percentage of earnings replacement than workers with higher earnings. Benefits are limited by the ceiling placed on the earnings on which a worker previously paid contributions. Only taxed earnings below this ceiling enter into the calculation of the average monthly earnings used in the benefit formula. Also, total family benefits are limited by a maximum amount.

2. A *minimum benefit* of $2,195 is provided workers (and survivors) who retire at age 65 and who would otherwise be eligible for very low basic benefits. A special minimum benefit (which is larger and increased annually according to the Consumer Price Index) is payable to those with 20 or more years of covered employment, the size of the benefit being dependent on the number of years of covered employment between 20 and 30.

3. A *dependent benefit*, equal to 50 percent of the worker's basic benefit, may be paid to a spouse and children under age 18 (and elementary or secondary school students under age 19); benefits for some spouses are reduced by federal, state, or local pensions payable to the spouse based on earnings in noncovered employment. Disabled children and divorced persons may also receive a benefit if certain specified conditions are met.

4. *Early retirement benefits* may be paid to beneficiaries at age 62–64, but these benefits are actuarially reduced (by 20 percent at age 62) to take into account the longer period over which they will be paid.

5. *Delayed benefit credits* are given to workers whenever they do not receive benefits after age 65. An additional 3 percent is added to benefits (for those reaching age 62 in 1979 or later) for each year between ages 65 and 72 that they do not get benefits. (Higher credits begin in 1990.)

6. A *retirement test* reduces benefits paid persons under age 70 (and their dependents) who earn more than a certain amount. Benefits are reduced one dollar for every two dollars earned above the exempt amount. The exemption for beneficiaries age 65 and over ($6,960 in 1984) increases automatically with increases in average wages.

*The $390 amount is adjusted annually to keep pace with average earnings.

7. *Survivors' benefits* are payable to a surviving spouse beginning at age 60 or, if disabled, at age 50, or if there is a dependent child (under 18) or if disabled, at any age. This benefit equals 100 percent of the basic benefit (see 1 above) for widows age 65 or over and disabled widows age 60 or over. Reduced benefits are paid to widows age 60–64 and to disabled widows age 50–59. Unmarried and disabled children, dependent parents, divorced wives, and remarried widows are also eligible for survivors' benefits when meeting certain specified conditions. Benefits for surviving spouses are reduced by government pension income (see 3 above).

Each of these components of the social security program is discussed in more detail below.

Benefit Levels   Benefits are based on a worker's yearly earnings (after 1950 or age 21, whichever is later) on which he or she previously paid payroll tax contributions. These earnings are adjusted upward by a wage index; the five years of lowest indexed earnings (or no earnings) are excluded; and the resulting total earnings are averaged to produce average indexed monthly earnings (AIME).

The law specifies a formula to determine the amount of benefit based on the worker's calculated AIME. The benefit formula for those reaching age 62 in 1983 is 90 percent of the first $254 of AIME, plus 32 percent of AIME over $254 and through $1,538, plus 15 percent of AIME over $1,538. The AIME dollar amounts in this formula change each year as part of a mechanism to stabilize replacement rates over time (see Chapter 6).

One of the best ways of evaluating the resulting level of pension benefits is to look at pension replacement rates. You will remember from Chapter 4 that a *pension replacement rate* specifies the proportion of a worker's prior earnings that is replaced by the pension he receives.

Table 13 shows the amount of earnings replacement provided a single person by social security at various earnings levels. Given the target rates (also shown in Table 13), we see that social security provides a significant proportion of the income required. The last column of the table shows the gap between the replacement rate necessary to maintain living standards upon retirement and the replacement rate provided by social security retirement benefits.

The Social Security Administration's Retirement History Study (Social Security Administration, 1976) provides us with comprehensive information on the actual amount of earnings replaced (in the recent past) by public and private pensions. Using these data, a Social Security Administration study (Fox, 1982) reports on the pension replacement rates achieved by social security recipients who were married and began receiving benefits during the 1968–1976 period (see Table 15, p. 106).

Minimum Benefits   Since its inception, the old age pension program has had a minimum benefit. In the original legislation the guarantee was $10 per month. Over the years the minimum benefit has been periodically increased and now equals $2,195 per year.

Table 13.   Target Replacement Rate Goals and Social Security, Single Person in 1980

Gross Preretirement Earnings	(1) Replacement Goal[a]	(2) Social Security Replacement[b]	(1) – (2) Gap
$ 6,500	79%	57%	22%
10,000	73	49	24
15,000	66	42	24
20,000	61	34	27
30,000	58	23	35
50,000	51	14	37

Source: Preston C. Bassett, "The Cost of Providing an Adequate Retirement Income." Background paper for the President's Commission on Pension Policy (Washington, D.C.: mimeo, 1980).
[a]The goal is to provide sufficient retirement income in order to maintain prior living standards upon retirement. For the derivation of the replacement rates see Table 12.
[b]Assume retirement at age 65.

Pechman, Aaron, and Taussig (1968) have succinctly summarized the major problem that arises when a minimum is provided:

> *If minimum and low benefits were paid exclusively to aged householders with little or no other money income, the case for sharply increasing the minimum would be overwhelming. In the absence of an income test, however, many beneficiaries receive minimum or low benefits because they have had limited attachment to occupations covered by social security, not because they have had low lifetime earnings. Former employees of federal, state, and local governments can enter covered employment late in life and acquire insured status sufficient to entitle them to low or minimum benefits.*

In the spring of 1981 the Reagan Administration proposed a number of social security amendments. These proposals included elimination of the minimum benefit, with the administration arguing that "the main beneficiaries of the minimum . . . are those with a modest work history in employment covered by social security." Congress passed legislation terminating the minimum but almost immediately restored the provision as a result of intense lobbying and a growing awareness that a significant number of low-income beneficiaries would be seriously harmed by the elimination.

Even before the Reagan Administration proposal, the Congress had recognized problems associated with the minimum. In 1972 it created a special minimum for long-term workers, and in 1977 it froze the regular minimum for future beneficiaries.

Under the provisions of the special minimum, persons with 20 or more years in covered employment have a guaranteed level equal (in 1984) to $17.86 per month times the years of coverage in excess of 10 years (but not exceeding $357 per month). In succeeding years the special minimum will be adjusted automatically for increases in the cost of living.

Dependent Benefits   In 1939 the social security program was amended to provide dependent benefits for wives over age 64 and for children under age 18.

Successive legislation liberalized these provisions and extended benefits to children age 18-21, disabled children age 18 and over, divorced wives, and "dependent" husbands meeting various eligibility conditions. In 1977 the Supreme Court further liberalized benefits by ruling unconstitutional the social security provision that men (unlike women) must prove they were financially dependent on their wives in order to get dependent benefits.

As indicated above, an eligible dependent can receive a benefit based on the related worker's earnings and work history. If a spouse also works and becomes qualified for benefits based on his or her own work experience, he or she receives either the dependent benefit based on the spouse's pension or a pension based on his or her own work history, *whichever is greater.* Thus, a wife may pay social security taxes without adding to the family's retirement income.* The problem is further aggravated by the fact that the husband and wife are treated as separate taxable units and consequently may collectively pay more social security taxes than a family with only a single worker earning the same amount. This occurs as a result of the taxable earnings ceiling that limits the taxed earnings of the single-earner family to the ceiling but taxes each earner of the dual-earner family up to the maximum.

As with the weighted benefit formula and the minimum, the justification for the spouse benefit is made on social adequacy grounds: on a given earnings history, two people are less able (than one person) to provide *for* retirement and need more income *in* retirement. Pechman, Aaron, and Taussig (1968) argue, however, that the greater amount a couple receives (currently 50 percent more than the single worker) is too large: "The benefits of single workers should be raised substantially, relative to those of married couples. A smaller increment than 50 percent is justified because, at any given earnings level, single persons now receive smaller benefits relative to their previous standard of living than do married couples."

Other arguments against the spouse benefit are (a) that a majority (but not all) of women in the future will be covered by social security on the basis of their own earnings, (b) that since few husband-wife families are poor, the spouse benefit is an extremely inefficient way to channel money to low income families, and (c) that as a result of rising earnings by women, most families are now characterized by the mutual economic dependence of husbands and wives (Munnell, 1977).

The treatment of women under social security provisions is currently receiving considerable attention (see p. 108). In the area of spouse benefits three approaches are most frequently proposed as changes:

1. Eliminating the spouse benefit and splitting the earnings of the husband and wife for purposes of calculating benefits (see Consultant Panel on Social Security, 1976, and U.S. Department of Health, Education, and Welfare, 1979).

---

*If a husband and wife both work, the working wife has several advantages not available to the nonworking wife. She can retire and draw benefits at 62 or over even if her husband works on. Survivors' benefits—lump-sum, children's benefits, and parents' benefits—may be paid on her earnings record. Also, before age 65 she may draw disability benefits on her own record.

2. Increasing the worker's benefit rate, at the same time reducing the spouse rate (see Ball, 1978b).
3. Extending coverage and benefits directly to nonsalaried household workers, as is currently done in West Germany (for example, see Task Force on Women and Social Security, 1975).

Early Retirement   Up until 1956 workers could not receive their old age pension until they reached the age of 65. The selection of age 65 for the receipt of benefits was a somewhat arbitrary decision of those who drafted the legislation. In large part the decision was simply to copy the age provisions of existing public and private pension programs, almost all of which used age 65.

In 1956 the social security law was changed to permit *women* workers to receive reduced benefits between the ages of 62 and 64; and in 1961 this option was extended to men. In both cases the reduction was to be the full actuarial amount. That is, persons receiving benefits before age 65 were to receive over their remaining lifetime amounts that—based on average life expectancy—would not exceed (on average) the total amounts received by those retiring at age 65.

From the very beginning, the early retirement option was exceedingly popular and has been exercised by large numbers of workers. The Social Security Administration reports that over half the men awarded initial retirement benefits each year since 1962 have received reduced benefits. Table 14 shows the rise in the proportion of new social security beneficiaries receiving reduced benefits. Over 70 percent of women and 60 percent of men do *not* receive full benefits.

Delayed Retirement   In 1939 the calculation of the social security pension was changed to include a 1 percent increase in benefits for each year that credited earnings were at least $200. "This provision thus gave an individual who postponed his retirement after 65 a larger benefit when he retired than if he began to draw his benefits at 65. This provision was the subject of much controversy and was repealed in the 1950 law so that higher current benefits could be paid without a cost increase" (Cohen, 1957).

In 1972 a provision was again added to social security that raised benefits for those who delayed retirement beyond age 65. Subsequent to the provision canceled in 1950, persons who continued to work beyond age 64 lost all pension benefits potentially available while they worked. The 1972 provision reduces the loss somewhat but does not totally eliminate it. For there to be no loss in the actuarial value of a worker's benefit would require that his benefit level be increased by about 9 percent a year, instead of the current 3 percent adjustment.

In 1983 Congress legislated future liberalizations in the delayed retirement credit. The credit will gradually rise from 3 to 8 percent over the 1990–2008 period.

The Retirement Test   The retirement test reduces or eliminates social security benefit payments if an otherwise eligible recipient has earnings above an exemption ceiling. Over the years officials of the Social Security Administration have acknowledged that this test generates the most questions and the most criticisms among people covered by the social security program. Further evi-

Table 14. New Social Security Worker Beneficiaries and the Proportion Receiving
Reduced, Early Retirement Benefits, 1968–1981

	Men		Women	
Year	Number (000s)	Early Retirement [a] %	Number (000s)	Early Retirement [a] %
1968	677	54	435	71
1969	691	53	449	71
1970	749	53	496	70
1971	752	57	507	73
1972	b	b		
1973	897	54	650	66
1974	766	63	606	69
1975	873	61	539	80
1976	808	66	569	77
1977	855	68	616	78
1978	754	70	578	77
1979	811	67	612	77
1980	850	65	621	76

Source: Table Q-3 published quarterly in the *Social Security Bulletin* (Washington, D.C.: U.S.
Government Printing Office).
[a]Reduced benefit awards currently payable as a percent of all awards moving to payment status
(currently payable regular awards plus those originally awarded as not currently payable that
moved to payment status).
[b]Data are not available.

dence of the controversy is that in every session of Congress since 1940, numerous bills have been introduced to eliminate or liberalize the test.

A past Advisory Council on Social Security (1975) gives the following rationale for the test:

> *The Council has reviewed the provisions of the retirement test and believes that
> the test is consistent with the basic purpose and principles of social security: to re-
> place, in part, earnings lost because of retirement in old age, disability, or death.
> Complete elimination of the retirement test is inadvisable.*
>
> *The retirement test has been criticized because it does not take into account a
> beneficiary's income from such nonwork sources as dividends, rent, or pension pay-
> ments. If the test took account of income other than earnings from work, it would
> no longer be a retirement test but an income test. If it became an income test, the
> fundamental idea that social security benefits are intended as partial replacement of
> earnings from work would be diluted or lost.*

While the reasoning advanced by the Advisory Council has also been the
official position of the Social Security Administration, it is important to recognize two other arguments that are frequently made in support of the test.*

First, since there are still many workers age 62 or older who do not receive
social security benefits and since most of them are working full time, repeal of
the retirement test would be relatively expensive and benefit most those who
need help the least. For example, about 93 percent of the increased benefits

---

*For a more detailed listing and discussion of arguments for and against the test, see
Schulz (1977) or Colberg (1978).

resulting from the liberalizations in the earnings test legislated in 1977 went to individuals at the top or in the middle of the earnings distribution (Esposito, Mallan and Dodoff, 1980).

Second, given the fact that relatively high rates of unemployment have been a frequent phenomenon in the American economy, the retirement test encourages older workers to retire and thereby opens up job opportunities for younger workers. Moreover, older workers with pensions are discouraged from competing for jobs with younger workers by offering their services at wages below prevailing levels.

The work-disincentive result of the retirement test arises principally from the fact that, in effect, earnings above the maximum are "taxed" at the relatively high rate of 50 percent. Studies have shown that some older workers have a strong aversion to loss of benefits at this tax rate (Campbell and Campbell, 1976). The effect of the test, therefore, is to discourage some workers from staying in the labor force and also to set a limit on part-time work activity so that earnings do not go beyond the maximum.

Whereas complete elimination of the retirement test would be costly and benefit many high earners, it can be argued alternatively that the test should be liberalized significantly to encourage and allow those people with low or moderate pension incomes to work in retirement. Various proposals have been advanced that would effectively exclude people with high earnings from the receipt of benefits but would not penalize low earners who wanted or needed to supplement their pension income. Complete *elimination* of the test is estimated to cost $6 or $7 billion in the first year (National Commission on Social Security, 1981), but substantial *liberalization*, while maintaining some earnings ceiling, could reduce the cost by 80 percent (Schulz, 1978).

The second argument—that older workers should retire to make room for younger workers—raises a number of very complex issues. Ideally, an appropriate mix of monetary and fiscal policy by the government could promote an expansionary economy with jobs for almost everyone—thereby avoiding the dilemma of the older versus younger worker trade-off. The problem that arises, however, is that as the economy approaches full employment, inflationary factors tend to push up the general level of prices. Economic policymakers are thus faced with the unpleasant trade-off of less employment to prevent more **inflation**. In addition to having to choose between inflation and unemployment (sometimes referred to as the problem of "fine tuning" the economy) there is the problem of the **recessions** and **depressions** that have occurred throughout the century. The result of these has been millions of unemployed workers.

The causes of downturns in the economy are varied. While it is generally agreed that increased economic sophistication now provides nations with the necessary tools to prevent or moderate economic instability, the application of this knowledge has been far from perfect. Given, then, the recurring instability and joblessness that have characterized the American economy, it is not surprising to find workers and unions supporting policies that promise to moderate the situation. The retirement test appears to be one policy that falls into this category.

In contrast, the recent aging of the population is a factor that may undermine future worker support for the retirement test. As the costs to the working population of providing pensions to a growing segment of the total population significantly increase, there is apt to be better recognition that there is a relatively high price tag associated with our present policies, which encourage or force people to retire. As indicated above, significantly liberalizing the test would probably encourage work without incurring the high costs of completely eliminating the test.

Responding to intense political pressure to completely abolish the test, Congress has instead retained it but has enacted three liberalizations:

1. Reduced the maximum effective age for the test from age 72 to 70, effective 1982
2. Increased the annual exempt amount to $6,000 (wage indexed upward in later years), effective 1982
3. Scheduled a reduction in the "take-back" rate from 50 to 33⅓ percent, effective 1990

Only one restrictive provision has been enacted in recent years. The 1977 social security amendments eliminated the monthly exemption test except for the first year of retirement. Under this monthly measure a beneficiary who did not earn over the specified monthly exemption, or render substantial services in self-employment in a month, received a benefit for that month *regardless of the level of his annual earnings.* Now only an annual test applies.

Survivors' Benefits   We are apt to forget that social security provides more than worker retirement pensions. Currently about 25 percent of the OASDI pensions being paid are to survivors and to disabled workers and their dependents—totaling about 9 million pensions in 1982.

When a worker protected by social security dies, a modest $255 lump sum payment is made to the surviving spouse (or if there is no spouse, to an eligible child). Qualifying widows, surviving divorced wives, children, and dependent parents are also paid monthly pensions. Conditions for receipt of a survivor's benefit vary considerably, depending on the relation of the relative to the deceased.

Probably the two most important categories are widows and children. A widow who was married to a fully insured worker for at least nine months and who has reached age 60 is entitled to a benefit of 100 percent of the worker's pension if payments begin at age 65 and a reduced benefit at an earlier age (71.5 percent at age 60). Benefits are subject to reduction if any earnings exceed the retirement test. Younger widows with eligible children, unmarried dependent children under age 18, and disabled children are entitled to a pension equal to 75 percent of the deceased's pension.*

Supreme Court decisions in 1975 and 1977 struck down provisions of the Social Security Act that prohibited men from receiving survivor benefits based on their wives' earnings. The number of widower benefits received by men

---

*Special benefits are available for disabled widows age 50 to 59.

remains relatively small. For example, in December 1980, for every widower receiving benefits there were 207 widow beneficiaries (Bondar, 1982). The main reason for the relatively small number of widower beneficiaries is that most men are entitled to higher benefits based on their own earnings records than the benefits based on the earnings of their wives.

The monetary value of survivors' benefits is often very large. Ball (1978b) reports, for example, that a male worker with median earnings in 1977 who dies at age 35—leaving a wife age 32 and two children age 3 and 5—"would have left his family the social security equivalent of an estate worth $129,265." And a study by Lucy Mallan (1975) found that if social security were omitted from the total 1971 income of widows under age 60 with children, the proportion with poverty incomes would double, rising from one-third to almost 60 percent.

Until recently one of the major factors resulting in low (and often inadequate) survivors' benefits has been the way earnings were indexed to calculate benefits. A survivor benefit was based on the amount of benefits that would have been payable to the deceased worker, as determined by applying a benefit formula to the worker's covered earnings. These earnings were indexed by a wage index reflecting the national wage trend. However, this wage indexing was applied to reflect nationwide wage increases only through the second year before the death of the worker. The benefit was calculated based on these wages and then indexed to take account of *only price changes in subsequent years.*

When the worker died long before retirement age, the benefit for which the widowed spouse ultimately became eligible in old age (or at disability) was based on outdated wages. Thus, the spouse who became widowed at a relatively young age but who did not become eligible for benefits for many years was deprived of the worker's unrealized earnings as well as the economy-wide wage increases that occurred after the worker's death.

The Social Security Amendments of 1983 changed this calculation procedure. Effective for newly eligible survivors after 1984, deferred survivors' benefits are wage indexed until the year the deceased worker would have been age 60. This will significantly increase benefits for many survivors.

Social Security Pension Reform

In recent years mounting criticism of the old age and survivors program has centered on five major issues:

1. The adequacy of benefits
2. Separating welfare from social security
3. The treatment of women
4. The retirement age
5. Financing current and future benefits

The last of these issues will be discussed in Chapter 6. In this section we discuss the other four.

Benefit Adequacy   Are benefits too low or too high? Until recently nearly everyone thought social security benefits were too low. A recent national survey by Peter D. Hart Associates Inc. (1979) for the National Commission on Social Security found "most Americans neither extremely satisfied nor totally dissatisfied with Social Security." The most frequent complaints, however, were about benefit levels. Although most respondents recognized that social security is intended to supplement other sources of retirement income, most felt that social security alone should provide enough income to meet retirees' basic needs and obligations.

Increasingly, however, arguments are made that social security benefits are now adequate—maybe even too large. The current controversy over benefit levels centers around the changes legislated by Congress in 1972.

Early in his first term (1969) President Nixon sent a message to Congress proposing changes in social security. The key recommendations were, first, a 10 percent increase in benefits; second, and more important, a proposal that the Consumer Price Index be used to adjust future benefits automatically and that a wage index be used to adjust the contribution and benefit base.

At the same time that the president proposed changes in social security, he proposed a welfare reform bill—the Family Assistance Act. The House Ways and Means Committee and the Senate Finance Committee held hearings that simultaneously considered both the social security and welfare reforms. The major focus of these hearings, however, was on welfare reform and not on social security. Therefore, most of the testimony did not even mention the social security proposals.

At about the same time the Social Security Advisory Council* reported. This council had been appointed in the early part of the first Nixon Administration, which had taken the position that aside from the changes recommended in its social security message, it would make no other legislative suggestions until the advisory council made its report. It argued that it would be premature for the administration to propose legislation while this very illustrious group, which was given the job of surveying the whole situation, was still deliberating.

This position, of course, set up expectations that something significant would come out of the council's report. Nothing did. The council looked at a number of incremental changes, mostly equity changes, and rejected most of the major benefit proposals people had made. Instead, an unusually large benefit increase (20 percent) was proposed by Senator Frank Church on the floor of the Senate and supported by the then powerful chairman of the House Ways and Means Committee, Wilbur Mills (at the time a presidential hopeful).

The council's only important recommendations were in the area of financing. The report argued strongly in favor of moving further toward a pay-as-you-go system (changing from a "three-year reserve" to a "one-year reserve") and strongly recommended that the actuarial assumptions for projecting benefit outlays and contributions be nonstatic—that is, assume that earnings levels will rise over time, that the contribution and benefit base will increase as earnings rise, and that benefits will be increased as prices rise. Both recommendations

---

*Under current law, a new council is appointed every four years. Its function is to review all aspects of the social security program and to recommend improvements.

facilitated the large benefit increases that were legislated, but the council itself never recommended the increases.

The increased benefit levels and indexing enacted in 1972 have caused some pension experts to argue that there is little need for future retirees to supplement social security. For example, Robert Ball, a former Commissioner of Social Security, writes: "At average wages, the [social security] replacement rate for the couple is approaching adequacy" (Ball, 1978a). Similar opinions have been voiced by other pension experts (see, for example, Bassett, 1978).

Perhaps the very strongest views on this point come from prominent conservative economist Martin Feldstein. Feldstein (1977) asserts that the high earnings replacement rates resulting at retirement from public and private pensions are "quite inappropriate for middle and higher income couples." Feldstein argues that retirement on social security now brings little decline in an average family's standard of living and that, furthermore, workers often receive additional income from private pensions. It is important to see how Feldstein reaches this debatable conclusion, since it is a view shared by others.

Feldstein and almost all recent discussants of social security reform focus on the replacement rate for a median (male) earner—that is, a hypothetical worker who earns the median annual wage *each year* of the working period. The social security benefit formula provides a retiring worker who has earned (each year) an amount equal to the median wage with a retirement benefit equal to about 46 percent of earnings just prior to retirement.* But if the worker has a nonworking spouse, the replacement rate jumps to almost 70 percent as a result of the additional spouse benefit. Given estimates that 65–75 percent of gross earnings for nonpoor families allows these families to maintain their living standards in retirement, we see that social security has the *potential* of providing most of the normal retirement needs for *these* average workers.

We then must add the contribution to retirement living of private pensions for those who are eligible. A study of 1979 **defined benefit plan** formulas (Schulz, Leavitt, Kelly, and Strate, 1982) indicates, for example, that these formulas often provide 25 percent earnings replacement for hypothetical long-service workers.

Combining the replacement rates from social security with those from private pensions raises the average pension replacement rate for the "average" one-worker couple to almost 100 percent. Can there be any doubt that we are overpensioning some workers today?

The truth is that the overpensioning characterization suffers from a number of major limitations. There is no doubt that severe economic deprivation faces far fewer retiring persons—at least as long as they stay well and avoid institutionalization. But the picture is not quite as rosy as the replacement rate percentages usually cited would suggest.

The statistic for median earnings before retirement selected by Feldstein and others for the hypothetical earnings calculations is an average for both

---

*This figure appears in almost all recent reports and publications discussing social security benefit levels and is based on methodology and estimates developed by the Office of the Actuary, Social Security Administration.

part-time and full-time workers at *all* stages of their earnings career (i.e., for all age groups). In estimating pension replacement adequacy, do we really want to use the earnings of men about thirty years of age as a measure of preretirement earnings for men *currently retiring*? That is what the statistic chosen is equivalent to. In contrast, men *close to retirement* have earnings that are much higher than the chosen statistic and, consequently, much lower replacement rates from social security.

In addition, the couple replacement rates of 70 percent (social security alone) and nearly 100 percent (with a private pension) are for a couple *with one worker, earning median wages, and retiring at age 65*. But not all those retiring fall into that particular category. To begin with, more than half of married women approaching retirement age are working in the labor force. The relevant replacement rates for many two-worker couples are very different from those for one worker; the higher earnings are not replaced proportionally by higher social security benefits. In fact, if the spouse doesn't earn enough to become entitled to a benefit greater than 50 percent of the other worker's benefit, there will be no increase in social security benefits. Thus, the pension replacement rate from social security for an "average" two-worker family will often be much lower.

An equally important consideration in the determination of actual (rather than potential) replacement rates is the age at retirement. The dramatic rise in the numbers of workers retiring before the retirement age of 65 has made early retirement almost the norm. Once again, because of the actuarial reduction provisions in social security (and reductions in most private pensions), the *actual* replacement rates of a great many retirees will be lower than the percentages originally cited.

While no individual is required to retire before age 65 and many retire early because they want to, numerous studies have shown that there is also a sizable group of early retirees without a meaningful option. These workers have little or no potential to engage in substantive employment activity because of poor health or structural unemployment problems.

Finally, as we discuss in Chapter 8, the private pension supplement that boosts the replacement rate for many is not available to all; many workers are never covered or lose pension credits before retiring. Failure to meet vesting requirements or plan terminations, for example, results in lost service credits for many workers, especially women (Thompson, 1978). Even those that are covered long enough to receive a pension do not achieve the long periods of service required for *large* private pension benefit amounts.

If we look at *actual* replacement rates for recently retiring workers we see how all these considerations affect pension adequacy levels. An important new study by Alan Fox (1982) provides estimates for couples, nonmarried men, and nonmarried women retiring over the 1968–1976 period. Fox calculates the proportion of after-tax earnings* replaced by pensions (also after taxes). The median replacement rate for social security benefits is only 43 percent for married

---

*Various definitions of earnings are used. The numbers reported here are based on "price-indexed estimated total earnings in the highest 3 years of the last 10."

Table 15. Total After-tax[a] Earnings Replacement Rates for
Social Security Recipients First Receiving Benefits in 1968–1976

Replacement Rate	Couples	Nonmarried Men	Nonmarried Women
0.1–19.9	1	1	0
20–39.9	18	32	18
40–59.9	44	44	50
60–79.9	27	14	21
80–99.9	7	4	6
100 or more	4	4	5
Total Percent[b]	100	100	100
Median	55	46	52

Source: Alan Fox, "Earnings Replacement Rates and Total Income: Findings from the Retirement History Study," *Social Security Bulletin* 45 (October 1982), Table 9.
[a]Includes federal, state, and local income taxes and FICA taxes, on both preretirement earnings and pension benefits.
[b]May not add to 100 percent due to rounding.

couples—in contrast to the 70 percent estimate by Feldstein. Even when private and government pension income is taken into account, replacement rates fall far below that level necessary to maintain living standards in retirement. Table 15 shows the replacement rates estimated by Fox using data from the U.S. Social Security Administration's Retirement History Survey. The data indicate that, despite improvements over the years, a gap still exists between the retirement income goals of most retirees and the benefits they get from social security. We will return to this issue in Chapter 8, when we discuss the role of private pensions.

Separating Welfare from Social Security   Pechman, Aaron, and Taussig argue in their book *Social Security—Perspectives for Reform* that the aged should be eligible for either an earnings-related pension or welfare payment—whichever is the greater. They argue further that the earnings-related pension should have a replacement rate that is roughly the same at all earnings levels between subsistence and the level of median earnings. They also recommend that there be no spouse benefits but that pensions be based on total family earnings instead.

The major point is that the social security system *should not operate both as a welfare system and a pension system.* If a person receives income in old age (including a social security pension) that places him in a taxable bracket, they feel that such a person should pay taxes (regardless of age). On the other hand, if the elderly person's income is too low, they argue, he should be eligible for a **negative income tax:**

> *The advantage of the dual system is its efficiency and flexibility. Either part of the system could be altered independently of the other. At present any effort to improve social security with respect to the income support function typically requires substantial improvements with respect to the earnings replacement function. For example, a program to raise minimum benefits to help the aged poor must in practice be*

joined with a general benefit increase, thereby making the cost of aiding the poor seem greater than it is. This is aggravated, of course, by the fact that the present system supplements income regardless of the income status of the beneficiaries. In many instances higher minimum benefits would be paid to individuals with adequate income. Under the proposed system the earnings related benefit could be set at any desired percentage of past earnings. Negative income tax allowances to those with low earnings histories would be sufficient to keep income above poverty level. Thus, policy makers and the public could identify immediately the cost of performing the two distinct functions of the system. [Pechman, Aaron, and Taussig, 1968]

The advantage Pechman, Aaron, and Taussig (and various other economists) see in separating the two issues is considered a drawback by others (see, for example, Brown, 1972, Chapter 4). Some writers in the field of income maintenance policy argue that when you separate the two groups (and hence make it very clear whom you're helping), it is very difficult to get sufficient political support for improving the situation of the poor. They argue that the only way one can get help for the poor is to piggyback it onto help for middle (and even upper) income groups. For example, one authority on social security, Wilbur Cohen, has argued that "in the United States, a program that deals only with the poor will end up being a poor program. There is every evidence that this is true. Ever since the Elizabethan Poor Law of 1601, programs only for the poor have been lousy, no good, *poor* programs. And a program that is only for the poor—one that has nothing in it for the middle income and the upper income— is, in the long run, a program the American public won't support. This is why I think we must try to find a way to link the interests of all classes in these programs" (Cohen and Friedman, 1972).

Another Brookings book by Alicia Munnell (1977) has updated the discussion of this issue and was the basis for a two-day social security conference in 1976. The conference gave major attention to whether the social adequacy function of social security should be reduced or transferred to the supplemental security income (SSI) program (described in Chapter 7). In addition to repeating the opposing arguments summarized above, there was general agreement that several serious problems had to be dealt with before SSI could assume a larger role.

Most conference participants felt that the SSI asset test was unreasonably stringent and needed a complete overhaul. Some participants pointed out that it would be difficult to reduce the current dollar-for-dollar SSI reduction for social security benefits (after a $20 **disregard**) to, say, 50 cents for each dollar so that low-wage workers would be insulated from a decline in retirement income as a result of a (more) proportional OASI formula. Supplementary state SSI programs in many, but not all, states would make it difficult to ensure uniformity of welfare programs in the face of large-scale changes in the relationship between OASI and SSI. And simply changing the federal SSI tax rate (i.e., the income offset rules) would not in itself be sufficient; state tax rates would also have to be changed. But that raises issues of state autonomy and whether states would be willing to bear the increased costs of the new program. Finally, a shift to an expanded SSI program would mean that more people would be subject to the much more stringent SSI earnings test. Munnell reports the conference viewpoint that "any attempt to encourage labor force participation of the elderly must take into account that with an expanded SSI program over 50 percent of the aged would be subject to the more stringent SSI test."

Still another approach to the matter is the "double-decker." The 1979 Social Security Advisory Council considered and rejected a double-decker social security plan. Under this plan each aged, disabled person, and surviving child would receive a flat grant of money (paid out of general revenue) that would be the same for all. In addition, as in the present system, a "second deck" benefit would be paid that was directly proportional to the past covered earnings of social security contributors. However, this second benefit would not be paid to dependents or survivors. (Variants of this type of plan are currently operating in Canada, New Zealand, and Scandinavia.)

In rejecting the plan on a split vote, the majority of the advisory council stated in their report that they believed the current system performed its functions well, and therefore there was "no need for the kind of radical changes embodied in the double-decker plan." Their specific objections to the plan included:

1. The resulting reduction of benefits for many dependents and survivors
2. Fear that the lower deck (financed out of general revenue) would not be adjusted over time for rising earnings and an eventual result would be lower benefits than under current law
3. The high costs of the lower deck and hence the large burden on general revenues
4. Fear that the lower deck would eventually be means tested
5. Coordination issues related to federal, state, and local pension plans

Four prominent members of the 1979 council (all economists) strongly supported the double-decker approach. They felt that the major objections raised by the majority of council members were attributable to the specific form of the double-decker they took as a model, rather than to the principles as such. In their supplementary statement to the report they argued that the double-decker (a) can effectively separate the adequacy and equity elements of the present system and permit separate adjustments of the two components, (b) would prevent high earners with limited coverage from qualifying for benefits on more favorable terms, (c) would reduce reliance on the means-tested SSI program, and (d) would help solve some of the adequacy and equity issues arising in connection with female and disabled workers.

Women and Social Security   There is widespread agreement that social security provisions related to women need to be reformed. As observed by Flowers (1977), "The social security benefit structure reflects a pattern of marital life and family obligations which is no longer typical in the United States." Benefits (and payments) are designed to provide family protection under an assumption that there are just two major family types: single workers and married couples consisting of lifelong paid workers and lifelong unpaid homemakers.

A number of important social trends have made that assumption increasingly unrealistic. First, female participation in the paid labor force has changed

Table 16.   Divorce Rates per 1,000 Population for Selected Countries, 1957–1975

Country	1957	1967	1975
United States	2.23	2.63	4.82
Sweden	1.20	1.36	3.14
U.S.S.R.	—	2.74	3.08
German Democratic Republic	1.33	1.66	2.47
Czechoslovakia	1.07	1.39	2.18
Finland	0.81	1.13	1.99
Canada	0.40	0.55	2.22
Federal Republic of Germany	0.77	1.05	1.73
Netherlands	0.48	0.59	1.47
Australia	0.65	0.82	1.76
Japan	0.79	0.84	1.08

Source: Extracted from United Nations, *Demographic Yearbook* (New York: United Nations, 1976 and 1977).

dramatically. Over half of the married women under age 60 are now in the labor force (Hayghe, 1978), and labor force participation for women age 25 to 54 is projected to rise even further—to about 70 percent in 1990. Moreover, increasing numbers of married women spend part of their lives solely as homemakers and another part in the paid labor force.

Second, there is a changing perception of roles within families. A government report (HEW Task Force on the Treatment of Women Under Social Security, 1978) describes these changes as follows:

> As more married women work and have broader employment opportunities, the homemaker role is more frequently viewed as a career choice in itself; the decision to have a spouse at home full-time is viewed as a conscious decision rather than a foregone conclusion. The idea that the homemaker role has economic value— though difficult to measure—is gaining acceptance. . . . Both the rising labor-force participation of married women and the changing perceptions of the homemaker role tend to lead toward a view of marriage as an interdependent relationship between spouses.

Third, there is a rapidly rising number of women who are divorced, separated, or widowed. Table 16 indicates that the United States has one of the highest divorce rates in the world. And there are currently about five widowed women for every widowed man in the United States (Lopata, 1977). Reporting on the economic consequences of families breaking up, the University of Michigan Survey Research Center's five-year study of American families found that "the economic status of former husbands improves while that of the former wives deteriorates" (Morgan et al., 1974). And almost half of women becoming widows find their income falling below the poverty line (Lopata, 1977).

In reaction to the many new issues that have emerged, increasing attention has been given to changing the way social security programs treat women. A number of other countries have already instituted major reforms, and many countries have legislative proposals actively under consideration. Canada, for example, has passed legislation at the federal level for a "child-rearing dropout" provision and "credit splitting" (both provisions are discussed below). While the former provision is not yet in effect, optional credit splitting at the time of a divorce is now available. Paltiel (1982) reports, however, that thus far very few people have utilized the option, despite widespread publicity concerning the provision.

In the United States, discussion has centered on three issues: the equity and adequacy of spouse and survivor benefits (see pp. 97 and 126), fairness of coverage of one-earner versus two-earner couples (see p. 126), and coverage of homemakers and divorced persons.

The first two issues are discussed in other parts of the book. With regard to homemakers, persons who stay out of the paid labor force to raise children or maintain a household currently accumulate no earnings credits for that period of their lives. If they later take a job outside the household, they find their average lifetime earnings depressed and hence receive lower social security benefits. Furthermore, American homemakers who do not work outside the home must depend entirely on the earnings records of their spouses for any social security benefits. Consequently, a divorce, disablement, or death *of a spouse* (especially in the early years) could result in the homemaker receiving very meager benefits or no benefits at all. Alternatively, the death or disability *of the homemaker* deprives the household of valuable services, but lack of homemaker coverage precludes any social security compensation.

Homemaker credits are used in several countries. In the United Kingdom, West Germany, and Japan, voluntary contributions by homemakers to the social security system are permitted. In Japan, where the system provides benefits in excess of the value of contributions paid, 80 percent of eligible homemakers participate (Lapkoff, 1981).

In the United States, several proposals have been introduced in Congress that would provide social security credits for people performing homemaker services in the family. A number of issues and problems have been raised in connection with these proposals, however. Disagreement arises over how these benefits will be financed: financing by general revenue, by a special earmarked tax, or by the covered person are all possibilities. Another issue is the difficulty in determining how much credit the homemaker should receive; suggestions range from having the Secretary of the Department of Health and Human Services determine the value to using the median wage for all paid workers (or all women workers). Other issues are who would be eligible, and how proper reporting of homemaker services would be assured.

An alternative approach would divide social security earnings credits of married couples equally between spouses. Retirement credits could be split and credit given on three alternative occasions: (a) as the credits are earned, (b) only in case of a marriage dissolution, or (c) at the time of retirement or disability. This type of approach is referred to as "credit splitting" or "earnings sharing." Although earnings sharing is a new idea for social security, the concept has been in use for a long time in community property states.

Various earnings sharing proposals have been developed and evaluated. The National Commission on Social Security was the last government-appointed task force to carefully study this option.* They concluded that the most serious problem was the fact that most plans that have been proposed would lower benefits for a significant number of future beneficiaries, even for some whom the plan was designed to help:

> It was the sense of the Commission that changes which erode the adequacy of the system do not help women. The Commission concludes that such changes could not be supported unless the unintentional disadvantages could be remedied at a cost which was deemed reasonable. To be fair to some women at the cost of reducing the protection of others does not achieve fairness. [National Commission on Social Security, 1981]

Instead the Commission chose "to concentrate on the incremental improvements" that it considered most urgent. It proposed that the special minimum benefit for long-term, low-wage workers be changed to allow credit for up to 10 child care years and that the earnings of deceased workers be wage indexed for purposes of calculating survivor benefits. The latter recommendation was legislated in 1983 (see p. 102). A bill which allowed up to two additional years to be dropped from the earnings history of persons leaving the work force to care for a child under 3 was passed by the Senate in the same year. The provision was dropped, however, in the conference agreement between the House and Senate.

The Social Security Retirement Age   Currently age 65 is when workers can retire and receive an *unreduced* retirement benefit. Over the years, however, there has been increasing support for raising the age. Increasing the retirement age around the turn of the century was recommended by three major commissions: in 1981 by the National Commission on Social Security and the President's Commission on Pension Policy and in 1983 by the National Commission on Social Security Reform.

The major reasons given to support this change are:

1. Americans are living longer and many are healthier.
2. Older workers will be in greater demand in future years.
3. Rising pension costs (especially in the next century) can be partially offset by reversing the trend toward earlier retirement.

Those arguing against an increase in the social security retirement age argue:

1. While life expectancy in later life is increasing, there is no evidence that general health and ability to work at later ages is improving.
2. A large proportion of people retire involuntarily (due to poor health, obsolete skills, and lack of job opportunities) and will not be able to respond to changes in social security by working longer.
3. The presumption that the economy in the future will be unable to support retirement at the current age is questionable.

It seems clear that the predominant factor that has motivated those favoring an increase in the age is a desire to reduce the long-run costs of social security retirement pensions. Faced with a serious shortfall in social security funds in

---

*The social security amendments of 1983 called for a report by July 1, 1984 on the impact of earnings sharing proposals, recommendations for implementation, and estimates of cost.

the short run and large projected deficits beginning around the year 2010, Congress began an urgent search for ways to bring the system into financial balance. One part of the solution voted by Congress in 1983 was an increase in the retirement age. Under the new law, future workers will have to be age 67 before receiving a full benefit. Individuals will still be able to retire as early as age 62 but will suffer a 30 percent reduction in their benefits. The change is scheduled to occur gradually, not beginning until 1999 and achieving its full impact in 2027.

Because this provision of the law is not scheduled to go into effect for many years, proponents and opponents alike see the intervening period as providing an opportunity for careful study of the consequences of the change. In fact, the 1983 legislation calls for a study and analysis of the law's implications "for those individuals affected by the change who, because they are engaging in physically demanding employment or because they are unable to extend their working careers for health reasons, may not benefit from improvements in longevity." And several members of Congress have filed bills to repeal the provision and have called for hearings on the issue.

Chapter Five Highlights

The Social Security Act passed in 1935 is considered a landmark in social legislation. This chapter—focusing on the old age and survivors' program—explained the major provisions and changing nature of the program as it has evolved over time:

1. Important changes in OASI have occurred with regard to coverage, benefit levels, eligibility ages, the retirement test, and indexing.
2. To reduce the number of people who would have to rely on needs-tested public assistance, Congress incorporated into OASI a large number of provisions that made it easy to qualify for benefits in the early years and raised the adequacy of benefits for low earners; critics today argue that these early decisions now raise serious issues of equity and cost.*
3. Despite increased benefit levels, there is still a large gap for most workers between OASI benefits and the income needed to maintain living standards in retirement.
4. The evolving roles of women in American society, widening life expectancy between men and women, and changing "marital" arrangements have all resulted in debate (but little action) on how best to reform social security with regard to its treatment of women.
5. One of the major policy issues of the next two decades is whether to increase the social security retirement age (now scheduled under law to begin rising in the year 1999).

Suggested Readings

Ball, Robert M. *Social Security Today and Tomorrow.* New York: Columbia University Press, 1978.

   A somewhat dated but very readable discussion of all major issues connected with social security.

*This point is discussed more extensively in the next chapter.

Burkhauser, Richard V., and Karen C. Holden. *A Challenge to Social Security: The Changing Roles of Women and Men in American Society.* New York: Academic Press, 1982.

    The best book to date on pensions and the treatment of men versus women.

Cohen, Wilbur, J., and Milton Friedman. *Social Security: Universal or Selective?* Rational Debate Seminars. Washington, D.C.: American Enterprise Institute, 1972.

    A debate between former HEW Secretary Cohen, who defends social security, and economist Friedman, who argues for its abolition.

Lubove, Roy. *The Struggle for Social Security, 1900–1935.* Cambridge, Mass.: Harvard University Press, 1968.

    An interpretive, historical analysis of the passage of the 1935 Social Security Act.

Munnell, Alicia H. *The Future of Social Security.* Washington, D.C.: The Brookings Institution, 1977.

    A good overview from an economist's viewpoint.

Rimlinger, Gaston. *Welfare Policy and Industrialization in Europe, America, and Russia.* New York: Wiley, 1971.

    A comparative analysis of the historical development of the social security systems in Germany, Russia, Great Britain, and the United States.

Schieber, Sylvester J. *Social Security: Perspectives on Preserving the System.* Washington, D.C.: Employee Benefit Research Institute, 1982.

    A comprehensive discussion of most aspects of social security.

Schorr, Alvin L. "Welfare Reform and Social Insurance." *Challenge* 20 (November–December 1977): 14–22.

    A leading spokesman against removal of the social adequacy function from OASDI presents his views on social security reform.

Tracy, Martin. "Removing the Earnings Test for Old-age Benefits in Canada: Impact on Labor Supply of Men Ages 65–69." *Aging and Work* 5 (1982): 181–190.

    This article examines the Canadian experience following the removal of the earnings test in 1975.

U.S. Social Security Administration. *Social Security Programs in the United States.* Washington, D.C.: U.S. Government Printing Office, various years.

    Describes the provisions of the OASDHI, unemployment insurance, workmen's compensation, temporary disability, and public assistance programs in the United States. It is revised periodically, so readers should make sure they have the most recent issue. At the time of this writing a new revision was scheduled for 1984.

Chapter Six

Social Security Financing: Who Pays? Who Should Pay?

In the article "The Young Pay for the Old," journalist Edwin L. Dale, Jr. (1973) wrote:

> A funny thing happened to your taxes on the way to 1973. Congress passed the biggest federal increase since the Korean war (and that one was temporary), and hardly anybody peeped except a few intellectuals. This was happening at the time of the "taxpayers' revolt" at federal, state, and local levels. . . .
>
> Before anyone wonders whether he missed some important news development, or has been somehow bamboozled, it is best to explain the mystery. The paradox is resolved in two words: social security . . . a $7 billion tax increase enacted in 1972 with scarcely a voice of protest.*

In 1977 Congress again found it necessary to schedule further increases in social security payroll taxes: "President Carter and Congress have a bear by the tail. Having decided . . . [in 1977] that the only way to rescue the social security system from bankruptcy was to raise an additional $227 billion in payroll taxes over the next ten years, they now have discovered—big surprise!—that this isn't very popular with the voters" (Rowen, 1978).

The 1978 report of the Social Security Trustees stated that the 1977 tax increase would "restore the financial soundness of the cash benefit program throughout the remainder of this century and into the early years of the next one." But by 1982 the balance of the OASI fund was less than the amount needed to pay benefits for the year, and interfund borrowing from the disability and health funds began. And in 1983 Congress had to pass another major social security financing package, including—for the first time—taxation of certain social security benefits.

For the public, one of the most important aspects of pension policy is the way these programs are financed; yet until recently there has been little controversy over these matters. Why suddenly has pension financing become front page news?

---

*© 1973 by the New York Times Company. Reprinted by permission.

Table 17.   Retirement Pension Expenditures, 1979

Type of Pension	Billions
OASI Benefits	$ 91
Private Pensions	32
Federal Employee Pension Benefits[a]	23
Veterans' Pensions and Compensation[a]	11
State and Local Government Pensions[a]	11
Railroad Retirement Benefits[a]	4
Total Benefits	$172

Source: Based on data in *Social Security Bulletin, Annual Statistical Supplement* (1981); Ann Kellman Bixby, "Social Welfare Expenditures, Fiscal Year 1979," *Social Security Bulletin* 44 (November 1981): 3–12; and Alicia Munnell, *The Economics of Private Pensions* (Washington, D.C.: The Brookings Institution, 1982).
[a]Data are for fiscal year.

Rising Pension Expenditures and Growing Controversy

Few people realize the magnitude of the expenditures involved in pension programs and hence the huge amount of funds that must be raised annually through taxes, worker "contributions," returns on pension reserves, and employer allocations for pension purposes. In 1979, $172 billion in pension benefits were paid to Americans (see Table 17). This amount, by way of comparison, was $54 billion *more* than national defense expenditures in the same year; almost 14 times the amount spent on "public assistance"; and more than the consumer population's expenditures that year on motor vehicles, gasoline, and oil. And in order to meet *future* expenditure obligations, 10,000 private, state, and local pension funds have amassed over $600 billion in financial assets (*Pension and Investment Age*, 1983).

In recent years there has been a sharp increase in criticisms of the techniques used to finance these pensions—especially those used for social security. Pension financing involves many complex issues, and, no doubt, part of the recent controversy arises because of the confusion and misunderstanding that generally prevail. Is the social security system bankrupt, as is frequently charged? Will younger workers get back less than they contribute to social security? Who pays for private pensions—the employer by tax-subsidized expense write-offs or the worker as a result of reduced take-home pay? Do public and private pension financing burdens fall disproportionately on the poor and treat racial minorities and women unfairly?

We will divide the discussion of social security financing into three broad aspects: (a) current social security financing practices and short-term versus long-term issues, (b) the equity of present practices, and (c) a review of various proposed changes in social security financing.

Financing Social Security

The OASDHI program is financed by a payroll tax that requires workers in covered employment (regardless of age) to pay a percentage of their earnings

Table 18.   Maximum Taxable Earnings
and Payroll Tax Rates, OASDI for Selected Years

Year	Maximum Taxable Earnings	Combined Payroll Tax Rate[a]
1937	$ 3,000	2%
1940	3,000	2
1950	3,000	3
1960	4,800	6
1965	4,800	7.25
1970	7,800	8.40
1975	14,100	9.90
1980	25,900	10.16
1983	35,700	10.16
1985	b	10.40[c]
1986–1987	b	11.40[c]
1988–1989	b	12.12[c]
1990 +	b	12.40[c]

Source: National Commission on Social Security Reform, *Actuarial Cost Estimates for OASDI and HI and for Various Possible Changes in OASDI and Historical Data for OASDI and HI* (Washington, D.C.: The Commission, 1982), and Social Security Amendments of 1983.
[a]The tax is split equally between employee and employer payments. The amount shown here combines the two. The health insurance tax is not included. Rates for the self-employed are different and not shown.
[b]The amount will be automatically determined by law on the basis of the annual increase in covered employment average earnings in prior years.
[c]As scheduled by the Social Security Amendments of 1983.

into the program and employers to pay an equivalent percentage based on their employees' earnings. In both cases the percentage paid is limited to the earnings of each employee up to a specified maximum. In the original legislation (and up to 1950) this maximum, called the *earnings base*, was $3,000. Between 1951 and 1972 the earnings base was increased periodically on an ad hoc basis. Then in 1972, legislation was passed that set the earnings base at $12,000 in 1974 and specified that the base was henceforth to rise *automatically* as average earnings rose. By 1984 the earnings base—through a combination of ad hoc and automatic increases—had reached $37,800.

Table 18 shows past and future increases in the payroll tax. As legislated by the Social Security Amendments of 1983, the OASDI combined tax is scheduled to reach 12.4 percent in 1990. An additional tax of slightly under 3 percent is imposed for the health insurance programs under social security.

It is important to understand that most of the revenues generated each year by these payroll taxes are used to pay benefits to nonworkers *in the same year*. Any surplus of revenue over expenditures is maintained as part of the reserves for future needs and is deposited in one of the four social security trust funds: OASI, Disability, Hospital Insurance, or Supplementary Medical Insurance. However, the size of these trust funds is never very large relative to future obligations.

Concerning reserves, J. Douglas Brown (1972) writes that "as originally enacted the old age insurance system would have accumulated in time a reserve of

$47 billion, more than the outstanding debt of the government in 1935." But before any benefits were actually paid by the new pension program, Congress quickly revised the contribution rates, postponing scheduled increases in the payroll tax. This action set the pattern for future financing action, with tax rates being set below the rates that would be appropriate for a private pension or insurance plan.

Over the years there has been considerable controversy over whether adequate financing of social insurance programs requires the accumulation of large financial reserves. Much of the discussion has centered on the extent to which public insurance programs require financing practices conforming to the traditional tenets of actuarial soundness associated with private insurance.

The term *actuarial soundness* refers to the ability of insurance programs to provide sufficient (i.e., legally obligated) payments to eligible recipients at the time they come due. A private insurance company, for example, must necessarily operate on the basis that it will not sell any new policies in the future. Therefore, it should always have sufficient funds on hand to meet its obligations for existing policyholders, even if they all surrender their policies at once. Similarly, private pension plans generally try to maintain reserve funds sufficient to meet current contracted obligations but, at the same time, often amortize (i.e., pay over a period of years, usually ten or more) the costs of unexpected new obligations and benefits provided for employee services rendered *before the pension plan began operation*.

There is now widely accepted agreement among pension specialists that social security programs do *not* require the accumulation of large amounts of reserves to be actuarially sound (see, for example, Myers, 1975). It is recognized that the taxing power of the government helps to guarantee the long-run financial integrity of such programs and that, unlike private insurance, it is appropriate to assume that the programs will operate indefinitely—with a consequent continuous flow of revenue. And perhaps more fundamentally, the fact that public insurance is usually compulsory and covers most of the population avoids the financing problems arising from a fluctuating number of participants.

This way of financing social security is known as the pay-as-you-go method. Benefits are paid to the current aged out of the payroll tax contributions of the current working population. In return, members of the working population know that they are promised benefits when they become eligible, financed out of the taxes of the future working population.

Thus, while OASDI reserves have increased in 32 out of 44 years (1937–1981), total reserves at the end of 1982 were equal to less than one year's disbursement. Given this small reserve, some people have argued erroneously that social security is a bankrupt program that does not have the money to pay its obligations. Without necessarily characterizing the situation as bankruptcy, others have seriously questioned the financial soundness of the program.

As we indicated above, the unfunded liability results in part from a decision by Congress not to operate a funded system (see Robertson, 1977). Part of the unfunded liability arises, however, from a related decision to grant significant pension benefits to persons reaching retirement age during the initial years of the program ("blanketing in"). To become eligible for social security benefits an individual must work a certain number of calendar quarters. Congress set the required quarters low for the older worker group, which resulted in their receiving benefits that far exceeded their few years of contributions.

Thus, ever since the social security system began, most retirees have received more benefits than they have paid in. New groups that were covered in the fifties and sixties also were granted these "windfall gains." And with liberalizations in the benefit structure, most retirees will also experience these gains—and for many years to come.

Why did Congress grant these generous (relative to payroll contributions) benefits for early participants in the system? First, because the early participants needed the benefits. Without them, a majority of the aged would have had incomes below the poverty level. Many had seen their lifetime savings disappear or decline dramatically during the Great Depression. Congress, aware of their economic plight, sought to ameliorate it without forcing people to confront the stigma of needs-tested public assistance.

Second, as we discussed in Chapter 5, Congress confronted by a nation with severe unemployment initially set benefit eligibility very low to encourage older workers to leave the labor force. And the periods of unemployment in the years that followed continued to encourage expanded coverage and liberal eligibility.

Finally, the growing social security coverage itself and the general economic growth of the post-World War II years resulted in surplus revenues for the system. These actual and projected surpluses made it politically and economically easy for Congress to be liberal with benefits.

The resulting policy—*not* to exclude persons with relatively few years of participation in the program and *not* to make them "pay their way"—was financed on a pay-as-you-go basis out of the rising earnings of the working population with only modest increases in taxes. But it has also added to the "unfunded" liabilities of the social security program.

In answer to critics of these nonfunding practices, five former secretaries of the Department of Health, Education, and Welfare and three former Social Security commissioners issued on February 10, 1975, a statement emphasizing why the government need not amass vast reserves to keep social security financially sound. In part, they argued:

> By earmarking the proceeds of social security taxes for the payment of benefits and depositing them in a trust fund for this purpose, by entitling the system insurance, by continuing actions to assure its financial soundness, and by innumerable pronouncements of congressional committees and individual spokesmen, Congress has made clear beyond question its pledge to the American people that the social security commitment will be honored. [*Ad Hoc Advisory Committee, 1975*]

Thus, we see that the main argument for nonfunding rests on the quality of the promise made by the government. To fulfill this promise requires that social security planning ensure that over the long run the flow of funds remains in a "satisfactory actuarial status." But what constitutes satisfactory actuarial status? An expert Panel on Social Security Financing—composed of economists and actuaries—argued that this means being able to predict with reasonable confidence (a) that future scheduled income and future scheduled outgo will be in harmony and (b) that future scheduled taxes required to support the program be within the limits of practical acceptability to the population paying the social security tax (U.S. Senate Committee on Finance, 1975).

Actuarial projections of future benefits and taxes are made annually by the Social Security Administration's Office of the Actuary. The projections and a general assessment of financial status are submitted in a report by the Social Security Board of Trustees to Congress each year. In the early years there was little concern expressed in these reports about any long-term financing problem. In the 1974 report, however, the actuarial projection forecast a significant actuarial deficit over the 75-year period 1974–2048. This projected deficit, higher than any previously forecasted, was *almost doubled one year later* when the trustees issued their 1975 report! This was the beginning of the concern about the serious financial problems that have plagued the system over the past decade.

Long-Term Financing The long-term financing concerns of the past decade have been the result of three major factors: (a) expanding pension expenditures, including costs arising from the automatic cost-of-living adjustment mechanisms legislated in 1972, (b) the post-World War II "baby boom," and (c) a dramatic decline in the birthrate.

In the early 1970s, long-term social security deficits were projected to increase dramatically. These increases were in large part related to the particular way social security changes in 1972 specified that pension benefits were to be automatically adjusted for inflation. Soon after this legislation was passed, various pension analysts demonstrated that the particular inflation adjustment mechanism used had the unintended effect of increasing the replacement rates of benefits for workers retiring in future years. The greater the rate of inflation, the greater the increase in real benefits, and hence the greater the future financial burden on social security.*

The result of what was generally acknowledged to be a mistake in indexing procedures was a dramatic change in *projected* benefits. The social security benefit structure promised (given forecasted inflation rates) to provide future generations of retiring workers with social security benefits that replaced much larger proportions of preretirement income than were originally intended. These replacement rates were projected to get bigger for successive cohorts of retiring workers. Thus, the replacement rates for some retirees in the twenty-first century were projected to be well above 100 percent of preretirement earnings.

Naturally, the cost of these rising benefit levels was also projected to rise. And, as a result, actuarial assessments of the financial status of the social security system (referred to at the end of the previous section) projected sharply rising system deficits in the next century and the need for greatly increased payroll tax levels.

*We do not present the relatively technical explanation for this result. Interested readers should see the monograph by Lawrence Thompson (1974).

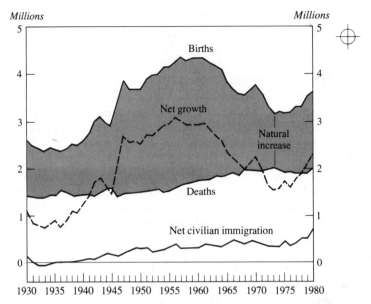

*Figure 16. Annual Levels of Births,
Deaths, Net Immigration, Net Growth, 1930–1976*

Source: Based on data in U.S. Bureau of the Census, "Estimates of the Population of the United States and Components of Change: 1940 to 1976," *Current Population Reports*, Series P–25, No. 706 (Washington, D.C.: U.S. Government Printing Office, 1977), Figure 1 and U.S. Bureau of the Census, "Population Profile of the United States: 1981," *Current Population Reports*, Series P–20, No. 374 (Washington, D.C.: U.S. Government Printing Office, 1982), Table 2–2.

Congress took action in 1977 to correct the indexing procedures and to roll back for future retirees most of the real benefit increases that had occurred over the five-year interim period as a result of the 1972 procedures. Thus, the projected deficits were significantly reduced by eliminating the unintended indexing increases. But the deficits were not eliminated, given two other key factors: the "baby boom" and declining fertility.

Figure 16 shows the number of births, deaths, and immigration during the 1930–1980 period. The steady rise in births after World War II (reaching a peak in 1957 at 4.3 million) will cause a rise in the retirement age population relative to the working age population. This will occur around the year 2010, when this baby boom population begins reaching old age. The drop in births in recent years causes the rise in the ratio to be even sharper, since the falling number of births reduces the number of persons who will be in the working population. The result is a large rise in social security retirement benefits that come due in the twenty-first century, without an increase in payroll tax revenues from workers, whose numbers will not be increasing.

Congress took major steps in 1983 toward eliminating the projected deficits of the next century. It passed legislation amending the Social Security Act that contained a number of provisions designed to have a positive impact on long-term financing. The most important was to impose for the first time federal income taxes on up to half of social security benefits for beneficiaries with income over a specified level. This provision will initially affect relatively few elderly persons, since most have "adjusted gross income" levels which, together with 50 percent of social security, fall below the specified level of $25,000 (an individual) or $32,000 (a married couple). Eventually, however, real and inflation-induced income increases will push a significant number of future elderly persons into the taxable range, since the initial legislation does not index the exemption level. One result will be more revenue for the system, since the 1983 amendments specified that this tax revenue be transferred to social security.*

Second, an eventual long-term financial impact will occur as a result of a legislated provision raising the social security normal retirement age (see p. 111). Unlike the taxing provision, however, the age increase is not scheduled to go into effect until late in this century.

Third, tax revenues will be increased significantly in the long run by mandatory coverage of nonprofit and new federal employees and an increase in the payroll tax for self-employed persons. In addition, a six-month delay in cost-of-living increases from July 1983 to January 1984 not only resulted in expenditure reductions in the short run but will also have a significant impact on outlays over the long run.

Despite the action taken in 1983, issues about long-term financing will continue to demand consideration. The lesson from our past experience is clear: unforeseen circumstances and constantly changing economic, political, and demographic considerations make it impossible to plan social security's financing future with any great certainty. As observed by Morrison (1982), for example, "as long as Social Security payments are financed by intergenerational transfers instead of by the contributions of the recipients themselves, the system will be vulnerable to demographic shifts—for example, unforeseen swings in future fertility—that legislation cannot fully anticipate."

What is also clear from past history, however, is that attention is constantly being given to the evolving finances of social security. The activities of various government groups (some mandated by law), numerous interest groups, academics, research institutions, and the Congress itself result in continuous monitoring of the situation.

Short-Term Financing Problems   In 1979 a survey by Louis Harris Associates (Johnson and Higgins, 1979) reported that more than four out of five workers did not have confidence that social security would be able to pay the benefits owed them when they retired. Perhaps more startling was the finding that about 40 percent had hardly any confidence at all that they would receive their entitlement.

These were startling statistics. But other surveys that followed the Harris survey produced similar results. What produced such anxiety with regard to

---

*The taxing of benefits is discussed again later in this chapter (see p. 133).

social security? Why does that anxiety continue today? Was it the projected long-term deficits discussed in the previous section?

Clearly media stories about the indexing problem in the 1970s and the specter of the baby boom generation eventually retiring have contributed to the anxiety many people have about the security of their promised social security benefits. It is probably the more immediate financing problems, however, that created the aura of crisis that has prevailed. Off and on over a period of ten years, the American public was told that the social security system was about to run out of money. If we want to understand the anxiety existing among Americans today, we must understand why social security finances over this period seemed to bumble along like those of a small corner grocery store on the verge of bankruptcy.

Starting in the mid-1970s, both high inflation and high unemployment rates rocked the country. As far as social security was concerned, there was both a decline in expected payroll taxes and an increase in benefit obligations. The result was unexpected funding deficits, with payment obligations exceeding revenue by billions of dollars. In 1975 a Social Security Administration study (Thompson and Van De Water) of these unexpected short-term deficits concluded that the deficits were "due almost entirely to [the] unforeseen adverse economic circumstances."

In later years the situation became even worse. The nation, during the late 1970s and early 1980s, was battered by poor economic conditions that were unprecedented in our postwar economic history. Along with double-digit inflation, record levels of agricultural and industrial bankruptcy, the near-destruction of whole industries, the agony of millions suffering long-term unemployment, and turmoil in financial markets, there were financial problems plaguing our pension programs. In fact, the pension problems were basically a result of the other problems. Social security reserves over this period continued to dip, despite various congressional actions.

As we discussed previously, social security, run on a pay-as-you-go basis, never accumulates more than a minimal amount of reserves. The reserves that accumulate are, in fact, there to be "nearly exhausted." That is, their function is to provide a cushion against adverse economic conditions that can never be fully and accurately anticipated by Congress and the actuaries who advise Congress. The terrible economic situation over this period was not anticipated, and hence the reserves were needed to meet the drains on the system.

While the short-term problems were real and serious, they were not unsolvable and were not a result of some basic flaw in social security's design. Yet many critics of social security seized on this situation to proclaim disaster and call for major changes in the system. Reacting to these critics, Henry Aaron (1981) argued, "It is intellectually dishonest, though it may be politically convenient, to use the short-run problems as the basis for making changes in the system that are more relevant to the long-run problem." In assessing the viability of social security in delivering promised benefits, it is important to keep the distinctions between short- and long-term development clearly in mind.

Financing Equity

Rising costs of social security now and in the future increase the importance of developing financing methods considered fair by the population. Our first question in assessing the equity of social security is: Who pays? In the United States the size of the payroll tax exceeds all other federal, state, and local types of taxes except the federal income tax. Thus, it is important to look at who pays the tax and the relationship between those taxes paid and the benefits ultimately received.

Who Pays?   Determining "tax incidence" or who ultimately bears the burden of any tax is one of the most complex issues in economics. Although the general population thinks it knows who pays taxes, economists disagree—especially about who actually bears the corporate income tax, sales taxes, and the property tax. Until recently, the payroll tax had received little attention from economists. Most people have assumed the worker bears the burden of *his* payroll contribution, but there has been great disagreement over the employer payments. A variety of recent economic studies indicate that most of the employer tax is ultimately paid by the worker in the form of wages that are lower than what they otherwise would have been (or, to a smaller extent, by consumers in the form of higher prices). In the most thorough study of the question to date, economist John A. Brittain's findings indicate that the worker generally bears all the tax. He found that given the level of productivity, the higher the employer payroll tax rate the lower the basic real wage—the wage rate being lower by the same amount as the payroll tax increase (Brittain, 1972). Not all economists, however, agree with the Brittain findings (see Feldstein, 1972, and Leuthold, 1975).

The payroll tax has been criticized as unfair by numerous people. There have been three major criticisms: (a) that the tax is regressive and a heavy burden on the poor, (b) that the tax is unfair to certain groups of beneficiaries, given the benefits they are likely to receive, and (c) that younger workers who are now paying taxes (and those who will pay in the future) are likely to get an unfair deal. We will examine each of these criticisms in turn.

First is the issue of a regressive tax structure and its impact on the poor. In general a regressive tax is one where the amount of tax paid is a *declining* proportion of income as incomes *increase*. Since the payroll tax is levied only on the "earnings base" and not on earnings above the maximum earnings ceiling, the tax is partly regressive. The proportion that contributions represent of total earnings falls *for earnings levels above the ceiling*.

During the 1950s and 1960s the maximum ceiling was low relative to average earnings. The proportion of total earnings in covered employment subject to the payroll tax fell from more than 90 percent during the early years of the program to a low of 71 percent in 1965. Thus, for example, in 1972, when the earnings base was $9,000, about one-quarter of the workers paying social security taxes had earnings that exceeded the maximum. With the significant increase and indexing of the earnings ceiling that began in 1973, the proportion of total earnings in covered employment had risen to over 90 percent.

What concerns many critics, however, is not the burden on workers with earnings near or above the maximum, but, rather, the tax burdens of low wage earners. The payroll tax contrasts sharply with the personal income tax, falling more heavily on persons with relatively low incomes. There are several reasons for this:

1. The maximum taxable earnings ceiling places a limit on the earnings subject to the payroll tax of high earners.
2. The payroll tax rate is constant, rather than increasing at higher income levels.
3. The payroll tax has no exemptions or deductions.
4. Income from interest, rents, and profits—the bulk of which is received by people in the higher income brackets—is not subject to the payroll tax.

Why should people with poverty-level incomes have to pay any taxes—including social security? The principal answer given by supporters of the current payroll tax is that the benefit structure of the program is heavily weighted in favor of low earners and that tampering with the tax structure threatens to turn the program into a welfare program—thereby undermining its general political acceptability. J. Douglas Brown (1973) in a memorandum sent to the U.S. Senate Special Committee on Aging gives some additional arguments:

> Overall, the advantages of uniform proportionate contributions toward one's social insurance protection are of great psychological, social and political importance. They clearly differentiate benefits as a matter of right from those available only on individual proof of need. They reflect a natural desire for self-reliance. They refute a criticism of dependency. They also are a factor in avoiding a class-conscious society in which some classes give and some classes get. Proportionate contributions are a force for political restraint in the evolution of a total system, both in respect to excessive demands for liberality in the benefit structure and the condoning of abuses in unwarranted payments.

Despite growing criticism, little change occurred in the payroll financing mechanisms until the 1980s. Beginning in 1984, a portion of social security cash benefits are taxed when total income of the recipient exceeds a specified level (see the discussion on p. 133).

Intergenerational Equity   From time to time people argue, and sometimes present calculations to show, that payments to social security by new entrants into the labor force will be much greater than the retirement benefits they can expect to receive subsequently. Such calculations almost always assume that currently legislated contribution rates and benefit levels will remain unchanged in the future, which is an unrealistic assumption.

A better way to investigate this question is to calculate **lifetime rate of return**. This method mathematically determines the rate of interest or rate of return implicitly earned on payroll tax contributions paid over a worker's lifetime. It is done by comparing the taxes paid (plus an imputed interest rate on them) to the benefits received during the entire retirement period. John Brittain, using 1966 tax and benefit levels, estimated projected yields for hypothetical *average* earners that ranged from about 3 to 6 percent, depending on assumptions with regard to economic growth, birth/mortality rates, the interest rate, and the age when entering the work force. Brittain (1972) concluded that "if the model and the official demographic projections are fairly realistic, new contributors will in the aggregate get neither a very good 'buy' nor a very bad one, but they will fare moderately well." Another study by Chen and Chu of 1974 retirees and entrants calculates similar lifetime rates of return. The rates for 1974 hypothetical retirees ranged from 6 to almost 17 percent. Entrants into the labor force in 1974 were estimated to have much lower rates of return, between 1 and 8 percent (Chen and Chu, 1974).

Both the Brittain and Chen/Chu studies calculate measures of individual equity for *hypothetical* case histories that are thought to be representative of the lifetime experience of various individuals. In contrast, Freiden, Leimer, and Hoffman (1976) calculate measures of individual equity for a sample of *actual* case histories. Using data from Social Security Administration records, they calculate rates of return for a sample of workers retiring between the years 1967 and 1970. Again, relatively large positive rates of return were found, with higher rates for those with histories of lower earnings.

Two recent studies provide additional findings in this area. Louise Russell (1982) finds that average rates of return on the payroll taxes paid by workers are positive for all cohorts (entering the labor force between 1960 and the year 2000) under a variety of alternative demographic and economic assumptions. In the most recent study of these issues, Pellechio and Goodfellow (1983) compare the worth of benefits relative to taxes paid by hypothetical workers who were age 25, 40, and 55 in 1983. Unlike earlier studies, Pellechio and Goodfellow are able to take into account the impact of the 1983 security amendments. Their study finds a substantial drop in gains from the system for younger generations, with many workers projected to receive benefits worth less than the payroll taxes they will pay. Aaron (1982), in a critique of an earlier but similar study by Pellechio, argues that "although their estimates are carefully prepared, they do not support the contention that social security is actually unfair, because they attach no value to important features of social security not available privately—such as complete indexing—and take no account of selling costs associated with virtually all private sector plans that provide similar benefits."

Thus we see that, just as in the case of who pays the payroll tax, determining the relative cost–benefit equity of social security is extremely difficult. The wide range of rates of return estimated by various researchers demonstrates the difficulty of giving an unequivocal answer to the question of whether social security is a "good buy"; results are highly sensitive to the assumptions made in the analysis. Also, these studies fail to include in the analysis the federal and state income tax treatment of social security contributions and benefits.

Brittain (1972), moreover, raises another question:

Why should one ask whether a person ultimately recoups in benefits the equivalent of his taxes when the same question is rarely asked about other taxes? . . . Since the taxes and later benefits assigned to a person are not at all closely related, as they are under private insurance, a strong case can be made for a completely separate analysis and evaluation of the tax and benefit structures on their own merits.

While many would agree with this point of view, others see social security taxes differently—as special earmarked taxes associated with a *compulsory* pension program, which necessitates analysis of who pays and who should pay.

Examination of the various findings, however, does help focus attention on possible differences between various population groups. Brittain, for example, notes that the wide spread in the rates of return indicates substantial income redistribution among categories of participants. For example, the college graduate who starts work at 22 may fare much better than the high school graduate who starts work at 18 if both earn the same average earnings over their respective work lives. Their social security benefits will be very similar, but the college graduate, entering the work force later, will pay less total payroll taxes over his career. Leimer (1979), however, cautions against giving too much weight to such hypothetical findings when evidence indicates that there are more offsetting factors in real life experiences (see p. 128).

Women and Social Security Financing   Certain specific groups have been singled out for attention by some critics of social security. The treatment of women has recently come under careful scrutiny.* In the financing area the most controversial issue has been the differential treatment of working and nonworking women. Currently, a spouse is entitled to a benefit equal to 50 percent of the working partner's pension—regardless of whether or not the spouse participates in the social security program. A spouse who works, however, may become eligible for a regular benefit on the basis of that work. In effect, the law stipulates that such a person can get only one benefit—50 percent of the spouse's pension or his or her own pension, whichever is larger.

An issue arising from this treatment of working spouses is the low rate of return on contributions of the spouse. A working wife may pay social security taxes toward retirement protection, but the resulting benefits of the family may be *no higher* if the spouse doesn't work a sufficient number of quarters to achieve eligibility. Moreover, because of anomalies in the benefit structure, a couple composed of two retired workers can receive lower total benefits than a couple with the same average lifetime earnings credits all earned by one spouse. For example, the annual 1979 benefit for a couple composed of two retired workers who each had average indexed earnings of $6,000 would be $3,173 each. In contrast, the benefit of a couple with one $12,000 earner would be $7,640—nearly $1,300 more annually than the two-earner couple (HEW Task Force, 1978).

---

*See, for example, the report of the Task Force on Women and Social Security listed in the Suggested Readings at the end of this chapter.

Although a working woman's retirement benefits may be little more or no more than a nonworking spouse's, she does receive certain protection under social security not available to a nonworking wife:

1. Disability protection
2. Benefits payable at or after age 62, even if her husband continues to work
3. Monthly benefits to her children if she becomes disabled or dies

As we discussed in Chapter 6, the economic role of women has been shifting over time (see also Kahne, 1975). As a result, a number of social security reform bills have been introduced in Congress over the years to deal with the working woman issue. Thus far, no legislation has been seriously considered. This and other matters, such as whether to have social security benefits for housewives, are likely to be hotly debated in the years to come. When the 1975 Advisory Council on Social Security recommended no major action in this area, Rita Campbell gave a dissenting opinion:

> It is my belief that because of the continuing trends in the increasing labor force participation rate of women, the declining labor force participation rate of men, the increase in divorce and decrease in marriages, and the decline in the birth rate, it is advisable to begin now to restructure the social security system to adapt to these socioeconomic changes rather than wait for dissatisfaction with the system to so increase as to force hurried changes which may be undesirable.

Differential Life Expectancies

Another issue that has been raised in relation to women, and also by various ethnic minority groups, is the extent to which differences in average **life expectancy** should be taken into account. Women, *on average*, tend to live longer than men; nonwhites, *on average*, have shorter life expectancies than whites. For benefit purposes, social security policy has largely ignored these or any other differences in life expectancies. Some private pensions, however, *have* paid differential pension benefits based on sex, causing certain women's organizations to challenge in the courts such differentials in benefits.

In contrast, some nonwhites argue that they *should* receive preferential social security benefits because of adverse life expectancy rates. For example, the 1971 White House Conference on Aging "special concerns session" on aged blacks recommended: "The minimum age-eligibility requirement for primary beneficiaries of Old Age, Survivors, Disability, and Health Insurance (OASDHI under social security) should be reduced by eight years for black males so as to erase existing racial inequities."

The average life expectancy *at birth* is different for whites versus nonwhites, in large part because of higher infant mortality rates for nonwhites, but differences in life expectancies at other ages are not nearly as great. At age 65, for example, there are almost no differences for men.

Ubadigbo Okonkwo has investigated "Intragenerational Equity Under Social Security" for subgroups of the United States population differentiated by race, marital status, education, and region of residence. Calculating "internal rates of return" by race, Okonkwo finds that returns are higher for all groups of nonwhite workers except nonwhite couples with 16 or more years of schooling. The highly favorable mortality experience of white female college graduates results in a more favorable internal rate of return for these couples. Okonkwo concludes:

> *In general, the progressivity of the social security benefit structure tended to redistribute lifetime earnings in favor of subgroups with low earnings, exemplified by nonwhites and workers with relatively few years of schooling. However, this redistributive effect was weakened, but not reversed, by the relatively smaller probabilities of survival experienced by these subgroups. [Okonkwo, 1975]*

Similar conclusions are reached by Leimer (1979). Specifically, Leimer examines the validity of the arguments made by some critics of social security that the disadvantaged (nonwhites, low earners, and women) get a poorer deal from social security (see, for example, Friedman, 1972; Aaron, 1977). Leimer uses the hypothetical worker approach; projected earnings streams for representative workers are based on cross-sectional age-earnings profiles derived from the 1973 Current Population Survey. Leimer's investigation suggests that in the future nonwhites, low earners, and women will generally fare better than their counterparts.

Prior hypothetical worker studies in this area have all found that entrants to the labor force at early ages have lower rates of return from social security because they contribute payroll taxes over a longer work life. Since going to college may delay entry into the labor force and result in higher lifetime earnings, most researchers have concluded that the actual impact of delayed entry into the labor force is very important. Leimer, however, analyzes data showing that workers with high ultimate education attainment have substantial earnings *during* the education period. This offsetting factor tends to reduce the importance of the delayed entry factor in actual case histories.

Viscusi (1979) in his book *Welfare of the Elderly* argues against public pension differentials based on life expectancy. He cites the widespread resentment that would probably be generated by an explicit set of different eligibility criteria or benefit levels. And he points out the administrative and practical difficulties in taking account of all differentials—smokers versus nonsmokers, drivers of safer cars, persons in occupations or industries with environmental settings that may affect health. Finally, he argues that these differentials are not as important as equalizing benefits per unit of need. "Once we accept the notion that the principal focus of Social Security should be on equalizing income for the periods one is alive, the need to adjust for differing lengths of lifetimes is not only unnecessary, but is also detrimental to this more fundamental objective."

Reform Proposals

Numerous proposals for changing the financing of social security have been put forth. This section will look at only four approaches: (a) the Buchanan proposal to change social security radically, (b) general revenue financing, (c) changing the payroll tax structure, and (d) taxing social security benefits.

*The Buchanan Proposal** Economists James Buchanan and Colin Campbell have written about the inequities they see arising from the social security system. In an article published in the *Wall Street Journal* they proposed that a new system of financing be devised that would, in effect, finance the "windfall gains benefits" of current and future social security recipients out of general revenue. Once this is done, they recommend that the payroll tax be set at a rate that would make it actuarially certain that the amount people paid into the program would equal, on average, the amount that is paid out to them.

In a later article Buchanan amplified the original proposal, calling for a radical change in the social security structure. The purpose of the proposed new program is "to embody the advantages of an intergenerational tax transfer program while at the same time incorporating most of the desirable features of a genuine insurance program" (Buchanan, 1968).

Buchanan refers to the advantages of an intergenerational tax transfer program. As originally described by economist Paul Samuelson (1958), there can be a "subsidy" in public social security programs that moves from one generation to the next as a result of population growth and economic growth. Buchanan seeks to establish a social security program that would embody that subsidy advantage but, at the same time, be more consistent with private insurance principles in terms of a *guaranteed* pension payoff based on law.

Buchanan proposes that the present payroll tax be repealed. In its place, individuals would be required to purchase "social insurance bonds." The pension benefits paid out at any particular time would be financed from revenues (purchases) of bonds sold during the same period.

Thus, when someone bought a bond for retirement, the purchase money would be immediately transferred to people who were currently retired. This would resemble the current practice of taking social security contributions and immediately paying them out to current social security pension recipients. If these bond revenues were insufficient to meet current benefit obligations, Buchanan proposes that general revenue financing be used to pay for the balance of benefits due. In this way, he argues, current bond purchasers would not be paying for the results of blanketing in certain groups (see p. 118) or for higher individual benefits that are not based on prior contributions.

If they wanted to, individuals would be allowed to buy more bonds than the compulsory amount. *In either case, however, individuals would be able to buy bonds from either private companies or government.* When the individual turns 65, the bonds mature, and he can then convert them into an annuity.

As far as the government bonds are concerned, Buchanan proposes that the return on them be the higher of either of the following: the interest rate on long-term U.S. Treasury bonds or the rate of growth of the nation's total economic output (gross national product). Thus, the private bonds—in order to compete—would have to promise (with a fair degree of certainty) a rate of return

---

*Three somewhat similar plans have been proposed: Browning (1973), Robertson (1981), and a plan proposed to the National Commission on Social Security Reform by economists Michael Boskin, L. Kotlikoff, and J. Shoven.

either better than the interest rate on long-term government bonds (if one didn't expect any growth in the economy) or equal to the rate of general economic growth.

Thus, Buchanan accepts the need for compulsory pension programs. He also agrees that there need not be reserve funding—accepting the validity of a nonfunded, pay-as-you-go government program. But he seeks to prevent inequities that occur as a result of combining benefits based on limited contributions ("blanketing-in" coverage and retroactive benefits) with benefits based strictly on contributions paid over a lifetime.

Buchanan tries to incorporate into the system an adjustment procedure that guarantees that the individual in the social security system will benefit from the general growth of the economy. Adjusting the bonds at the same rate as the changing gross national product also takes care of the problem of inflation, for this procedure will automatically adjust for general price increases in the economy. Thus, one would have both a price adjustment and a real growth adjustment factor built into the social security system.

Buchanan argues that such a program would have much wider acceptability than the current system because of its "individualization." The current system, he argues, is politically acceptable because people think of themselves as paying contributions to it and getting back benefits when they retire based upon *their* contributions. It is not a welfare system; it is a system of forced savings in the minds of most people. But Buchanan is worried that increasingly people will find this rationale unacceptable—given the current divergence between individuals' contributions and the amount paid back. He argues that future generations will be less and less certain that they're going to get their money's worth; they may lose faith in the system. The advantage of Buchanan's plan is that the individual gets his own piece of paper with a guaranteed rate of return. He argues that this is a much stronger guarantee than the *implicit* promise of benefits to be paid inherent in the current system.

Buchanan argues that his proposed program also insulates social security from political interference and from *excessive and inequitable* spending on the part of Congress. Congress would not be able to manipulate the system so easily, taking some from one population group and giving more to other groups. Instead, a straight one-to-one relationship would exist on an individual basis—just as in private insurance.

Some critics of the Buchanan proposal argue, however, that it is very important for a government pension program to be able to redistribute income. Indeed, many people think that it is quite justifiable to redistribute income through a social security program.

A more fundamental concern is that the proposal calls for a radical change. The current program has strong support both from a broad segment of the population and within Congress. It is questionable whether the Buchanan proposal would have any chance of acceptance because it is so completely different and does not build on what we have at present. The tendency is for legislation to develop incrementally, and major changes that are proposed still have to embody in some way prior legislation.

Apart from the political feasibility of such a major change, it is questionable whether the resulting gains obtained in equity are worth the great cost. There are major developmental, administrative, and information costs associated with a radical shift to this or a number of other completely new programs that have no established consumer acceptability or understanding.*

General Revenue Financing   Other people concerned about the financing of social security have also recommended the introduction of general government revenues to help support the costs. Like Buchanan, many of them see the blanketing in of large groups of persons during the initial years as a burden that need not be financed by the payroll tax. Unlike Buchanan, however, most people call for general revenue financing without abandoning the basic structure of the current social security system.

General revenue financing was first suggested by the Committee on Economic Security, a presidential committee whose recommendations formed the basis of the original Social Security Act. The idea was also supported by the first Advisory Council on Social Security in 1937–1938 and the one in 1947. Later advisory councils, however, did not see an immediate need for this additional source of financing or opposed general revenue financing as destructive of the insurance principles embodied in the program.

In 1944 Congress (over presidential veto) froze the payroll tax and authorized an appropriation from general revenue to the trust fund for "such additional sums as may be required to finance the benefits and payment under this title." Rather than representing an enthusiastic endorsement by Congress of the concept of general revenue financing, this action was really a by-product of the division in Congress over when and how large social security reserves should grow. Ignoring the 1947 Advisory Council on Social Security's recommendation for a "government contribution," both the House Committee on Ways and Means and the Senate Finance Committee in 1950 stated that the system "should be on a completely self-supporting basis," and Congress in that year repealed the general revenue provision.

Many who agree with the idea of general revenue financing favor restricting these payments to help meet the costs of "windfall benefits" (i.e., those given without contributions equal to the actuarial value of these benefits). In a working paper prepared for the U.S. Senate Special Committee on Aging, Nelson H. Cruikshank, as president of the National Council of Senior Citizens, presented such a proposal:

> *Workers already close to retirement age when the [social security] system was first started, or when coverage was extended to their employment, received full benefits even though the contributions they and their employers paid would finance only a small part of the benefit. While this was sound public policy and kept many old people off relief, it did mean that these benefits had to be financed from future contributions. There is no justification for expecting presently covered workers to pay for this "accrued liability"—estimated in the long run to amount to one-third of the total cost of the program—through a regressive payroll tax. A far fairer method*

*See Browning (1973) for a discussion of income distribution problems associated with the Buchanan plan and a proposed alternative.

would be to finance this share from general revenue sources to which all taxpayers contribute and through a more progressive tax structure. [U.S. Senate Special Committee on Aging, 1970]

During the debates leading up to the 1977 social security amendments, President Carter proposed an alternative mechanism: to limit general revenue contributions to the amount of social security revenues lost as a result of an unemployment rate in excess of 6 percent. When workers lose their jobs they (and their employers) do not pay payroll taxes on their behalf, causing a shortfall in projected revenues. Through this proposed mechanism, general revenue financing would not be open-ended but would be used only when economic activity falls significantly short of full employment levels. The proposal was not accepted by the Congress, however, when they considered the 1977 amendments.

As the costs of social security increase and the burden of low earners also rises, the pressures for change in this area have risen. The 1979 Advisory Council on Social Security, for example, unanimously recommended "that the time has come to finance some part of social security with nonpayroll tax revenues." Their suggestion: finance the hospital insurance program entirely through earmarked portions of the personal and corporation income taxes. Reporting soon after the advisory council, the National Commission on Social Security Reform also recommended general revenue financing for half of the hospital insurance program costs. In addition, it recommended a cap on future payroll tax rates of 18 percent (9 percent each for employees and employers), with general revenue making up the difference.

When the Congress developed its financing legislation in 1983, it did not adopt any provision to move the medical program toward general revenue financing. It did adopt, however, a more restrictive general revenue provision.* To help meet short-term funding short-falls, it authorized an immediate and one-time transfer of about $20 billion from general revenue to cover benefits that will be paid to veterans of World War II and the Korean War. Military personnel during this period were credited with tax contributions to social security that they did not actually make. This general transfer in effect accelerates payments from general revenue to cover these costs.

Thus, opposition to any major expansion of general revenue financing still seems to be strong in Congress. A variety of arguments have been raised against general revenue financing. The major ones are:

1. That it would encourage excessive increases in benefits
2. That it tends to integrate social security into the annual budget review process and to make social security more "political"
3. That it is contrary to the insurance and contributory principles of the program, which promote the political acceptability of social security
4. That it would turn social security into a welfare program, with an associated congressional and public decline in support

Changing the Payroll Tax Structure A variety of proposals have been made to change the payroll tax. The principal approach is to make the payroll

---

*The taxation of benefits legislated in 1983 may also be viewed as a kind of general revenue transfer (see p. 133).

tax rate progressive. One method is to provide individual lump-sum exemptions to the tax in the same way as exists in the current income tax law. The late union leader Walter Reuther, for example, proposed in 1967 a $600 exemption per earner. Other proposals would allow exemptions for dependents, and some propose a "standard deduction" amount equal to that in the federal income tax law.

Alternatively, it has been proposed that the payroll tax be integrated with the income tax. The present tax withholdings for both social security and income taxes would continue, but at the end of the year the total amounts collected would be added together and applied to satisfy the individual or couple's income tax liability. An excess of taxes over liability would be the basis for a tax refund. To accomplish this would require higher taxes.

Arguments against the above two proposals are similar to those against general revenue financing, but another type of reform proposal actually became law in 1975.

The 1975 Tax Act contained a one-year provision known as the "earned income credit" or "work bonus" for low-income workers *with children*. Under this provision, an eligible individual was allowed a tax credit equal to 10 percent of earned income up to $4,000 a year (a rough approximation of his or her combined payroll tax). The tax credit was reduced (till it reached zero at income levels of $8,000) by 10 percent of "adjusted gross income" (or, if greater, the earned income) that exceeded $4,000 per year.

The major justification for the amendment was to remove the work-disincentive effect of social security taxes on low-income workers. In 1975 this credit offset most of the total payroll taxes paid on earnings of $4,000 or less.

Again, some of the opposition to the work bonus amendment was based on its weifare character. Senator Sam J. Ervin, for example, charged in one floor debate over the credit that "it is robbery to take social security money and use it for welfare purposes." In addition, the Nixon Administration came out against an early version of the work bonus, arguing that the provision would create serious administrative problems and that it would complicate the development of sound income maintenance policy by "adding yet another program to the many present assistance programs." The Ford Administration, using similar arguments, also argued against the provision.

Despite this initial opposition, the earned income credit has been continuously renewed in all subsequent tax legislation. In fact, the 1978 tax "reform" law extended its application to the first $10,000 of earnings. However, the provision has still not been extended to workers without children, a liberalization recommended by many.

Taxing Social Security Benefits The 1979 Advisory Council on Social Security made a major recommendation designed to make social security financing more equitable. A majority of the council recommended including half of social security benefits as taxable income under the federal income tax:

> The . . . *tax treatment of social security was established at a time when both social security benefits and income tax rates were low. In 1941 the Bureau of Internal*

> *Revenue ruled that social security benefits were not taxable, most probably because they were viewed as a form of income similar to a gift or gratuity.*
>
> *The Council believes that this ruling was wrong when made and is wrong today. The right to social security benefits is derived from earnings in covered employment just as is the case with private pensions.* [*Advisory Council on Social Security, 1979*]

When the advisory council's recommendation was announced, there was an immediate outpouring of criticism from Congress. In less than two months, nine bills (one with 241 cosponsors) were introduced in the House to reaffirm tax exemption of benefits and within seven months resolutions opposing taxation were passed in both Houses.

With this history in mind, it is somewhat hard to believe that three years later Congress actually passed legislation to tax social security benefits. With a short-term financing crisis confronting it, Congress moved quickly on a group of recommendations proposed by a new commission, the National Commission on Social Security Reform, a commission that included key leaders of Congress in the social security area. Their recommendations included changes designed to deal with both short- and long-term financial problems.

The strategy developed by congressional leaders was to get Congress to vote on the changes as a package, allowing no amendments. As expressed by Ways and Means Chairman Dan Rostenkowski, "Voted on separately, very few of the controversial elements of our bill can survive. But taken together, the sacrifice they demand is fairly spread." Timothy Clark (1983) interprets what happened:

> *With a single-minded concentration rarely found on Capitol Hill, leaders of Congress pushed the legislation first through the House and then through the Senate. . . . Faced with the choice between legislation that appeared to distribute its painful burden evenly and the alternative of possible failure to agree on a substitute set of reforms, Congress was quick to grasp the former.*

Beginning in 1984, a portion of social security and railroad retirement benefits are included in taxable income. This provision applies, however, only to taxpayers whose "adjusted gross income," combined with 50 percent of their social security benefits, exceeds a base amount. The base is $25,000 for an individual, $32,000 for a married couple filing a joint return, and zero for married persons filing separate returns. The amount of benefits included in taxable income is the lesser of one-half of benefits or one-half of the excess of the taxpayers' combined income over the base amount. The proceeds from the taxation of benefits are transferred to the appropriate social security trust funds.

Chapter Six Highlights

Financing issues associated with social security are many and complex. Some of the major points we emphasized in this chapter were:

1. As social security expenditures grow, there is increased controversy over how to finance current and future benefits and the equity of various financing provisions.
2. It is important to distinguish between long-term financing problems arising from demographic factors and short-term problems resulting

from a pay-as-you-go financing system confronted by cyclical instability of an *unexpected* magnitude.

3. Researchers do not agree on the existence or extent of financing inequities related to younger workers, women, and/or minorities.

4. General revenue financing of a portion of social security continues to be looked upon unfavorably by Congress, but the historic opposition to taxing benefits collapsed in 1983 when Congress was confronted by a serious OASI financing crisis.

Suggested Readings

Aaron, Henry J. *Economic Effects of Social Security*. Washington, D.C.: The Brookings Institution, 1982.
> Chapter 6 contains a perceptive discussion of pension equity considerations and an assessment of prior studies.

Congressional Budget Office. *Financing Social Security: Issues and Options for the Long Run*. Washington, D.C.: CBO, 1982.
> A good overview of the issues.

Fisher, Paul. "The Social Security Crisis: An International Dilemma." *Aging and Work* 1 (Winter 1978): 1–14.
> Discusses the impact of the worldwide recession of the 1970s on social security financing in various countries. The study reports on action taken by countries in the areas of migrant ("guest") workers, unemployment insurance, early retirement policies, and financing schemes.

Munnell, Alicia H. "Is It Time to Start Taxing Social Security Benefits?" *New England Economic Review* (May/June 1982): 18–27.
> Written before taxation of benefits began, this article gives a good economic analysis of the issues involved.

Myers, Robert J. "Financial Status of the Social Security Program." *Social Security Bulletin* 46 (March 1983): 3–51.
> A detailed review of past and future financial operations.

Subcommittee on Fiscal Policy, U.S. Joint Economic Committee. "Issues in Financing Retirement Income," Paper No. 18 in *Studies in Public Welfare*. Washington, D.C.: U.S. Government Printing Office, 1974.
> The best available summary of the financial history of social security and the issues as they have been discussed over the years. It also contains a comprehensive bibliography of congressional documents, monographs, and journal articles on social security financing.

U.S. Senate Special Committee on Aging. *Women and Social Security: Adapting to a New Era*. A working paper prepared by the Task Force on Women and Social Security. Washington, D.C.: U.S. Government Printing Office, 1975.
> An excellent summary of the various issues, including a discussion of various proposed changes in women's benefits.

Chapter Seven

Health, Disability, and SSI Benefits

As is the case with pensions, the future of health care services and policy is being debated amid growing concern about government deficits and the growing financial burden of federal health programs. Medicare and Medicaid expenditures alone reached $64 billion in 1982 and are projected to reach about $75 billion in 1985. Many analysts now express the fear that health care costs are out of control.

On the other side are the elderly themselves who are confronted with the prospect of paying large amounts out-of-pocket despite existing government programs. Many health expenses (especially long-term care) still fall directly on the individual or his family. Thus, "the fear of a long and costly final illness haunts many old people. To end one's life as a ward of the state, or to drain the resources of one's children, is an all-too-frequent prospect for old persons in America" (Brown, 1972).

In this chapter, we look at the health care system for the elderly, how it is financed, and the problems remaining to be resolved. We also discuss two other important government programs—disability and SSI.

Medicaid and Medicare

Major legislation to help individuals meet health costs was passed in 1965: hospital insurance and supplementary medical insurance (collectively known as Medicare) and a medical assistance program (Medicaid). We will look first at Medicaid.

An amendment of the Social Security Act in 1950 had provided for federal financial participation in providing medical care to public assistance recipients, and in 1960 another amendment authorized additional federal matching for medical care payments for Old Age Assistance recipients. The Medicaid program, enacted in 1965 as Title XIX of the Social Security Act, greatly expanded beyond these prior actions the access of low-income people to health care.

Medicaid is not a program limited to aged persons. About 23 million people were eligible for Medicaid services in 1980. All states cover recipients of Aid to Families with Dependent Children (AFDC); about 30 percent cover all aged, blind, and disabled recipients of Supplemental Security Income (SSI); the other states limit coverage of SSI eligibles to persons who meet restrictive medical assistance standards. In addition, about two-thirds of the states cover medically needy persons who are aged, blind, disabled, or members of AFDC families ineligible for cash assistance but not able to afford medical services. Needy individuals excluded are single people who are neither aged nor disabled, couples without children, and in many states, two-parent families with children.

A wide measure of discretion is allowed states under the Medicaid legislation with regard to what income and asset means tests will be applied to various individuals. Consequently, actual practice among the states varies greatly.

Participating states are required to provide both inpatient and outpatient hospital services, skilled nursing home or home health care services, and physicians' services. Other services—such as drug therapy, dental care, and physical therapy—are provided at the option of the state.

Medicaid provides federal funds appropriated from general revenue to states establishing qualifying medical assistance programs. All states now participate. The federal cost-sharing ranges from 50 percent to 80 percent, based on a formula that varies the percentage in accordance with a state's per capita income. In the fiscal year 1980, expenditures were $15.6 billion from federal funds and $12.0 billion from the states.

The Medicare program is very different from Medicaid. It arose from three principal premises (National Commission on Social Security, 1981):

1. That the cost of medical care was not something that could be budgeted in preparing for retirement, because it varied greatly from time to time and from person to person. Therefore, insurance against this cost was necessary to retirement security.
2. That for most retired people, the premium cost of adequate health insurance was too high to pay out of retirement income or savings. Therefore, a new prepayment approach and government aid were required to make health insurance in retirement feasible.
3. That adequate and affordable private-sector health insurance was generally available only through group coverage. But retired people usually could not be brought together into groups suitable for such coverage.

The "hospital insurance" program (sometimes called Part A) provides benefits financed by *compulsory* payroll taxes and covers all persons age 65 or over entitled under either OASDI or the railroad retirement system and most disability beneficiaries under age 65.* Hospital insurance benefits are also available to *noninsured* persons who were over age 65 in July 1966 and to other persons age 65 and over who voluntarily enroll and pay a premium rate that meets the entire cost of their protection.

---

*Certain workers and their family members with kidney disease also receive benefits.

"Supplementary medical insurance" is a *voluntary* program financed by participant premiums ($12.20 per month in 1982) and a matching but much higher contribution ($37) by the federal government out of general revenue; with certain minor exceptions, any person age 65 or over in the United States can participate. It is often referred to as Part B.

The hospital insurance program provides a variety of hospital and post-hospital benefits (subject to certain deductible and cost-sharing charges). Reimbursement for services provided are made on a "reasonable cost basis" directly to hospitals, skilled nursing facilities, and home health service agencies. With regard to the major type of expenditure, hospitalization, an individual is entitled to inpatient hospital benefits for the first 90 days in a spell of illness and for an additional "lifetime reserve" of 60 days that can be used on an elective basis. In addition, 20 days of skilled nursing care are provided without cost to eligible persons for each spell of illness, and 80 days following are provided on a cost-sharing basis. Finally, certain home health services can be provided under a plan established by a doctor (while he is providing care to the individual). These services may include part-time or intermittent care by a visiting nurse or a physical, speech, or occupational therapist. Full-time nursing is not included, nor is such care as housekeeping, meal preparation, shopping, and so forth.

The supplementary medical insurance program covers certain nonhospital medical costs, primarily the cost of physician services. In general the program reimburses 80 percent of "reasonable charges" after an initial deductible of $75 per calendar year (with certain carry-over provisions). There are, however, two very different administrative procedures available for reimbursing covered services. If a doctor accepts "assignment" and therefore agrees to bill for no more than "reasonable charges," he is paid directly by the government (after taking into account any deductible and coinsurance). If the doctor does not accept assignment, the beneficiary must pay the doctor's actual charges, present an itemized bill from the doctor to the government, and be reimbursed on the basis of "reasonable charges" (which may be lower than the actual charges). In actuality, a great many doctors will not accept assignment—some because of strong personal views against dealing with government agencies and having fees "dictated" by them, others because it is the American Medical Association's recommended action, and still others because of alleged delays in receiving payments. In recent years the proportion of physicians accepting assignment has fallen from 85 percent to about 50 percent.

When it was enacted, Medicare was visualized as a fairly comprehensive program, comparable to the better private health insurance plans available. But as a result of rising health costs and increases in coinsurance payments, a large gap has developed between the costs of health care and the protection provided by Medicare. The program pays for about three-quarters of hospital bills, 55 percent of doctors' bills, and only 2 percent of nursing home bills. National statistics for 1981 show that Medicare accounts for about 45 percent of total health care spending by those age 65 and over. Another 19 percent is paid for by Medicaid (and other public programs). The rest—36 percent—comes from private health insurance and out-of-pocket payments by patients and their families.

Regarding the specific benefit provisions of Medicare and Medicaid, numerous reforms have been suggested. The fact remains, however, that since their enactment about 20 years ago, very little has changed.

Long-Term Care

The tragedy of old age is not the fact that each of us must grow old and die but that the process of doing so has been made unnecessarily and at times excruciatingly painful, humiliating, debilitating and isolating through insensitivity, ignorance and poverty. [Butler, 1975]

At no time are older persons more sensitive to the issue Robert Butler raises in the above quote than when they confront the issue of long-term care.

Probably one of the greatest fears of old age is what will happen at the onset of severe and chronic illness or loss of capacity. The independence of living arrangements and lifestyles so cherished by most Americans is threatened (and often lost) when physical and/or mental capacities diminish. In addition, as we explain below, the financial burden of dealing with this issue falls heavily upon the individual and his or her family. The costs of long-term care can wipe out the resources of all but the very rich. And finally, but certainly not least in importance, is the emotional strain placed upon individuals and their families in making decisions on how to meet the new medical, service, and financial demands.

Summarizing the current state of affairs, Callahan (1981) observes:

In long-term care we have the answer—a coordinated, comprehensive system of services which is case-managed and cost-effective. Now what is the question? There are a number of candidates: How can the cost of long-term care services be controlled? How can families be helped so that they do not give up caring for a disabled older person? How can an older person's functional abilities be maintained and/or enhanced? How can this country care for a growing population of very old women?

As Callahan also observes, there is one fact that seems relatively clear. The majority (but not all) older persons with severe health and physical limitations prefer to remain out of an institutional care facility if at all possible. Hence, the major effort over the past decade or so has been to develop alternatives to institutionalization.

Yet the fact is that at present our programs and policies are heavily biased toward institutional care. Most public money for long-term care currently goes for institutional care. And the inadequate availability of community care services (and restrictions under public programs in the use of those available) encourage overutilization of institutional options.

In addition to the problem of institutional bias, it is generally recognized that the following major long-term care problems exist (Callahan and Wallack, 1981):

1. The general quality of care is typically poor.
2. Services and financing are fragmented.
3. There remain large amounts of unmet needs and a geographic maldistribution of available benefits.

4. Costs have been rising rapidly and public expenditures are not under acceptable control.
5. There is an absence of adequate case management (i.e., no centralized mechanisms for information, referral, prescription, allocating resources, and so forth).
6. The current situation places heavy burdens on individuals and families.

As yet no consensus has emerged in the United States as to what action is appropriate to deal with these issues.

Long-Term Care Providers   Hospitals still provide a significant amount of long-term care to the aged. While most hospitals are designed for short-term stays, many (especially city and county hospitals) treat patients requiring more than 60 days of care. Also, while the numbers have declined significantly, many elderly still receive care in psychiatric hospitals and residential treatment centers.

The trend has been to move the elderly from hospitals and mental institutions into other care facilities. The most common option is use of nursing homes. Over the past few decades there has been phenomenal growth in the number of such facilities, most being occupied predominantly by older people. Currently about 1.5 million persons with chronic conditions reside in over 20,000 of these homes.

The growth of nursing homes is not the result of satisfaction with the services provided. The quality of care provided in many of these homes has been notoriously poor. For example, a 1978 government report cited the overuse of medications, the administration of drugs by untrained staff, the rarity of physician visits, and poor quality staffing with high turnover (U.S. HEW, 1978).

The average cost of care in a nursing home with skilled staff is over $20,000 per year. Medicaid pays for a little over 50 percent of all nursing home costs in the United States today. In order for individuals to become eligible for this financial help, however, they must first impoverish themselves. And all those who qualify must then give up all future income (except a small personal allowance) in order to help meet the costs of care.

Two alternatives to nursing homes for some people are day-care programs and home care. Day care is designed for people who do not require 24-hour institutional care and provides a protective environment and treatment as needed.

However, in many ways it is home care that is the most attractive option to institutionalization. Ideally, support for the elderly is provided in these programs by making available a wide range of community services to allow elderly persons to remain in their homes. Unfortunately, most publicly funded programs do not provide the full range of services needed; and, as with nursing homes, individuals are required to "spend down" almost all of their wealth in order to achieve eligibility for the services.

Finally, it is important to emphasize that over the years—and still today—it is the families of the chronically ill elderly who provide the largest amount of care. Currently over 3 million families provide major assistance to the impaired elderly living outside institutions; this includes physical, personal, and financial help. It has been estimated that "70 percent of the elderly rely mainly on relatives to meet their personal and physical care needs in case of disability rather than on agencies" (Morris and Youket, 1981).

Financing Health Care

Health costs and, consequently, program costs have risen rapidly over the years. In early 1983 the White House issued statistics to support President Reagan's "health care incentive reform proposal." "This year," said the fact sheet, "Medicare and Medicaid will spend more *every two weeks* than they did during the *entire year* of 1966, their first full year of operation" (White House, 1983).

In 1950 the average stay in a hospital was eight days at a cost to the hospital for the entire period of $127. In 1981 the average stay had declined slightly but the hospital cost had soared to $2,168. And the cost for some illnesses can be a great deal higher. For example, Roger Evans of the Battelle Human Affairs Research Centers estimates that currently it can cost about $80,000 to care for a person with end-stage cardiac disease (*Newsweek*, 29 August 1983). By 1982 the percent of our gross national product represented by health care services had risen to almost 11 percent, compared to 6 percent in 1965.

Not surprisingly a disproportionate share of health care services go to the elderly. The personal health care costs of older persons are between two and three times higher than what one would expect from aggregate statistics for people of all ages (Zook and Moore, 1980). Here again, however, differences among the elderly are important. Many of the aged are healthy and rarely use health care services, while others require extensive services. In fact, only 9 percent of the elderly account for 70 percent of all Medicare payments (for the aged), and 40 percent of the aged receive no Medicare reimbursed services in any particular year (Davis, 1982).

Medicare is financed by a payroll tax (currently 1.3 percent) for Part A expenses, payments by the federal government from general revenues to help finance Part B (and some transitional expenses connected with Part A), and co-insurance payments by eligible individuals for both Part A and Part B. The rising costs of the program are a result of four principal factors:

1. The general inflation in health care costs, with health costs rising much faster than the CPI
2. Increased number of persons receiving services
3. Expanding medical technology and increased utilization of expanding services
4. The high cost of institutionalization

In an attempt to deal with the resulting rising costs, Congress passed important legislation in 1983. The Social Security Amendments of 1983 specified a major change in the way the government pays claims for inpatient hospital services. Medicare now pays a fixed amount (determined in advance) for various expense categories. Hospitals must consider these reimbursements as payments in full and are prohibited from charging beneficiaries any additional amount, apart from any statutory deductible and coinsurance amount.

This new procedure was instituted in an attempt to reduce the costs of the hospital insurance program. Estimates in 1983 projected a saving of about $34 billion over the 1983–1999 period. Still, most policymakers in the health area agree additional changes will have to be made if health care costs are to be kept within reasonable limits.

Other Social Security Programs

In previous chapters we have referred to a number of programs other than health and retirement pensions that have an important impact on the economic welfare of the aged. It is appropriate at this point to discuss two of them, since they are important complements to health and pension programs.*

Disability   Over 16 million noninstitutionalized Americans between the ages of 20 and 64 have *limited ability to work* because of chronic health conditions and impairments. And more than three times that number suffer from one or more chronic health conditions. Approximately half the disabled (8 million) are unable either to work altogether or to work regularly (Krute and Burdette, 1978).

In general, whatever the degree of impairment, the chance of disability increases with age, as shown in Figure 17. The figure also shows how the prevalence of *total* disability rises sharply with age. Among persons age 20–34, total disability occurs at a rate of 22 per 1,000 population. The rate approximately doubles for each succeeding 10-year age group—reaching 190 per 1,000 for those 55–64.

The social security disability programs discussed below are only two of a great many disability programs; there are more than 85 public and private programs dealing with disability (Berkowitz, Johnson, and Murphy, 1976). Table 19 shows the growth of expenditures for the major programs. Coordination problems among these various programs create a number of adequacy and equity issues related to attempts to help physically impaired individuals.

Social security's Disability Insurance program (DI) and the Supplemental Security Income program (SSI)** provide benefits to people who have severe long-term disabilities. Disability protection under the DI program is currently provided to: (a) disabled insured workers and their dependents, (b) disabled widows and widowers of insured workers, and (c) the adult (18 or older) sons and daughters of insured disabled, retired, or deceased workers who become disabled before age 22.

Disability protection as part of Social Security was not legislated until 1956. Although it had been proposed repeatedly, major groups opposed it. Early social security advisory groups disagreed about the predictability of disability program costs and about whether one could administratively determine eligibility for this type of benefit (i.e., distinguish legitimate disability from malingering).

---

*Not discussed are unemployment insurance, the food stamp program, and special veterans' benefits.

**SSI is discussed in the last section of this chapter.

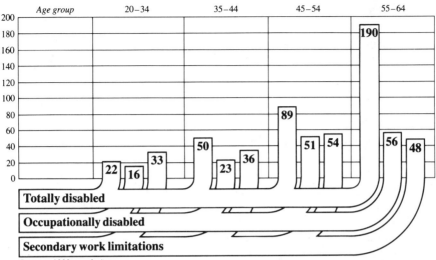

Figure 17. Disability by Age, 1972

Source: *Work Disability in the United States—A Chartbook* (Washington, D.C.: U.S. Government Printing Office, 1977).

Table 19.   Expenditures of Major Disability Programs: 1955, 1965, 1975, 1980

Program	Year			
	1955	1965	1975	1980
	(millions of dollars)			
Disability Insurance (DI)	0	1,573	8,414	14,899
Supplemental Security Income				
State	0	0	70	100[a]
Federal	135	417	3,072	4,912
Workers' Compensation				
Disabled and Dependents'	521	1,074	3,205	n.a.[b]
Survivor	70	140	360	n.a.
Hospital and Medical Care	325	600	2,030	n.a.
Black Lung				
Social Security Administration	0	0	948	1,032
Department of Labor	0	0	9	808[a]
Veterans' Programs	1,982	3,026	5,583	8,100[a]
Railroad Disability Programs	155	190	451	650[a]
Government Employee Disability Programs	355	751	2,702	5,000[a]
Vocational Rehabilitation	42	211	1,036	99
Rehabilitation Services (DI)	0	0	91	n.a.
Medicaid	0	0	14,177	n.a.
Medicare	0	0	14,781	n.a.
Total	3,564	7,982	56,927	n.a.

Source: Based on Richard V. Burkhauser and Robert H. Haveman. *Disability and Work: The Economics of American Policy* (Baltimore: The Johns Hopkins University Press, 1982), Table 3.1. Used by permission of Johns Hopkins University Press.
[a]Estimated by Burkhauser and Haveman from incomplete data.
[b]Not available.

When the first major legislative proposals for disability protection were debated in 1949 and 1950, strong criticism and opposition were voiced by the American Medical Association, the United States Chamber of Commerce, the National Manufacturers Association, and representatives of private insurance organizations. After the defeat of the 1949–1950 bill, strong opposition continued in succeeding years to the various new proposals that were introduced—including the disability freeze amendment of 1954* and the social security disability benefits finally legislated in 1956. All the disability proposals were attacked as potentially costly, difficult to administer, and the beginning of "socialized medicine." Given this strong opposition over the years, the ultimate passage of disability legislation in 1956 is viewed by many as a major development in the legislative history of social security in the United States.

Some historical perspective is important in understanding the current problems and criticisms of inadequacy surrounding the DI program. The strong opposition of major groups to the program and fears about administering the program (discussed above) influenced Congress to severely restrict the scope of the program passed in 1956. Key features of the original program that reflected these concerns were:

1. Establishment of not one but three different tests of insured status
2. A very narrow and severe definition of disability
3. Benefits unavailable to anyone under age 50 or for any dependents
4. A separate trust fund created to help monitor program costs
5. Vocational rehabilitation mechanisms created to move people off the disability rolls

The costs of the program in the early 1960s, however, proved to be much lower than had been anticipated, encouraging an immediate liberalization of the program. Expenditures then began to grow faster than revenue by the mid-1960s. In response, Congress tightened the definition of disability in 1968. Even under the revised definition, however, claims mushroomed, with the number of disability beneficiaries tripling between 1965 and 1978 to a total of about 5 million disabled workers and their eligible dependents.

During the same period, the costs of the program grew from $1.5 billion in 1965 to $11 billion in 1977. If not for a legislative reallocation in 1977 of OASDHI payroll tax revenues—less to the retirement (OASI) and health (HI) programs and more to disability (DI)—the disability program would have exhausted its reserves and been faced with a financial crisis. While some part of the increased costs resulted from program maturation (i.e., more workers meeting the years-of-coverage requirements), much of the increase came from unanticipated increases in claims (Cardwell, 1976).

DI's financial problems in the 1970s caused policymakers to take a long, hard look at the program. The result was legislation passed in three different

*A provision that prevented periods of disability from reducing or wiping out retirement and survivors' benefits by "freezing" the individual's rights at the time of disablement. For a good discussion of the legislative history of this and other disability provisions, see Cohen (1957, Chapter 4).

years (1977, 1980, and 1981) that was designed to address the financial problems of the program and, at the same time, to improve its operation.

Currently the financial condition of the program is satisfactory. The number of disabled-worker beneficiaries *peaked* in 1978 at 2.9 million and then began to fall—by the end of 1982 standing at 2.6 million (or 10 percent below the 1978 level).

As stated above, multiple tests of insured status were built into the disability laws. To be eligible for social security disability payments a worker must be screened on three levels: (a) determination of insured status, (b) assessment of physical condition and level of functional impairment, and (c) determination of ability to work. To achieve insured status, the worker must have 1 quarter of work coverage credit for each year since 1950 (or since age 21, if later) and 20 quarters of coverage during the 40-quarter period prior to disability. Disability, for purposes of benefit entitlement, is defined as "inability to engage in any substantial gainful activity by reason of any medically determinable physical or mental impairment which can be expected to result in death or which has lasted or can be expected to last for a continuous period of not less than 12 months." This strict disability definition excludes many people with relatively severe incapacities. Surveys find that two-thirds of the self-described severely disabled do not receive social security disability payments (Van De Water, 1979).

The DI program is administered under a unique federal–state partnership; program administration is carried out by each state and is paid for by the federal government under negotiated agreements. The determination of an applicant's disability is by a state agency whose primary function is to develop medical, vocational, and other necessary evidence, evaluate it, and then make a decision. The principal reason for establishing the federal–state relationship was that it was deemed essential that the disability program be linked with an effective vocational rehabilitation program in each state. But because of the extremely small number of workers rehabilitated (only 20,000 over the 1967–1976 period), some now argue that the principal reason for having the federal–state arrangement is no longer completely valid and that the relationship should be modified. After a review of the disability program, the U.S. General Accounting Office, for example, recommended in 1978 that the disability determination process be brought under complete federal management (Ahart, 1978). Congress, instead, passed legislation in 1980 requiring the Secretary of Health and Human Services to enter into new agreements with each state. Each agreement requires states to follow performance standards and administrative requirements issued by the secretary.

Like retirement benefits, the disability pension is based on average indexed earnings (excluding the disablement period) and is calculated using the same formula and the same minimum benefit level. Initially the social security disability benefit was reduced dollar-for-dollar by any workmen's compensation benefits received by the same worker. Then in 1958 this deduction was removed and considerable controversy followed. Turnbull, Williams, and Cheit (1967) report that with the deduction removed, "it became possible in some states for a seriously injured worker to receive combined benefits that would exceed his wages prior to his disability." Faced with the criticisms of those who feared the encroachment and possible supplantation of federal disability insurance for state and private programs, Congress reintroduced an offset provision in 1965. However, controversy continued to arise over the issue of program coordination and how to "cap" the benefit level. The most recent action related to this issue occurred in 1981 when Congress passed a disability "Megacap." The new provision specified that a person's disability benefits (including any benefits for the spouse or children) were to be reduced (if necessary) so that the sum of all benefits payable under certain federal, state, and local public programs do not exceed 80 percent of the person's average current earnings (a concept defined in the law). The intent of Congress in passing this new provision was to reduce the overlapping and duplication of public disability programs and to avoid work disincentives arising out of the old law.

The Supplemental Security Income Program   A new cash-assistance program for the needy aged, blind, and disabled went into operation at the beginning of 1974. This Supplemental Security Income program (SSI) replaced federal grants to three programs: the state-administered programs of old age assistance, aid to the blind, and aid to the permanently and totally disabled. The SSI program is administered by the federal government and financed from general revenues. It establishes uniform eligibility requirements and benefits levels for the whole nation. In addition, states are encouraged (and some are required) to supplement the federal benefits with their own payments. In cases where they do, the states have the option of administering the supplementary payments themselves or contracting with the federal government.

Eligibility for this program requires meeting both an income and an assets test. Nonexcluded assets may not exceed $1,500 for an individual and $2,250 for a couple. The major assets excluded from the test are (a) the value of a home, (b) the value of household goods and personal effects up to $2,000, (c) an automobile (up to $4,500), and (d) life insurance (cash surrender value up to $1,500).

Congress increased SSI benefits in 1983, in part as a way of offsetting the six-month delay in benefit cost of living increases legislated at the same time. As of July 1, 1983, SSI guaranteed recipients a monthly income of $304.30 ($3,652 per year) if single and $456.40 ($5,477 per year) if a couple.

These guarantee levels are adjusted yearly for inflation, beginning in January, 1984. Benefits are reduced by 100 percent of all *unearned* income and by 50 percent of *earned* income above certain "disregards." Unearned income of $20 per month is disregarded, and an individual can also earn up to $65 per month before benefits are reduced.

There are now about 3.8 million people (1983) receiving SSI payments. Surprisingly, more than half of these recipients are disabled persons—not aged. The number of aged participating in the program has declined over time—down from 2.3 million in 1975 to 1.5 million in 1983. Total expenditures totaled a little over $9 billion in 1983.

When SSI was legislated, its supporters argued that it would reduce many of the traditional problems associated with other programs to help the poor—that it would produce more efficient program administration, less stigma to recipients, and more adequate benefits using a national standard. During the first years of the program the Social Security Administration had difficulty coping with the new responsibilities and the additional workload suddenly thrust upon it as the chief administrator of the new program. In 1977, three years after its operations began, the SSI program was described by the U.S. Senate Committee on Finance staff as follows: "The early months of the program were characterized by near total administrative breakdown, primarily as a result of insufficient and inaccurate planning and inadequate resources. The crisis stage has passed, and steady improvements in administrative capabilities are taking place" (U.S. Senate Committee on Finance, 1975).

An analysis (Schieber, 1978) of the first year of program operations indicated that comparatively few people were moved out of poverty by SSI; but most of the individuals transferred into SSI from abolished programs did experience an increase in income levels (after adjusting for general price increases). As intended, the greatest income increases accrued to persons who had been the poorest before SSI was implemented.

A major question has arisen because of the low participation level of eligible persons in the SSI program. *The Social Security Administration estimates that 30–35 percent of the aged eligible for SSI do not participate in the program.* Findings from a study (Drazaga et al., 1982) investigating nonparticipation indicate that the two key reasons why many aged do not participate are lack of knowledge about it and stigma.

The study found that 45 percent of nonparticipants had not even heard of the SSI program. But large numbers of those who knew of SSI still did not participate, indicating a reluctance to become involved in a means-tested program.

That some people are reluctant to participate in a means-tested program is illustrated by a surprising occurrence arising out of a recent Social Security (SSA) study of nonparticipation. After the study was completed, SSA sent a letter to about 300 of the nonparticipants in the study. The letter stated that the individuals might be eligible for SSI payments and encouraged them to contact their local SSA office. But even personal letters from SSA did not substantially increase participation. Only about 10 out of the 300 individuals contacted subsequently applied for and received payments! Thus, while an earlier study by Tissue (1978) indicates that most SSI *participants* do not find SSI stigmatizing, there seems to be a significant minority of nonparticipants who do and never apply.

Another major issue associated with SSI is the asset test. Studies show that most low-income elderly have few assets (see, for example, Friedman and Sjogren, 1981). Yet the asset test for SSI is so stringent that some people with inadequate incomes are denied assistance because of small amounts of savings and other resources. The National Commission on Social Security (1981) reported that in 1977 approximately 58 percent of applicants were denied SSI payments due to excess resources but had savings averaging only $2,834. This average slightly exceeds the asset test, but as the commission points out, a savings account of that amount "would earn annual interest of less than $250."

The commission recommended in its final report that the asset test be eliminated. They argued that this action would simplify program administration, while providing SSI to many more needy persons. Various other groups studying the program have made a number of other recommendations for improving SSI, but thus far Congress has not changed the program significantly from the original provisions legislated in 1972.

Chapter Seven Highlights

The programs discussed in this chapter complement the retirement pension programs providing the bulk of income for older persons no longer working. Some important points to remember:

1. The cost of health care services for the elderly is now a major item in the federal budget and is growing rapidly—many say too rapidly.
2. Families in the United States remain the major providers of long-term care to chronically ill elderly persons, providing about 70 percent of personal and physical care needs.
3. Because of strong opposition (in the past and currently) to government disability programs, the disability programs under social security determine participant eligibility using a very narrow and severe definition of disability that excludes many people with relatively severe incapacities.
4. SSI is a means-tested program designed to provide needy aged, blind, and disabled persons throughout the fifty states a more uniform minimum income level.

Suggested Readings

Arling, Greg, and W. J. McAuley. "The Feasibility of Public Payments for Family Caregiving." *The Gerontologist* 23 (June 1983): 300–306.
    A paper dealing with the issue of how to encourage and support family caregiving.
Burkhauser, Richard V., and Robert H. Haveman. *Disability and Work: The Economics of American Policy*. Baltimore: The Johns Hopkins University Press, 1982.
    An up-to-date discussion of disability issues.
Callahan, James J., and Stanley S. Wallack. *Reforming the Long-Term Care System*. Lexington, Mass.: Lexington Books, D. C. Heath, 1981.
    This study explores major options for financing and organizing long-term care: block grant, national long-term care insurance, disability allowances, case management, and the social/health maintenance organization.
Grimaldi, Paul L. *Supplemental Security Income*. Washington, D.C.: American Enterprise Institute, 1980.
    A careful review and analysis of SSI issues.
Lando, Mordechai, A. V. Farley, and M. A. Brown. "Recent Trends in the Social Security Disability Insurance Program." *Social Security Bulletin* 45 (August 1982): 3–14.
Shanas, Ethel, and G. L. Maddow. "Health, Health Resources, and the Utilization of Care" and Karen Davis. "Health Policies and the Aged: Observations from the United States." In R. Binstock and E. Shanas, eds., *Handbook of Aging and the Social Sciences*, 2nd ed. New York: Van Nostrand Reinhold, 1984.
    Two articles that review current research in the health and the aged area.

Chapter Eight

What Role for Private Pensions?

Pension plans set up by private industry or employee groups did not appear in the United States until the end of the nineteenth century. The first company pension plan was established by the American Express Company in 1875 but provided benefits only to permanently incapacitated workers over age 60 who had at least twenty years' service. Thereafter, plans were established in the railroad industry and by a few firms in other industries. However, a congressional study reports that such pension schemes "were by and large slow in developing and [that] there were probably fewer than ten plans in operation by the end of the 19th century" (U.S. House Committee on Education and Labor, 1972).

The Civil Service Retirement Act was enacted in 1920, providing pension coverage for the first time to federal civilian employees. A year later the implementation of private plans was encouraged by the Revenue Act of 1921; this legislation exempted from income taxation both the *income* of pension and profit sharing trusts and the *employer contributions* to these plans.

Although between 3 and 4 million workers were covered by private pensions prior to the establishment of social security, coverage was concentrated in only a few industries; benefits were very limited; less than 15 percent of the work force was covered; and payments were made only if certain very stringent age and service requirements were met. It was not until the 1940s and 1950s that the growth of private pensions mushroomed. Coverage rose from about 4 million employees in the late thirties to roughly 10 million in 1950, 20 million in 1960, and 35 million in 1979.

Various factors have been cited as responsible for this rather dramatic increase in private pension coverage:

1. Continued industrialization of the American economy, together with a movement of workers out of agriculture, which stimulated increasing interest in alternatives other than the family for providing retirement security.
2. The introduction of private pensions by some employers as a way of creating employee loyalty and discouraging job shifting, since most early plans called for the worker to lose his rights to the pension if he left the firm.

3. Wage freezes during World War II and the Korean War that encouraged fringe benefit growth in lieu of wages.
4. A series of favorable tax inducements offered by the federal government beginning with the Revenue Acts of 1921 and 1926. Probably the most important inducement was offered in the Revenue Act of 1942. Coming at a time of sharp personal and corporate federal income tax increases, the 1942 act (a) treated employer contributions to qualified pension plans as tax deductible, (b) excluded plan investment income from taxation, and (c) deferred taxes on participant beneficiaries until actually received in retirement.
5. A favorable decision by the Supreme Court in 1949 supporting the National Labor Relations Board's decision that pensions were a proper issue for collective bargaining.
6. The report of the Steel Industry Fact-Finding Committee in 1949, which included a recommendation that the industry had a social obligation to provide workers with pensions.
7. Growing recognition by unions of the inadequacy of social security benefits and the need for supplementation.
8. The development of multiemployer pension plans—particularly in the construction, transportation, trade, and service industries.

In years past there have been numerous serious problems related to worker protection under private pensions. Workers lost benefit rights as a result of unemployment, company mergers, plant closures, or firm bankruptcies—often after long years of service. Many workers did not know about, or understand, the sometimes very stringent age and service requirements that had to be met to actually receive benefits. Pension reserve funds, supposedly put aside to guarantee benefits to workers, were sometimes mismanaged or misused. Benefits, when actually paid, were often inadequate.

A great deal of attention was given these problems by investigating groups and legislative committees in the 1950s. Congressional concern for the protection of employees' private pensions eventually caused the enactment of the Welfare and Pension Plan Disclosure Act. This act, however, placed primary responsibility for policing the plans on the participants themselves. Dissatisfaction and problems continued. Finally in 1974 Congress passed much stronger, more comprehensive legislation: the Employee Retirement Income Security Act (**ERISA**). This legislation, which is summarized later in the chapter, was a major step in providing protection to covered workers against benefit loss.

This chapter, then, focuses on the progress made in developing private pensions into a viable institution for providing income in old age. The role that private pensions will ultimately play in the economics of aging depends on the resolution of a number of remaining issues: extending coverage, protecting benefits, and dealing with the problem of inflation. To these issues we now turn.

Who Is Covered?

The total number of workers covered under private pension plans has increased from about 4 million workers in 1940 (12 percent of the private wage and salary labor force) to 35 million workers (48 percent) in 1979. The major increases occurred in the 1940s and the 1950s, averaging about 12 percent and 7

Table 20.   Which Workers Were Not Covered by Pension Plans in 1979?

In 1979, 49.4 million workers were not covered by a pension plan:

Sex:	54% of these were *men*; 46% were *women*
Hours Worked:	71% of these worked *full time*; 29% *part time*
Age:	68% were *over age 25* and 51% of noncovered were over 25 and had one or more years of service with their employer
Sector:	8.2 million were employed in the *public sector*
	38.1 million were wage and salary workers in the *private sector*

Of private sector noncovered wage and salary workers:

Industry:	78% worked in *three main industries*:
	• 32% in trade
	• 28% in service
	• 18% in manufacturing
Earnings:	30% earned less than $5,000 in 1978
	36% earned between $5,000 and $10,000 in 1978
	19% earned between $10,000 and $15,000 in 1978
	15% earned over $15,000 in 1978
Firm Size:	79% were in firms with fewer than 100 employees
	8% were in firms with 500 or more employees
Union Status:	About 90% were not members of unions

Source: Based on President's Commission on Pension Policy. *Coming of Age: Toward a National Retirement Income Policy*. Report of The Commission (Washington, D.C.: The Commission, 1981), Chart 6.

percent a year respectively. The growth rate slowed in the 1960s and 1970s to a little over 3 percent a year.

In 1979 (the latest year for which government data are available), almost 50 million workers did not participate in a pension plan on their current job. Table 20 shows who these uncovered workers are. Some are younger, part-time, low-wage workers and/or individuals working for small businesses. But many others are full-time workers with moderate or average earnings.

Sixty percent of those uncovered work in two industries: trade and service. *But the two key factors in understanding coverage are union status and the size of the employing firm.* Almost all workers without pension coverage are non-union and work for firms with a relatively small number of employees.

It has been especially difficult to extend private pension coverage to employees in small firms. Among the factors that have been cited for this difficulty are:

1. The high costs per employee of establishing and maintaining a private plan
2. The lack of pressure in these companies from employees or unions
3. The fact that small business firms are often relatively young and, on average, short-lived
4. The fact that small employers tend to view pensions as personal costs
5. The personality of the small business owner who tends to emphasize individual self-reliance in financial matters
6. The often unstable and insecure financial status of many small businesses and competitive pressures for cost-cutting

As a result of these and other factors, a sizable proportion of the American work force in small firms is not likely to be covered by private pensions.

Private Plan Characteristics

It is difficult to generalize about the provisions of private pension plans because of the large number of different plans with widely varying characteristics. There are about one-half million corporate pension plans in the United States. These can be generally divided into *single employer* and *multiemployer* plans. Multiemployer plans usually require employers to make contributions into a central fund (typically a specified percent of payroll or cents-per-hours-worked), and employees can qualify for benefits from the fund by meeting eligibility requirements through employment in the various firms participating in the program. Reciprocity agreements among some of these multiemployer plans (and a few single employer plans) allow workers to move between plans. Another important difference between the two types of plans is in their administration. Single employer plans are generally managed by the employer alone; multiemployer plans are almost invariably administered by a group of trustees, with equal representation from labor and management (in accordance with terms of the Taft-Hartley Act).

Another common way of classifying private plans is to distinguish between *contributory* and *noncontributory* plans. Contributory plans require that the employee pay part of the cost, whereas noncontributory plans are financed solely by the employer. In the United States, most covered workers (80 percent) participate in noncontributory plans—in part because employ*er* contributions are tax free but under current federal laws employ*ee* contributions (unless sheltered by special arrangements) are not. Also, noncontributory plans do not require the employer to put aside money for *each* worker at the time benefit rights accrue. And employers can use actuarial assumptions that permit them (a) to take account of employee turnover (reducing current pension expenses) and (b) to raise the level of funding of the plan over an extended period of time (see p. 161).

Multiemployer plans cover about one-third of all covered workers. These multiemployer plans tend to be concentrated, however, in particular industries (mining, construction, trade, transportation, and service) and, in these industries, affect more than 50 percent of all covered workers.

In surveying the specific provisions of various pension plans, there are four key characteristics that are generally considered most important: the benefit formulas, vesting and portability requirements, the availability of survivors' benefits, and early retirement options.

Benefit Determination   While there is a great deal of variation among private plans in the way benefits are calculated, three major types can be identified:

Defined Benefit Plans:

1. *Dollar amount times service*—benefits are determined by multiplying a specified dollar amount by the number of years of employed service credited under the plan.
2. *Combined service/earnings formulas*—benefits are based upon (a) the employee's earnings over a specified period of employment (e.g., career, high five of the last ten, or last ten years of earnings) and (b) years of service.

Defined Contribution Plan:*

3. *Money-purchase arrangements*—periodic contributions are set aside according to a predetermined, or agreed upon, formula (usually a percent of earnings). Pensions are paid out based on the accumulated funds (contributions plus investment income) in individual employee accounts.

The overwhelming proportion of workers covered by *single employer plans* belong to plans that use the defined benefit formula basing benefits on earnings. In contrast, only a small proportion of workers under *multiemployer plans* participate in plans using earnings-based formulas. Instead, most multiemployer plans use the "dollar amount times service" formula. Defined contribution plans are most common in small businesses and nonprofit organizations.

In recent years, however, an increasing number of *new* plans have been the defined contribution type. Since defined contribution plans have been more popular with small employers and since most new plans are small, this is not a surprising development. Some benefit experts have speculated that rising regulatory and financing issues associated with defined benefit plans are causing employers to rethink pension design and to view defined contribution more favorably. However, a 1983 decision by the Supreme Court, ruling invalid the common practice in defined contribution plans of providing women (who on average have longer life expectancies) with lower benefits, may discourage some adoptions. A divided Court held that this practice by employers violates the law against sex discrimination.

Another important trend has been a shift to basing benefits on earnings just prior to retirement. The major advantage of this type of formula is a built-in adjustment for inflation *prior to retirement*, since earnings over time are usually adjusted upward for cost-of-living increases.

An important feature of many benefit calculations is the attempt of some private plans to integrate private pensions with social security. Some plans deduct (typically) 50 percent of the social security benefit from the amount computed according to the private plan formula. Other plans use a formula that provides higher benefits on earnings above a certain specified amount, often the social security maximum earnings ceiling.

---

*Deferred profit sharing plans are often listed as defined contribution plans. For the reasons given in the next section, we exclude them.

Table 21.   1979 Median Private Pension Benefit and Replacement Rates[a]
for a Hypothetical Worker with 30 Years of Service, by Sex and Industry

	Women		*Men*	
Industry[b]	*Benefit*	*Replacement Rate*	*Benefit*	*Replacement Rate*
Manufacturing	$3,284	35%	$4,999	27%
Transportation, Communications, and Utilities	4,432	34	6,935	34
Trade	1,794	26	4,097	24
Finance, Insurance, and Real Estate	2,647	26	5,605	30
Service	1,792	23	3,609	23

Source: James H. Schulz, T. D. Leavitt, L. Kelly, and J. Strate, *Private Pension Benefits in the 1970s* (Bryn Mawr, Pa.: McCahan Foundation for Research in Economic Security, 1982), Table 7.
[a]Rates of estimated median benefit to average earnings in the year before retirement.
[b]The mining and construction industries are omitted because of small sample size.

A study (Schulz et al., 1982) of pension benefits levels in 1979 estimates the pensions received by long-service employees retiring in various industries. Median private pension replacement rates for workers with 30 years of service and average earnings were 27 percent for men and 34 percent for women. The rates varied from a low of 23 percent for men and women in the service industry to a high of 35 percent for women in manufacturing (Table 21).

Vesting and Portability Requirements   **Vesting** and **portability** are related pension concepts but are not identical. Vesting refers to the provision in pension plans that guarantees that those covered by the plan will receive all or part of the benefit that they have earned (i.e., accrued), whether or not they are working under the plan at the time of their retirement. Through vesting, the pension rights of otherwise qualified workers are protected whether they are discharged, are furloughed, or quit voluntarily. Prior to ERISA (which established a variety of controls over private pensions), vesting provisions were often nonexistent. Where vesting was available, eligibility conditions varied greatly, and many workers lost their pension rights—sometimes after long years of service and sometimes just prior to retirement. The 1974 law required all plans covered by the law to provide minimum vested benefits meeting one of three alternative standards. In fact, most companies have adopted the same option: vesting of 100 percent of accrued benefits after ten years of service. Hence, those workers who change jobs before accumulating ten years of service receive no pension credits.

Another problem is that vested benefits left in a pension plan after a worker voluntarily or involuntarily leaves the firm are not adjusted upward if the pension plan's formula for *continuing* workers is changed either to compensate for inflation or to provide a higher level of real benefits.* "Portability" of pension

---

*Also, vested benefits left in plans with earnings related formulas do not reflect the rise in earnings that would occur if the worker remained employed by the firm.

rights permits employees to transfer the money value of these rights into another plan and, hopefully, by this process to reduce the inflationary losses that arise when benefits are left behind. Unfortunately, although portability has received a lot of public attention (and is often confused with vesting), the administrative, financial, and actuarial complexities of setting up such arrangements have discouraged any significant action in this area. The multiemployer plan, however, reduces the problems associated with job change by introducing limited portability (i.e., within the boundaries of the plan) through a centralized pension fund.

The 1974 pension reform law permits a separated employee to transfer *tax free* the value of a vested benefit into an "individual retirement account"* if permitted by the plan or to another plan if permitted by both plans. In fact, an employer with a noncontributory plan has a positive financial incentive not to agree to this transfer, since he can earn interest or dividends on any "funded" money he keeps and need not pass on any of these earnings to the former employee.

Survivors' Benefits   The survivor benefits of private plans are of four types:

1. *Joint and survivor annuity.* Regular payments are made during the combined lifetimes of retiree and spouse. It is typically calculated by reducing (15–20 percent) the worker's benefit to pay for the additional costs of survivor protection. Survivor benefits are typically 50–75 percent of the worker's benefit amount.
2. *Early survivor annuity.* This is a regular payment for survivors of workers who die *before* retirement, elected by the employee while working and paid for through reduced benefits.
3. *Preretirement automatic death benefit.* This benefit (like [2] above) is provided by the employer to the survivors of those workers who die before retirement. The key difference is that the protection is provided automatically by the employer, with no reduction in the worker's accrued retirement benefits.
4. *Postretirement automatic death benefit.* This benefit is also automatic but is typically a small lump sum amount, provided to help meet immediate burial expenses.

There is great variation in the provisions various private companies have made for dealing with problems arising from the death of an employee; private pensions are just one of a number of mechanisms. Some employers also provide financial assistance to employees' survivors through group life insurance and profit sharing plans.

Death protection through private pensions was not a high priority item in the early years of pension planning. Consequently, until recently some pension plans made little or no provision for the survivors of workers. In 1974, before ERISA became effective, for example, about 20 percent of the workers covered by defined benefit plans were in plans with no survivor provisions of any kind. The most common type of survivor benefit in those private plans that did have provisions was the joint and survivor equity.

---

*Individual retirement accounts (IRAs) are discussed in the next section.

ERISA now mandates that all pension plans subject to its provisions give certain workers, at a minimum, an opportunity to elect a 50 percent **joint and survivor option** covering *some* of the preretirement years. This preretirement option must be offered at the initial age the worker becomes eligible for early retirement benefits, or ten years before normal retirement, whichever comes later. In both cases, the cost of these options may be imposed on the worker through a lower amount of pension paid out. In addition, plans must provide all workers with this type of survivor protection *at the time of retirement* (unless it is specifically rejected by the worker).

Even though ERISA requires employees to offer survivor benefits, the decision to provide these benefits legally rests with the worker alone. Some workers, without the knowledge of their spouse, do not elect the extra protection; in other cases, the worker and spouse together decide to opt for the bigger retirement benefit, gambling (for that is what it is) that the survivor benefit won't be needed. A recent unpublished study done for the U.S. Department of Labor, for example, found that in 1978 only 38 percent of married workers (both men and women) elected one of the survivor benefit options available from their private plan (Myers, 1982).

In summary, the existing data indicate that the most important means of providing survivor protection through private pensions continues to be the joint and survivor option, typically at the cost of a lower benefit paid to the retiring worker (which discourages its election). Survivor benefits provided over and above the joint and survivor option are not widespread, are of generally limited duration, and are often of small magnitude.

Some firms do have life insurance and/or supplemental plans which add to the level of benefits provided, but, nevertheless, current benefits often do not reflect the needs of employees and their survivors. For a large number of long-term employees, there remains the very real possibility that many years of employer contributions in his or her name provide little or no survivor protection.

Early Retirement Options   During the past two decades we have witnessed a tremendous push toward early retirement. Increasing numbers of workers are retiring early under social security. Federal employees can retire on full benefits at age 55 with 30 years of service; in fact, the President's Commission on Pension Policy reported that 59 percent of retiring male civil service employees (fiscal 1978) were age 60 or younger. Most state and local government employee plans also have very liberal retirement provisions; early retirement is usually possible after 20 to 30 years of service—often as early as age 50 or 55.

Less well known are the retirement options provided under private pension plans. The generous provisions of the big plans—for example, in the auto industry—are well known (see Chapter 3). In the rubber and metal industries, special "early retirement benefits" supplement regular pension benefits until the plan's normal retirement age or until age 65, when the retiree becomes eligible for unreduced social security benefits.

Few data are published on the hundreds of thousands of plans in other industries. A study of pension plans by the U.S. Bureau of Labor Statistics

(1980), however, found that more than half of covered workers were eligible to receive *normal* retirement benefits *before* age 65. And almost a third were eligible for normal benefits at age 60 or earlier!

Another study of defined benefit plans covering about 23 million workers in 1974 (Schulz et al., 1980) shows that 70 percent of these workers were eligible for early retirement benefits at age 60 (provided service requirements, if any, were met). Over half could retire as early as age 55, and 15 percent were in plans with even earlier eligibility ages (or no age requirement at all).

But these numbers do not tell the whole story. More than 90 percent of all workers covered by private pensions are in plans having early retirement options. When a worker retires early, that is, before the "normal" retirement age, the benefit is usually reduced. A large number of employers, however, encourage their employees to retire early by absorbing some of the costs of paying pensions over a longer period of time. Thus, while some plans reduce benefits by the full actuarial discount, many plans, in effect, give actuarial bonuses to workers who retire early.

The study of defined benefit plans in 1974 indicated that powerful economic incentives are provided in many plans. For example, there were about 7 million workers in 1974 covered by plans permitting their retirement at age 60 with less than a full actuarial reduction in benefits.

Thus, we see that social security is not the sole force pushing workers into retirement. Certainly social security income, when it becomes available, encourages workers to retire. But for many workers it is military, federal, state/local, or private plans that make it possible to retire at increasingly early ages.

Alternative Types of Coverage

Private pension plans vary greatly. In fact, there is disagreement among experts over just what type of arrangement should be called a pension. In this section we look at three such controversial arrangements.

Profit Sharing Plans   Most estimates of pension coverage include workers who are covered only by a **deferred profit sharing plan.** Yet profit sharing plans are very different from the traditional private plans we discussed in the previous section. Contributions into profit sharing plans vary with the amount of a particular company's profits and are more directly tied to the vicissitudes of the economy. Hence, profit sharing plans—less certain with regard to ultimate payout—are a more debatable way of providing retirement benefits for the millions of workers with *only* this type of coverage. In contrast, pension plans described in the previous section make a pension promise that is generally independent of fluctuations in the economy or the prosperity of a particular business enterprise.

The pension history at the Sears and Roebuck Company is a good example of the problems that can arise. In the 1970s over 20 percent of Sears' common stock was owned by Sears employees through the company's profit sharing plan. In the good profit years of the 1960s and early 1970s, employees realized huge investment gains through this plan. But when business conditions became poor, the price of Sears' stock fell dramatically, the potential gains from the plan declined dramatically, and workers became very angry. Sears responded by creating a regular pension plan to complement the profit sharing plan, thereby giving more security to workers approaching retirement.

Today millions of workers covered only by profit sharing plans still face the issue raised by the Sears example: How secure is their retirement income promise? A study (Profit Sharing Research Foundation, 1978) of the largest profit sharing plans reports, for example, that only 58 percent of the companies surveyed also had a regular private pension for their employees' retirement security.

Individual Retirement Accounts   Perhaps the most important mechanism created to deal with the private pension coverage issue is the **Individual Retirement Account (IRA)**. In a message to Congress on December 8, 1971, President Nixon first proposed that pension legislation be enacted that would contain saving incentives. The legislation was ultimately enacted as part of the private pension reform legislation (ERISA) that became law in September 1974.

President Nixon's proposal, and the subsequent law, permitted wage and salary earners to set up their own individual retirement plans (IRAs) if they are not covered by any qualified pension plan. In addition, the 1974 pension-reform legislation liberalized existing limitations on contributions to retirement plans for the self-employed (generally called Keogh or HR 10 plans).

In 1981 Congress legislated a major liberalization of the IRA program. Originally IRA participation was limited to employees without pension plan coverage. The legislation passed in 1981 allows every worker to invest up to $2,000 yearly—even if covered by a group plan. Thus, a working couple can invest $4,000; a family with only one worker can add $250 for a nonworking spouse to the $2,000 amount.

When President Nixon proposed the original IRA legislation he argued that it would encourage people to save and that public policy should reward and reinforce this type of activity. In transmitting the legislation, he said:

> *Self-reliance, prudence, and independence are qualities which our government should work to encourage among our people. These are also the qualities which are involved when a person chooses to invest in a retirement savings plan, setting aside money today so that he will have greater security tomorrow. In this respect pension plans are a direct expression of some of the finest elements in the American character. Public policy should be designed to reward and reinforce these qualities.*

The president also argued that this legislation would be responsive to the inequity that existed between those people who were covered by private pensions and those who were not. People covered by private pensions receive favorable tax treatment because contributions made by the employer on their behalf are not taxable. These private pension contributions are only taxable at the time they are paid out, usually at much lower tax rates because retirement income levels are lower than those of work periods.

These were the president's two principal arguments in favor of such legislation. Other people have argued that by encouraging people to save for retirement individually, one allows them to control their own investments and decide what they want to invest in and the amount of risk they want to take. If you are a member of a private pension plan you usually have nothing to say about the investment policy of the plan. Often the gains of good investment accrue only to the employer. If you are sophisticated about financial matters and economics, you might be able to do better with the same amount of funds, especially if you are willing to take some risks.

And, finally, it has been argued that this approach is an alternative to increasing and expanding the social welfare programs that currently exist to help older people. Such tax incentives, it is argued, give people the option to build upon their social security base and give them the freedom to choose how to do it.

The proportion of lower paid workers who will take advantage of this opportunity for tax-sheltered saving, however, is likely to be smaller than that of more highly paid persons. The fear that such tax-exemption proposals would turn into tax loopholes for higher income people was the principal argument voiced in Congress against the legislation when it was proposed.

Thrift Plans   Another mechanism that helps workers prepare for retirement is the company thrift or savings plan. Individual accounts are set up for participating employees, with employers matching some proportion of contributions by the employee. Unlike most pensions, however, an employee can usually withdraw funds from thrift plans before retirement.

Sixty-one of the top 100 industrial corporations have these plans (Bankers Trust, 1977). Company contributions are a deductible business expense. Also, the employee pays no income tax on both the company's contributions and the *earnings* on his own (and the company's) contributions until the funds are taken out of the account.

Thrift plans are not necessarily alternatives to a pension plan. Most companies with such plans also provide a pension plan for employees. Some companies, however, just have thrift plans.*

Private Pension Legislation

Benefit formulas, vesting, survivors' provisions, and early retirement options are four of the most important aspects of private pensions, but there are still others that have great significance for evaluating private pensions and determining public policy toward them. One of these areas concerns the danger of lost pension rights as a result of inadequate pension funding, misuse of pension funds, or the termination of plans because of plant closures, bankruptcy, or other reasons.

A great deal of attention has been given to this area by investigating groups and legislative committees. Congressional concern for the protection of employee benefit funds caused the enactment of the Welfare and Pension Plan Disclosure Act in 1959 but placed primary responsibility for policing the plans on

---

*Not discussed are Tax Reduction Act Stock Ownership Plans (TRASOP) that allow companies to make contributions for employees, primarily in the company's common stock.

the participants themselves. The Employee Retirement Income Security Act of 1974 set up a more comprehensive set of safeguards—establishing participation, vesting, funding standards, plan-termination insurance, and extensive reporting and disclosure requirements. The following are the major provisions of the act:

1. Plans must minimally vest benefits using one of three alternatives.
2. Plan-termination insurance is established.
3. Funding standards are established and fiduciary standards are strengthened.
4. Individual retirement accounts (exempt from federal income taxation) may be established.
5. Disclosure regulations permit participants to request once each year a statement from the plan administrator of total benefits, both vested and nonvested, that have accrued and the earliest date on which unvested benefits will become nonforfeitable.
6. The Social Security Administration receives reports from employers (through the Treasury Department) of vested benefits due separated workers; Social Security notifies employees of all vested pension rights at the time they apply for social security benefits.
7. With the consent and cooperation of their employers, employees may transfer upon separation vested pension rights on a tax-free basis from one employer to another; or the employee may transfer the funds to an individual retirement account.

Passed by both houses of Congress by wide vote margins, **ERISA** is an attempt to provide greater certainty that private pension promises will be fulfilled. But the legislation does not deal with all private pension problems. Critics have been quick to cite the problems they think still remain:

1. A large segment of the private work force still remains uncovered.
2. Very few private pensions automatically adjust pension benefits *during* retirement for inflation.
3. State and local government pension plans were excluded from the 1974 law.
4. The lack of "portability" in pensions may result in a reduction in mobility and, for those who move, a reduction in the value of pension rights relative to what the value would be if they did not change jobs.
5. The proportion of survivors with benefits remains relatively low, and those benefits paid are often small.
6. Private pension provisions may discourage the hiring of older workers because it typically costs more to provide such workers with a specified pension benefit.

While the drafters of the 1974 private pension legislation admitted in debate that the legislation did not deal with all the problems, they argued that it was a major step forward. And they pointed out that the legislation itself calls for further study of many of the unresolved issues.

Financing Private Pensions

In 1963 the Studebaker Corporation, a small producer of automobiles, went out of business. The company had established, fourteen years before, a pension plan that ultimately covered about 11,000 employees. When the company closed its South Bend, Indiana, plant, there were assets worth $24 million in the pension fund. But these assets were insufficient to meet all the pension rights that had been accumulated. The result: about 4,500 workers received an average of only $600 apiece, or 15 percent of the value of their rights. And those workers who had accumulated years of service but had not achieved pension vesting status got nothing.

Because of the number of workers affected and the prominence of the industry, the Studebaker case immediately became a favorite example cited by those persons calling for private pension reform. Studebaker (and dozens of others) illustrates the major goal *and also the major hazard* of private pension financing—to ensure that there are adequate funds so that promised benefits are, in fact, paid.

Prior to the 1974 pension reform legislation, most private plans financed pensions on a reserve basis, with a few operating on a partial or full pay-as-you-go basis. Now all plans covered by the 1974 act are required to meet its minimum funding standards.

In reviewing financing practices it is useful to group plans into three categories: (a) noninsured or trusteed plans, (b) insured plans, and (c) multiemployer plans. The majority of plans are noninsured or trusteed plans whose reserves are either self-administered by the individual company or administered by a trustee, in most cases commercial banks. Significantly, the great bulk of these reserves are administered by only about twenty-five banks. Insured plans are administered by various insurance companies. Multiemployer funds, usually the result of union collective bargaining, are usually jointly run by the union and employer trustees.

Less than a quarter of private plans require employee contributions to the plan; the rest are financed entirely by the employer. A major reason for the prevalence of noncontributory plans is that employee contributions from earnings are subject, with certain exceptions, to federal income taxes. In contrast, the money employers put into a pension fund is not subject to any taxes. In addition, employee contributions greatly complicate the administration of a plan—requiring the establishment of a pension account for each worker and policies regulating these accounts. And, as we indicated earlier, noncontributory plans usually reduce employer pension costs during the early years (p. 152).

Although most firms have established reserve funds to be built up over the years as their pension liabilities grow, many of the pension rights granted under the plans remain in jeopardy as a result of "past service credits." When new plans are established or old plans liberalized, the usual practice is to give workers full pension credits for their years of work prior to the plan's establishment or liberalization. While the pension liabilities for these past service credits accrue immediately, employers usually adopt a payment schedule for funding these liabilities that in the past extended over a ten- to forty-year period (and sometimes longer). As long as this unfunded liability remains, a plan that terminates will be unable to pay all of its promised future pension benefits. This is what happened in the Studebaker case. And, in fact, many plans have terminated over the years—with a resultant loss of pension rights to thousands of workers.

The 1981 funding status of large firms in the United States has been studied by the pension consulting firm of Johnson and Higgins (1981). The analysis covered 386 of the Fortune 500 industrial corporations and 168 of the largest 200 corporations in banking, retailing, transportation, and utilities. There was wide variation in funding status among companies, but overall assets covered about 90 percent of plan liabilities.

Some plans, however, still have sizable unfunded liabilities. Munnell (1982b) screened Standard and Poor's 1980 data on 6,000 companies in order to isolate those companies with unfunded pension liabilities in excess of 30 percent of their net worth. Munnell identified 86 firms, with Chrysler Corporation at the top of the list with unfunded liabilities of $1.2 billion and International Harvester with $1.1 billion.

What happens to workers when a plan terminates without adequate funds? Number ten on Munnell's list was Braniff Airlines. In the spring of 1982 it shut down.

Even before Braniff filed for bankruptcy, there were dramatic reductions in the numbers of employees working for the company. A few years before there were about 15,000 employees working for Braniff. That was in their heyday. Just before filing for bankruptcy, there were only 9,500 employees left.

Thus, a significant number of people left Braniff—were forced to leave Braniff, in most cases —prior to the bankruptcy. What happened to the pension rights of these particular employees? And after Braniff filed for bankruptcy and terminated its pension plans, what happened to the workers still employed who were covered by the plan and had expected to receive benefits?

One thing is certain. Those people who had fewer than ten years of service working for Braniff Airlines—whether they had left before the bankruptcy or whether they were working at the point of bankruptcy filing—got nothing. However, ERISA requires that employees with more than ten years of service, which is the most popular alternative of three plan vesting provisions, receive benefits when they retire.

Those former Braniff employees retired and receiving pensions and those eligible for vested benefits were protected by the Pension Benefit Guarantee Corporation (PBGC). This government organization, part of the Labor Department, was set up under ERISA to guarantee (within limits) the continued payment of benefits to retired workers and the future payment of benefits to vested workers. When a plan terminates without sufficient funds to meet these obligations, the PBGC takes over the plan and assumes responsibility for paying the benefits. Each company or union with a plan covered by ERISA must make contributions (insurance premiums) to the PBGC to cover the costs of providing this insurance protection (see p. 164). And it is these contributions, if needed, that will help pay the costs of the Braniff pensions. Currently PBGC guarantees benefits up to a maximum of $1,517 per month (1983).

Unfortunately, vested benefits, under present pension practice, do not adjust for inflation. Thus, all former Braniff workers who were vested (either vested when they left prior to bankruptcy or vested when the plan terminated) face many years of uncertainty. If inflation continues to be relatively high, the real value of those vested benefits will be eroded, raising the serious question of whether the benefits will be worth anything when the employees ultimately retire. For example, a Braniff worker vested at age 42 and retiring at age 62 may get a benefit equal to only 38 percent of its value when Braniff went bankrupt. This assumes that inflation over the intervening period will average 5 percent; if inflation were to average 10 percent over the period, the worker's pension would be worth only 15 percent! Thus, many Braniff employees, even though they are vested and will receive vested benefits, may lose rather significant amounts in contrast to what they would have had if Braniff prospered and they had been able to stay with the company.

The problems associated with vesting and inflation erosion of vested benefits are not solely related to terminating plans. Braniff is just an example. Any job change—for example, one made to take advantage of a better opportunity by moving from one job to another—subjects the worker to similar costs.

The Future of Private Pensions

Plan termination is not the only problem arising in connection with private pensions. As we have indicated previously, private pensions are now a major source of retirement income for many people. The amount of income ultimately received varies greatly depending on an individual worker's employment experience, his preretirement earnings level, the size of the firms he works for, and the industry of employment (Thompson, 1978). Coverage under a private plan and receipt of a pension are obviously no guarantee that a plan benefit will be adequate. There are plans that provide excellent benefits, and there are plans that provide very low benefits.

If private pensions are to become a truly effective supplement to social security, three problems must be solved: (a) coverage must be extended, (b) benefits receipt must become less risky, and (c) benefits must not be so vulnerable to inflation. In this section we discuss the first two problems; the third is discussed in the next chapter.

Coverage ERISA did not obligate any employer without a pension plan to establish one. Thus, ERISA contained no provision beyond the tax incentives provided in the federal tax laws to encourage the expansion of existing private plan coverage. Rather, the principal focus of ERISA was on expanding the supervision and regulation of private plans by the federal government and creating tax exempt individual retirement accounts (IRAs).

This expanded regulation costs money. In addition to the costs to taxpayers for the federal supervisory agencies and their staffs, considerable new regulatory costs are imposed on the businesses with pension funds. These costs arise from the necessity of providing information to the government in order for it to carry out its various supervisory roles. Because of the complexity of the regulations, businesses must often either develop staff or hire outside consultants to provide them with the expertise necessary to ensure compliance with the ERISA law. Businesses have been complaining strongly before congressional committees about both the high costs of reporting required information to the government and the costs of simply understanding the law. Some plans have been terminated because of the increased administrative burdens and costs, and some pension experts say that employers without plans are increasingly reluctant to start new ones.

Thus, when we look at the coverage trend over the last couple of decades, we see a slowing down in coverage beginning *prior* to ERISA. This slowdown results primarily from the fact that almost all the workers in large, relatively affluent corporations have become covered. Noncoverage is now concentrated among nonunion, small employer groups (Table 20). A profile of these small employers would include the business proprietors found on any typical small-town Main Street or any large city neighborhood shopping center: the small retailer, the local restaurant, the service station, repair services, the barber and beauty shop, the doctor and dentist, the auto dealer—and many, many more small employers of wage and salary workers. The profile would likewise include partnership operations such as law firms, consulting engineers, accounting firms, real estate firms, and small manufacturing plants operated as corporations or by self-employed owners.

Legislation passed by Congress in recent years has encouraged the development of a variety of options: "simplified pension plans" (the Revenue Act of 1978), Employee Stock Option Plans (ESOPs), and IRAs. We will have to wait and see what impact this new legislation has on the coverage problem. In the meantime, large numbers of workers without private coverage will continue to rely primarily on their social security benefits for retirement protection.

Pension Risk   In August 1978 the Professional Drivers Council, a dissident Teamsters union group, charged that millions of dollars were being drained from the union's pension funds because of mismanagement and corrupt practices. The dissident group claimed that, among other abuses, multimillion-dollar loans had been made to individuals and groups with questionable backgrounds or to entities running deficits when the loans were made (BNA, 21 August 1978). That same month a U.S. district court ruled that a $20 million loan by pension trustees of Teamsters' Local 281 violated ERISA regulations; the money was loaned to finance a thousand-plus room hotel and gambling casino in Las Vegas. Earlier, a reform group called Miners for Democracy acted to displace the United Mine Workers' leadership—charged with illegal financial transactions and the use of union pension funds for personal gain. Although such abuse cases affect a minority of workers covered by private pensions, there has been a continuous history of such incidents. The result has been to depress the level of benefits in certain instances and threaten the actual financial viability of certain plans.

As we discussed in the prior section, Congress created the Pension Benefit Guaranty Corporation (PBGC) to protect workers if plans not fully funded terminate due to corruption, a merger, or bankruptcy. PBGC was there to step in

when the poor economic conditions of the 1970s and 1980s caused plan terminations to increase. In fiscal 1981, for example, there were 5,000 plan terminations. This was a 25 percent increase over the previous year and the highest rate
of terminations experienced since the immediate period after ERISA was enacted in 1974. Most terminating plans can meet their obligations; however,
many cannot. By 1981, the PBGC had to take over 659 plans with benefits owed
to about 71,000 workers.

In 1983, the head of the PBGC went before a congressional committee and
said the agency would run out of funds unless Congress increased the premium
on single-employer plans from $2.60 per participant to $6. He stated that
PBGC liabilities due to terminating plans were far higher than had ever been anticipated. This statement shocked both the Congress and the business community paying the premiums, since this was the first time the agency had publicly
revealed its severe financial problems.

The possibility of rapidly escalating premiums has caused many employers
to call for changes in the reinsurance program. They argue that companies with
fully funded plans are, in effect, subsidizing unfunded plans as a result of legal
loopholes that allow companies to dump their unfunded pension liabilities on
the PBGC. Legislation is currently being considered that would revise the insurance program to make it more financially viable. The magnitude of the problem
is illustrated by a statement made recently by George Swick, retired president of
Buck Associates, a major actuarial and pension consulting firm. Swick consid-
ers the plan insurance problems so serious that he has called for a complete rethinking and restructuring of the plan insurance program. Thus, a mechanism
that we thought was in place and was able to do the job is now being called into
question, even by recognized authorities in the pension industry.*

A somewhat different risk issue arises because women are not as likely as
men to receive private pension benefits. A federal Task Force on Sex Discrimination (U.S. Department of Justice, n.d.) recently pointed out that women, because of their home and family responsibilities, are likely to accumulate far
fewer total years of service with any one employer. Aspects of ERISA that the
task force thought created problems were:

1. Workers under 25 may be excluded from coverage, although the 20 to
   24 age group has the highest female participation rate.
2. Coverage is not required for employees who work less than 1000
   hours per year, although a high proportion of women work part-time
   or part-year.
3. "Breaks in service" by women are likely to exceed current allowable
   limits.
4. Vesting requirements are too long.
5. In defined benefit plans, even vested rights, if acquired through service early in an employee's working life, may be worth little at retirement (see p. 154).

---

*Because of space and the complexity of the issues, we have not discussed a number of
major problems that have also arisen in connection with insuring multiemployer plans.

With regard to spouses, the task force observed:

> *The retirement income protection provided for most women as wives of workers covered under private pension plans is generally both insecure and inadequate. . . . [ERISA] has done little to change the fact that most women, as housewives, are only one man away from poverty. [U.S. Department of Justice, n.d.]*

Legislation that addresses many of these issues was considered by Congress in 1983 and was expected to pass in 1984.* The Senate bill reduces the minimum age requirement from age 25 to 21, reduces the minimum age for vesting credit from age 22 to 18, liberalizes "break in service" rules, and tightens standards for survivors benefits.

Government Employee Pension Plans

Our discussion of pension plans would not be complete without mentioning one other category: federal, state, and local plans for government employees. These plans have many characteristics similar to the private plans discussed above but are unique in some respects.

Federal Plans   Most civilians working for the federal government are covered by the civil service retirement pension program. In 1980 there were 1.2 million beneficiaries receiving about $15 billion in pension, survivor, and disability benefits under this program (Office of Personnel Management, 1981). Benefits are computed on the basis of length of service and the average of the highest three consecutive years of earnings. An automatic cost-of-living adjustment is made to this benefit. Federal employee fringe benefits now comprise a third of the government's compensation payments (Marcou, 1978). The major item in this outlay is the payments for pensions.

"Of all pension plans, probably none is better than the military's" (Aspin, 1976). This pension is based on salary during the final year of service and is automatically adjusted for general price increases. Benefits equal to half of basic pay are available at any age after only 20 years of service and equal to 75 percent of basic pay after 30 years. Military personnel do not contribute toward these pensions. Not surprisingly, costs have risen dramatically in recent years. About 10 percent of the defense budget currently goes to meet these pension obligations.

Until 1984 federal civilian employees were not covered by social security. The relatively low number of quarters needed to qualify for social security in the past encouraged them to seek dual coverage. Many federal employees worked part time while employed by the government and/or retired (perhaps early) from government employment, took a new job to obtain social security

---

*Two similar bills passed the full Senate and the House Education and Labor Committee in November 1983.

eligibility, and eventually obtained a minimum (or better) social security benefit. In fact, among those age 62 or older, the proportion of civil service annuitants eligible to receive social security retirement benefits was 63 percent in
1979 (Social Security Administration, 1982). Over the years, the cost and inequity of providing social security benefits to federal pensioners was con-
demned by many, and recommendations were frequently made to cover all government employees. It was not until 1984, however, that all *new* federal
employees were covered.*

The Civil Service Retirement System is financed mainly from government
revenues; however, employees are required to contribute 7 percent of pay. Full
retirement benefits are payable under several combinations of age and service:
age 55 with 30 years; age 60 with 20 years; or age 62 with 5 years.

Benefits are quite generous. A worker employed for 35 years with a final
salary over $30,000 will receive enough from his federal pension alone to main-
tain his or her standard of living in retirement (Hartman, 1983). In fact, Robert
Hartman argues in his recent book *Pay and Pensions for Federal Workers* (1983)
that up to now federal pensions have been much better than those in the private
sector and, as a result, too costly to the taxpayers. Moreover, he argues that
many aspects of the system are inequitable, favoring highly paid and long-term
workers and those people who return to government service late in their career.
Over the years Hartman and many others (e.g., the Universal Social Security
Coverage Study Group, 1980) have called for major changes in this pension
program. Now that social security coverage has been introduced for new employees, a new retirement plan is being implemented.

State and Local Pension Plans   There are almost 7,000 plans covering government employees in the states. These plans are similar in many ways to private
employer plans. James A. Maxwell (1975) has summarized some of the differences: "Overall, the state and local government pension systems provide more
generous benefits than do private systems. The normal retirement age and service requirements are more generous. . . . And they are more likely to have generous disability and survivor coverage. . . . (Most) require employee contributions, whereas most private plans do not."

Tilove's study (1976) of state and local plans emphasizes two other important comparisons between private and public employee plans. In a sharp rever-
sal from earlier years, Tilove found that vesting provisions in public plans had
improved greatly and compared favorably with private plans. And while automatic postretirement benefit adjustments are almost nonexistent in private
plans, they are quite common in state plans.

With regard to inflation protection, a study (Schulz et al., 1984) of the 76
major teacher and state-employee retirement plans found that 41 plans in 1982

---

*At the time of writing, the details of the new combined social security/government pen-
sion for new employees were not known. The discussion that follows describes the plan for workers
hired before 1984.

had automatic adjustment mechanisms, with annual ceilings on these adjustments of 2 to 5 percent. Only two of these plans did not have ceilings: Maryland, for employees hired before 1980, and New Jersey, which adjusts pensions for 60 percent of the change in the CPI.

State and local governments are free to choose whether to cover their employees under social security. Consequently, about 70 percent of state and local employees are currently covered by both social security and a state or local pension plan. Again, for workers not covered by social security, dual coverage is often achieved by early retirement from state or local service followed by work for a nongovernment employer.

A recent study (The Urban Institute, 1981) of 100 representative state and local plans found their benefits to be quite generous and, in some cases, to be excessive. The study found considerable variation, however, among the various plans studied. For workers age 65 with 30 years of service and a gross income of $10,000, the highest replacement rate in the sample of plans studied was 149 percent and the lowest was 52 percent.

Congressional interest in federal regulation of state and local plans was a major issue when ERISA was passed in 1974. These plans were formally exempted from the ERISA legislation, however, since it was not clear that Congress had the constitutional authority to regulate the states in this area. However, legislation has been introduced in Congress to establish minimum reporting, disclosure, and financial responsibility standards for state and local plans. Supporters of the legislation believe it is constitutional and will improve the security of pensions for employees in the states. Strong opposition to the legislation has come from state and local government organizations. They maintain that regulation is unnecessary and argue that such action would be an undesirable invasion of states' rights.

Financing Government Employee Plans

Unfortunately, data on the actuarial status of the thousands of government plans (or even a representational sample of them) are difficult to obtain and also difficult to interpret when available. A study by James A. Maxwell (1975) of the pension plans in the 29 largest cities "shows that many of them are in trouble." Using the ratio of current payments to assets as a rough indication of the financial strength or weakness of a fund, Maxwell also identifies four states where plan financing is weak: Delaware, Massachusetts, West Virginia, and Maine.

Another recent study by a Congressional Pension Task Force (U.S. House Committee on Education and Labor, 1978) surveyed plans covering 96 percent of all employees in public employee plans. The Pension Task Force reported serious deficiencies regarding the extent to which information is reported and disclosed to interested parties. They found that plans often did not operate in accordance with generally accepted financial and accounting procedures. And, most importantly, they found that "there is an incomplete assessment of true pension costs at all levels of government due to the lack of adequate **actuarial valuations** and standards."

The financial problems of many public employee retirement systems are serious. The Pension Task Force reports that one-third of the plans did not have actuarial valuations over the five-year period investigated (1971–1975); 75 percent of the plans basing contribution rates at least in part on actuarial funding methods were found to understate current pension costs and unfunded accrued liabilities; and 40 percent of the total federal, state, and local pension systems fail to meet the funding test "which many pension experts consider a bare minimum."

Tilove's assessment of the situation in 1976 was that significant improvements had occurred in the funding situation of state and local plans but that funding was in fact poorest where it is most needed:

> *The cases most in need of attention are the systems of the financially distressed urban centers and of the many smaller cities and counties that have no real assurance of future ability to pay. It is their fiscal difficulties that have kept many on pay-as-you-go, and that is precisely why they should begin to fund on an actuarial basis—so that they may confront the long-term implications of their pension decisions and, by the same policy, assure the ultimate security of their employees.* [*Tilove, 1976*]

In many ways, state and local pension financing falls in between social security financing and private pension plans. Like the federal government, state and city governments are not likely ever to cease operations, and pensions are protected by law and the taxing powers of the government. But, like private business, states and cities are not assured of a continually growing financing base. Some states and cities may experience a net loss of businesses or population and/or their tax base. These shifts are difficult to predict and can cause serious problems if pension costs (based on past promises) are rising while the government's tax revenues are growing very slowly or falling.

Because pension benefits can be liberalized without any substantial increases in current costs, some people fear that pension plans will be liberalized without due regard to the future financing implications. It is argued that the political process is particularly susceptible to this problem because the conduct of state and local politicians is often "determined by relatively short-run considerations. The impact of failing to adhere to actuarial principles will frequently fall upon a different mayor and a different city council. In these circumstances, concessions that condemn a city to future impoverishment may not seem intolerable" (Wellington and Winter, 1971). Despite the large number of state and local funds, the magnitude of fund assets, the growth of benefit levels, and the fears of many professionals regarding state and local pension financing, very little attention has been given to the impact of these plans on the economic status of the current and future aged. Individuals covered by these plans, and relying on them for retirement security, should be aware of this gap in our knowledge. State and local taxpayers should probably be more sensitive to the long-term costs of these pensions and support an increase in the availability of information in this area.

Chapter Eight Highlights

Private and government employee pensions play important roles in the United States. Some key points to remember are:

1. While government employee pensions were in place relatively early in this century, private pensions didn't develop rapidly until the 1940s and 1950s.
2. Still not covered by private plans are many working for small businesses; the uncovered are also more likely to be nonunion, female, part-time, lower paid, and in the trade, service, or manufacturing industries.
3. Most pension-covered workers are in noncontributory defined benefit plans with ten year vesting, optional survivors benefits, and nonindexed benefits based on years of service and final years of earnings.
4. The 1974 Employee Retirement Income Security Act (ERISA) set up a comprehensive set of minimum standards, financial safeguards, and disclosure requirements, seeking to ensure that benefits promised to workers would actually be realized.
5. The major private pension issues being debated are (a) the adequacy of coverage, (b) how to reduce the risk of pension loss, and (c) the extent to which benefits should be protected from inflation.
6. Government employee pensions are generally more liberal than private plans, but there is increasing concern about the financing provisions for these plans.

Suggested Readings

American Council of Life Insurance. *Pension Facts.* Washington, D.C.: yearly.
    A good source of up-to-date statistics on both private and public plans. Also provided is a succinct summary of pension history and legislation and an excellent selected bibliography.

Bankers Trust Company. *Corporate Pension Plan Study—A Guide for the 1980's.* New York: Bankers Trust, 1980.
    Bankers Trust periodically issues summary descriptions of a wide variety of plans. This publication is a good source of information on the details of plan characteristics.

Beller, Daniel J. "Coverage Patterns of Full-Time Employees under Private Retirement Plans," and Gayle Thompson Rogers. "Vesting of Private Pension Benefits in 1979 and Change from 1972." *Social Security Bulletin* 44 (July 1981): 3–29.
    Detailed analyses of pension coverage and vesting are presented in these two articles.

Employee Benefit Research Institute. *Economic Survival in Retirement: Which Pension Is for You?* Washington, D.C.: The Institute, 1982.
    A collection of conference papers focusing on the differences between defined benefit and defined contribution plans.

McGill, Dan M. *Fundamentals of Private Pensions.* 4th ed. Homewood, Ill.: Irwin, 1979.
    A comprehensive and authoritative book that traces the historical development and regulation of private pensions, explains plan design, reviews funding procedures, and discusses actuarial practices.

Munnell, Alicia H. *The Economics of Private Pensions.* Washington, D.C.: The Brookings Institution, 1982.
    Examines the interaction of private pensions and tax policy, saving, financial institutions, and corporate financing.

Schieber, Sylvester J., and P. George. *Retirement Income Opportunities in an Aging America: Coverage and Benefit Entitlement.* Washington, D.C.: Employee Benefit Research Institute, 1981.

> A good discussion of the issues related to measuring private pension coverage. Also provided is an overview of "the retirement income system" in the United States.

U.S. Subcommittee on Retirement Income and Employment, House Select Committee on Aging. *National Pension Policies: Private Pension Plans.* Hearings. Washington, D.C.: U.S. Government Printing Office, 1978.

> Testimony by government, academic, and business experts on the role and problems of private pensions.

Chapter Nine

Economic Security Today and Tomorrow

Years of economic deprivation among the elderly in the United States called forth a variety of public and private programs to alleviate the resulting hardship. OASDI, private pensions, government employee pensions, Medicare and the SSI program currently involve expenditures of over $400 billion per year.

Our nation's very positive response to the economic plight of the elderly and the problems of old age, however, has triggered great controversy. Some argue that the benefits are still insufficient, while others argue that the economic burden of providing even the benefits promised is becoming excessive.

At the heart of this controversy are two major questions: what should be the mix of public and private programs and how should these programs be financed? As OASDI, private pensions, government employee plans, and health programs grow in size and cost, it is clear that we must clarify the way we intend them to relate to each other, the level of benefits to be provided by each, and who will ultimately pay the costs. In addition, we must be clear about what responsibilities before and during retirement remain the individual's (or his or her family's).

The Pension System—Stability or Change?

Writers frequently described the country's provisions for retirement as a three-legged stool with social security, private pensions, and individual saving comprising each leg. However, the information provided in prior chapters indicates that the legs of that stool have changed. The evidence is clear: the overwhelming bulk of the population does not save sufficiently for old age. Home equity accounts for the bulk of most people's wealth, but these assets are not readily or willingly converted to spendable funds when people grow old.

It is *collective* saving through various pension programs that currently makes the big difference; wealth in the form of accrued future benefits constitutes the overwhelming proportion of assets for most Americans today. Thus, the three-legged stool for retirement provision is more appropriately viewed as composed of the three basic parts of the pension system currently operating in the United States: OASDHI, private pensions, and government employee pensions. Together these three programs provide most of the income and health services going to people who are retired.

In prior chapters we have discussed how provision for old age in the United States has evolved into a mix of multifarious collective pension structures. *For better or worse, this pension system is now in place, and its basic structure is not likely to change significantly in the years to come.* That is, we are not likely to see a shift to providing much more of our retirement income through social security (as in West Germany, Italy, and Belgium, where most comes from social security). Nor, for reasons we discuss below, are we likely to see the role of private pensions greatly increased. And despite all the pleas and advocacy of some to the contrary, it is doubtful that we will see a significant shift to self-reliance through individual saving as an important retirement provisions mechanism. Some people advocate such a shift, together with an expanded needs-tested income support program. Such a program would likely be a broadened and more developed version of the SSI program that is currently a part of social security. Again, there does not seem to be much political support for such a change.

The stability of the existing situation does not mean, of course, that all the major issues of providing retirement income are resolved. This is hardly the case, as anyone who has gotten this far in the book (or who, for that matter, has read the newspapers) knows all too well. Discussions about health and pension programs and how best to provide for old age have never been more numerous, except perhaps during the social security debates of the 1930s. It is not unusual today to hear or read clarion calls for the fundamental rethinking of how we should provide for retirement. And there is no dearth of proposals for major structural changes in our current health and pension systems, especially government programs.

Regarding pensions, most experts would agree that the present public-private pension system is in some sense a nonsystem with gaps, flaws, inequities, and inadequacies. However, it also contains the basic elements of stability that will ensure its long-term continuity. These elements (described more fully in prior chapters) are:

An evolving retirement policy based primarily on *collective* financing—reducing the magnitude and complexity of *individual* retirement preparation

The institutionalization of retirement: rising retirement expectations and benefits as a matter of right, not need—eliminating social stigma from retirement income receipt

Individuals being subject to "forced saving" through private and public group plans, countering the tendency for individual economic myopia

Benefits related to preretirement earnings, which is a necessary prerequisite for developing "adequate" pension income

A heavy reliance on government taxes for financing social security and tax incentive mechanisms to encourage provision through private pensions

Universal involvement of the population in pension programs and the development of a large number of organizations (governments, corporations, banks, insurance companies, and so forth) providing pension services—both helping to ensure broad-based political support for existing programs

It is important to reiterate that this growing stability does not mean that our system for providing income in old age has no major problems. In prior chapters we have stressed, for example, the still precarious economic state of most people covered only by social security, the economic problems of many widows, the conflicting actions around encouraging early retirement while facilitating later retirement, and the plight of those workers whose private pension plans are inadequate or inequitable. Thus, although a basic retirement income provision system is in place, we will need to improve it over the years to come.

Coping with Inflation

A major challenge that continues to face many of the elderly is the need to deal with inflation. Recently, inflation has been very high—at unprecedented levels. But what is more worrisome is the evidence indicating that these high inflation rates are not a temporary phenomenon. A number of fundamental changes that have taken place in our economy will make it difficult to return permanently to the very low inflation rates of old. Instead, we probably face recurring periods of rapidly rising prices.

The world is now going through a long-term transition with regard to energy sources and the costs of energy. Until a new cheap energy source is developed, we face the threat of continuing pressures on prices from the energy component of the goods and services we produce.

Perhaps more fundamental are the implications of our current economic structure. Large businesses, unions, and governments, together with public and private economic security provisions, have created an institutional environment that effectively insulates most industries from price and wage reductions. At the same time, this environment often encourages wage and price increases that are not justified by productivity gains.

Finally, there is no evidence that the American electorate appreciates the need for higher taxes to meet the rising need for public goods and services in an increasingly affluent and complex society. As John Kenneth Galbraith (1958) pointed out some years ago:

The line which divides our area of wealth from our area of poverty is roughly that which divides privately produced and marketed goods and services from publicly rendered services. Our wealth in the first is not only in startling contrast with the meagerness of the latter, but our wealth in privately produced goods is, to a marked degree, the cause of crisis in the supply of public services. For we have failed to see the importance, indeed the urgent need, of maintaining a balance between the two.

The result is a continuing tendency for the government to run deficits as social problems generate pressures by citizens through various interest groups for action while the collective polity (of these same citizens) remains stingy with its hard-earned income. The tax and spending "solutions" to our economic problems and government deficits promoted by President Reagan are but one dramatic example of our long, vacillating history with regard to the national mix of private versus public goods and services.

One recent tax reform—indexing federal income tax brackets for inflation—creates great uncertainty for the future. The new law (scheduled to go into effect in 1985) eliminates the increase in individuals' taxes that, in prior years, resulted from inflation increasing people's incomes and pushing many into higher tax brackets. But in turn, this loss of revenue to the government contributes to its financing problems and practically insures there will be budget deficits in the future—deficits that could be inflationary.

The Vulnerable Elderly   The promise of continuing inflation in the years to come demands that we think seriously of appropriate safeguards for the most economically vulnerable of our population. There are two major sources of elderly income that are still highly vulnerable to inflation: financial assets and private pensions. Most financial assets—bonds, checking accounts, savings accounts, and insurance policies—do not adjust when the general level of prices changes. Others, which have at times adjusted better, require considerable financial sophistication or have much higher associated risk: real estate, corporate stock, and gold. The recent development of money market funds and similar financial securities offers some help for the small saver but again does not offer complete security from inflation over any particular short-run period.

At present, the most serious problem with regard to inflation and the elderly is the vulnerability of the *near-poor* aged. The overwhelming proportion of elderly live on incomes *above* the official poverty level but below $15,000 a year. Many of these elderly families depend on their financial savings and their private pensions to provide the margin of support necessary for a modest but more comfortable lifestyle. How can these people be helped?

Purchasing Power Bonds   Some people have argued that saving, particularly personal saving, is discouraged by the uncertainty of not knowing future rates of inflation. Another way of saying this is that people are discouraged from saving by the certainty of knowing that inflation is bound to take place at some rate and that their savings are likely to become devalued over time.

Various proposals have been made for the creation of a different type of financial asset, a constant purchasing power bond. These bonds would be sold by the government to people to protect their savings from inflation. The basic idea of constant purchasing power bonds is that people should be able to buy these bonds from the government to save for retirement or other purposes. They might or might not receive interest from them. Economist James Tobin has argued, for example, that people might even be willing to buy these bonds at a zero rate of interest—as long as there was a firm guarantee that their value would not depreciate from inflation. Having been purchased for a stated amount, the bond would be redeemable at some point in the future for that amount, *adjusted for any inflation that took place over the intervening period.* Thus, the value of the bond would remain constant in real terms and actually increase if there was a rate of interest associated with it.

Henry Wallich (1969), himself an advocate of the bonds, summarizes the *opposition* to them as follows:

> The case against purchasing power bonds every good official can recite in his sleep. If you escalate government obligations, people will say that you are throwing in the towel against inflation. Investors will stop worrying about inflation if they are protected. And the government with its unlimited resources would be competing unfairly with private borrowers who could not take the risk of assuming this kind of open-ended debt.

Milton Friedman (1971) argues against this sort of reasoning:

> The government alone is responsible for inflation. By inflation it has expropriated the capital of persons who bought government securities. Often at the urging of high officials who eloquently proclaimed that patriotism and self-interest went hand-in-hand (the good old government savings bond). The right way to avoid this disgraceful shell game is for the government to borrow in the form of purchasing power securities. Let the Treasury promise to pay not $1,000, but a sum that will have the same purchasing power as $1,000 had when the security was issued. Let it pay as interest each year not a fixed amount of dollars but that number adjusted for any rise in prices. This would be the precise counterpart of the escalator clauses that have become so popular in wage contracts.

The late Senator Pat McNamara from Michigan, when he was chairman of the Special Committee on Aging, introduced legislation in the early sixties to allow the government to sell purchasing power bonds to individuals up to a certain maximum amount, on the condition that the individuals would be willing to hold the bonds until retirement. The proposed legislation specified that if the bonds were cashed in before retirement, there would not be an escalator adjustment; instead, individuals would only get back the original amount plus a stipulated amount of interest. Senator McNamara introduced the bill over a period of many years, but hearings were never held on the proposal.

The principal opposition to purchasing power bonds is centered in the U.S. Treasury Department. In addition to the reasons cited by Wallich, the Treasury worries about possible destabilizing effects on the bond markets of introducing this new type of bond and the possibility of making more difficult the government's debt financing. In this particular area—debt management and federal debt issue—the Treasury is politically very powerful. Thus far, it has been persuasive in preventing Congress from seriously considering legislation of this sort.

Private Pensions and Inflation   There are almost no private pension plans that automatically adjust pensions during retirement for increases in the Consumer Price Index. Some plans adjust benefits on an ad hoc basis every few years, but these adjustments usually lag far behind the rise in prices.

Some people have recommended "retiree bargaining" as a way of dealing with this problem. However, the Supreme Court ruled in 1971 (*Allied Chemical and Alkali Workers* v. *Pittsburgh Plate Glass*) that retirees are not "employees" within the meaning of the National Labor Relations Act and, therefore, that benefits for retirees are not mandatory subjects of union bargaining. This means that if a company does not want to discuss increases in retirees' pensions, there is no way a union can legally force it to do so. Thus, for example, a few years ago major companies in the electrical manufacturing industry refused to bargain with unions seeking to improve what they saw as the serious financial plight of many retirees (Fitzgerald, 1978).

It is not likely that many private plans will ever voluntarily adopt full indexing provisions similar to social security. The uncertainties involved in funding such provisions are extremely high, and the costs of such provisions would make private plans unattractive to both employers and workers.

But that does not mean that there are no meaningful options. Two options immediately suggest themselves. Workers could be offered benefits when they retire that are initially at a lower level than otherwise and that increase annually by some predetermined and guaranteed amount.* This option is not likely to be very appealing to most workers, however. Retirees have shown a strong inclination to opt for money now and to postpone worrying about the future. Such an option, however, would provide a way of collectively combating this myopic tendency that most of us exhibit in greater or lesser degree.

Perhaps a more feasible response to the problem is adding automatic adjustment mechanisms to plans at employers' expense but with limits or ceilings placed on the increases.** Limits could be specified in terms of a maximum percentage increase, a specific dollar limitation, or a specified fraction of the movement in the CPI (e.g., 50 percent). Alternatively, increases could be limited to retirees of a certain age or period of years in retirement.

Many other variations or specifications of this option are possible. The important point is that private companies can respond to the inflation problem *without exposing themselves to unknown and unlimited costs.* Thus, for example, a typical plan with a postretirement adjustment every three years of 2 percent less than the increase in the CPI would cost a firm about 2 percent of payroll at a 7 percent inflation rate ceiling (Cooper, 1980). This does not seem like an unreasonably excessive cost, and the level of protection, while not total, is quite good.

Will We Pay the Price of Economic Adequacy?

Throughout the book we have discussed the growing costs of income support for the elderly. It is now common for people to point out the growing proportion of the federal budget that is spent on the elderly. For example, Barbara Torrey (1982), an economist at the federal Office of Management and Budget, begins her paper "Guns vs. Canes: The Fiscal Implications of an Aging Population":

> *The share of the federal budget devoted to the older population . . . has expanded substantially from approximately 2 percent in 1940 to 25 percent today. Over the*

---

*The pension fund for most college teachers (TIAA/CREF) currently offers an option similar to this.

**Ultimately the increased benefits paid out by these mechanisms would be paid for (in most cases) in terms of lower wage increases, lower improvements in other fringe benefits, or higher prices.

next fifty years this older population is expected to more than double in size. . . .
Even if no further responsibilities are assumed by the federal government, this pop-
ulation increase alone will put inexorable fiscal pressures on future federal budgets.

More recent numbers developed by Storey (1983) for fiscal year 1981 show that
$173 billion in federal outlays directly benefited the aged that year and repre-
sented 26 percent of all federal spending. However, social security programs financed by payroll taxes (OASDHI) accounted for 77 percent of these expenditures, or $133 billion.

Social security was included in the federal budget for the first time in 1969.
This inclusion of the operations of the social security trust funds in the federal
budget has been criticized by many social security experts. They argue that social security operations were put into the budget primarily for political reasons.
The surpluses being generated in social security during the 1960s and early
1970s had the effect of helping to "balance the budget." In fact, when the accounting procedure was introduced in 1969, the expected social security surplus
for that year permitted President Johnson to send a balanced budget to Congress, instead of one with a deficit. In recent years, when social security has often had a deficit, some government officials have tried to blame the very much
larger total budget deficits on "out of control" nondiscretionary programs like
social security. As shown in Table 22, however, the size of the two deficits are
very different. As we discussed previously, operating on a pay-as-you-go basis,
social security taxes and expenditures must be kept in close balance. Unlike the
federal budget, social security cannot generate large deficits.

Critics of the "unified budget" argue that these "artificial" and sometimes
manipulative accounting procedures actually hinder the budget making process. Thus, the 1981 National Commission on Social Security recommended
that the social security trust funds be removed from the unified budget.

Changes in how social security is counted in federal expenditures would no
doubt reduce some of the scare statistics so frequently quoted today. However,
it would not change the fact that providing adequately for the retirement period
is an expensive proposition. As the retirement age continues to decline, we face
the prospect of providing individuals with income and services for a 20- to 30-
year period outside the labor force. Increasingly, people are developing expectations that retirement can and should be an enjoyable period of life and that economic resources should be sufficient to avoid the limitations imposed on
retirement living by financial stringency. Unfortunately, if individuals only begin to worry and seriously plan for their own retirement shortly before the
event, the magnitude of the financing problem becomes insuperable for most.
The best and easiest way of accumulating the resources necessary for retirement
is to begin very early. But historically most people have shown a reluctance to
think about retirement until it is *almost* a reality or until it *is* a reality. The result
has been a great deal of poverty among the aged.

Pension systems and, before them, families have stepped in to provide
needed economic support for many of these people—often preventing destitu-
tion. The level of support has often been very low. Yet (as we discussed previously) the rising financial burden imposed on the working population, even at

Table 22.   Deficits: All Federal Programs vs. OASDHI

Fiscal Year	Total Federal Operations	OASDHI Only
1968	− 25.2	+ 3.5
1969	+ 3.2	+ 5.9
1970	− 2.9	+ 4.9
1971	− 23.0	+ 2.2
1972	− 23.4	+ 3.6
1973	− 14.9	+ 5.2
1974	− 4.7	+ 4.1
1975	− 45.2	− 0.1
1976	− 66.4	− 2.3
1977	− 45.0	− 5.1
1978	− 48.8	− 3.1
1979	− 27.7	+ 0.3
1980	− 59.6	− 3.3
1981	− 57.9	+ 3.1
1982	− 110.6	− 8.8

Sources: *Social Security Administration, Annual Statistical Supplement, 1981* (Washington: SSA, n.d.); *Social Security Bulletin* (July 1983); and *Economic Report of the President* (various years).

these low levels of support, has created political concern, and there is particular concern regarding the future burden.

There is considerable debate over what the future costs of social security will be. Despite the lack of agreement, it is clear that rather sizable amounts will be required. How willing are people to finance the required levels of support?

It seems to me that one of the best answers is provided by the individuals *now covered* by good private pensions and social security. The combined reduction in their take-home pay to provide social security and a good private pension is quite large (about 16–20 percent). Yet there is little complaining from this group, probably in large part because these costs are taken out before they ever get their earnings check. We can also look at the European experience, shown in Table 23. Other industrialized countries have payroll taxes for OASDI that average over 17 percent. Despite these high rates, there has been relatively little political opposition in these countries to this level of taxation for pension purposes. Rather, as in the United States, there has been concern in Europe about rising government deficits caused by record high unemployment and inflation.

Recent data indicate, in fact, a willingness of American workers to pay for better benefits. A 1977 survey by the University of Michigan Survey Research Center found that a great many wage and salary workers expressed a willingness to trade increments in pay for better retirement benefits. In the survey, 54 percent of workers preferred an improvement in retirement benefits over a pay increase (Staines and Quinn, 1979). The Peter D. Hart (1979) poll for the National Commission on Social Security asked people their choice between higher social security taxes or lower future retirement benefits. Higher taxes were clearly favored by the majority (63 percent).

Table 23.   Social Security Tax Rates in Selected Countries, 1981

Country	Combined Employee-Employer Tax	
	All Social Security Programs	OASDI Only
Austria	43.70	21.10
Belgium	37.87	15.11
Canada	8.44 [a]	3.60 [b]
France	47.55	13.00 [c]
West Germany	34.40	18.50 [d]
Italy	55.02	24.46
Japan	22.07	10.60
Netherlands	57.65	34.90 [e]
Sweden	35.20	21.15
Switzerland	17.72	9.40
United Kingdom	21.45	n.a. [f]
United States	18.00	10.70

Source: Alicia Munnell, "A Calm Loo, at Social Security," *New York Review of Books* 30 (March 17, 1983). Used by permission of the author.
[a]Excludes work injury insurance.
[b]Invalidity pension financed through sickness insurance.
[c]Includes only the Canadian Pension Plan and excludes the Old-Age Security Program financed out of general revenue.
[d]Invalidity and survivors' benefits financed through sickness insurance.
[e]Disability insurance also includes work-injury compensation.
[f]Not available.

Some people—such as Peterson (1982) and Robertson (1981)—see social security expenditures out of control and too costly to maintain in what they foresee as a no-growth economic environment. If nothing is done, they predict that payroll taxes will reach unbelievably high levels and that workers will rebel at such high taxes.

Certainly we must be sensitive to both the economic and political realities associated with retirement costs. The recent years of economic chaos are a vivid reminder of the uncertainties that lie ahead. We must constantly monitor developments and seek to anticipate problems. Some of the problems that must be dealt with—such as escalating health costs and the baby boom phenomenon—can be clearly seen. Most future developments, both negative and positive, are hidden from our view. The debate, consequently, often centers around two points of view: the pessimist sees the glass half *empty* but the optimist sees it half *full*.

Despite this dilemma, it is foolish to think we can escape the cost of providing an individual with an adequate retirement income by keeping the cost of social security down. If we do not provide for older Americans through taxation, then we will do so by other but less visible means—for example, by reducing a worker's take-home pay to finance private pensions or by transferring income within the family from the young to the old. Older people are no longer willing to live as paupers in their retirement. They expect to be provided for, one way or another.

Certainly the days of cheap social security, like the days of cheap gasoline, are gone forever. We will have to do some very hard thinking and some belt-tightening. But there is no rational justification for the hysteria that is being promoted today by some people who are attacking social security.

In 1961, then Secretary of Health, Education, and Welfare Abraham Ribicoff stated that he thought the limit to public acceptance of the social security payroll tax was 10 percent. We have passed through that ceiling without difficulty. Now people worry about the high rates in the year 2010 or 2020. But as economist Martin Feldstein (1975) has pointed out:

> *An increase in the social security tax rate to 16 or 20 percent would be a substantial increase. . . . There are some who believe that such high rates would create an intolerable burden on low-income and middle-income families. This is a false argument that ignores the substantial increase in real earnings that these families will enjoy at the same time that tax rates rise. Even a tax rate increase of 10 percentage points over the next 50 years is only an increase of 0.2 percent per year. The higher tax would absorb only one tenth of the annual real wage growth of 2 percent. Stated somewhat differently, with a 2 percent annual rate of growth, real wages would rise by 200 percent between now and 2030, and the higher social security tax would absorb no more than 10 percentage points of this 200 percentage point increase in real wages.*

Thus, it is important to remember the political acceptability of gradual increases in tax rates. This suggests that better pensions should be phased in over a period of years—similar to the way many other countries have introduced the major improvements in their programs. And it is probably wise to anticipate the demographic bulge and consequent sharp rise in costs beginning around the year 2010 as a result of the World War II baby boom.

Also, there is a need for a greater awareness of the intra- and intergenerational equity issues. As the costs of aged retirement living increase, more attention should be given to these issues in order both to maintain public confidence in and support for the programs and to use with maximum effectiveness the money allocated.

One of the most important issues we must deal with is the trend toward increasingly early retirement. It is certainly natural for many people to want to retire as early as possible. The evidence shows that as one gets older, the desire to continue working is clearly not as strong as it was once thought to be by many sociologists (see Chapter 3). There are many people who enjoy the new lifestyle retirement provides. But as society responds to the pressure for bigger pensions at earlier ages, pension costs rise at dramatic and staggering rates. For example, actuaries point out that pension costs increase by about 50 percent once the *normal* age of retirement is reduced from age 65 to age 60. Some private pension plans today allow people to retire below the age of 60 with no serious penalty. The cost of earlier retirement is measured not only by the costs of the pension benefits paid out, but also by the reduced economic output resulting when fewer workers remain in the work force.

Apart from the natural desire of many people to retire at an earlier age, there has also been a systematic, institutionalized pressure in this country to encourage older workers to leave the labor force. The Social Security Act itself imposes a severe retirement test on workers. More recently, private pension systems and early retirement policies have been instrumental in encouraging, and even forcing, workers to retire at increasingly earlier ages. Unions and management have responded to chronic unemployment in this country by devising pension systems that encourage one part of the labor force, the older workers, to leave in order to make room for another part, the younger workers.

What economists call "the lump of labor fallacy" is at the heart of this kind of thinking. There are those who believe there is a fixed number of jobs in the economy; so if younger people enter the labor force, older people must leave it. We do not need to accept such reasoning, however; the number of jobs in the economy is not fixed. We can provide jobs for younger and older people if we are willing to undertake the policies necessary to promote and ensure full employment while restraining prices. Full employment policies would reverse the trend toward early retirement.

Unfortunately, however, this solution does not appear to be a politically viable one—at least not in the near future; the political record of equivocation speaks for itself. Full employment without high inflation probably requires some major changes in the structure of the American economy and the rules under which it operates. Such changes are unlikely to occur in the near future, given "the privileged position of business" and the insecure position of unions (Lindblom, 1977).

Instead, we must look at more marginal, less effective solutions. Stopgap measures such as offering bonuses for delayed retirement, abolishing mandatory retirement policies, liberalizing the social security retirement test, and promoting full-time and part-time work among older people are being tried. But these attempts alone *will not have a major effect* on the trend toward early retirement.

We may have to do something more dramatic; we may have to raise the Social Security eligibility age and regulate the early retirement policies of private pensions. As unattractive as government action is in this area, it may be necessary in order to combat the very serious alternative of increasing early retirement. In this country the large and very prosperous corporations cover most of the workers with private pensions. When these large companies introduce an early retirement policy, competitive pressures force other less prosperous and smaller companies to follow suit.

One thing is clear about future costs. The major economic issue is not whether—in the face of other public expenditure problems such as urban blight, national defense, and pollution—we can have better pensions and services for the aged. The issue is whether we want a higher standard of living in our retirement years at the expense of a lower standard in our younger years. While trade-offs must be continually made in the short run, rising incomes in retirement are closely related over the long run to sacrifices in consumption made in the earlier years. Whether we like it or not, the "economics of aging" begins for most of us quite early in life.

Suggested Readings

Binstock, Robert H., Martin A. Levin, and Richard Weatherly. "Political Dilemmas of Social Intervention." In Robert H. Binstock and Ethel Shanas, eds., *Handbook of Aging and the Social Sciences*, 2nd ed. New York: Van Nostrand Reinhold, 1984.

    An excellent discussion of the problems of implementing social policies and programs.

Crystal, Stephen. *America's Old Age Crisis*. New York: Basic Books, 1982.

    A clearly written and thoughtful perspective on the aging dilemma, with an emphasis on pensions, family support, and long-term care.

Estes, Carroll L., and R. J. Newcomer (and associates). *Fiscal Austerity and Aging*. Beverly Hills: Sage Publications, 1983.

    Federal–state responsibilities and relationships are examined in the light of the fiscal austerity of the 1980s.

Heclo, Hugh. "Toward a New Welfare State?" In P. Flora and A. J. Heidenheimer, eds., *The Development of Welfare States in Europe and America*. New Brunswick: Transaction Books, 1982.

    A comparative view of political and economic developments, both past and present, as they relate to developing welfare programs and policies.

Myles, John F. *Old Age in the Welfare State: The Political Economy of Public Pensions*. Boston: Little Brown, 1984.

    A penetrating discussion of old age and the role of pensions.

Peterson, Peter G. "Social Security: The Coming Crash." *New York Review of Books* 29 (2 December 1982) and "The Salvation of Social Security." *New York Review of Books* 29 (16 December 1982), Munnell, Alicia H. "A Calm Look at Social Security." and P. G. Peterson. "A Reply to Critics." *New York Review of Books* 30 (17 March 1983).

    A provocative exchange of views on social security that emphasizes the funding controversy.

Glossary

Actuarial valuations   Cost projections that take into account (for pensions) the number of employees retiring and dying each year, labor force turnover, the benefit formula, plan expenses, and investment income.

Age Discrimination in Employment Act   Originally enacted by the federal government in 1967 "to promote employment of older persons based on their ability rather than age; to prohibit arbitrary age discrimination in employment; and to help employers and workers find ways of meeting problems arising from the impact of age on employment." The original act prohibited discrimination based on age against persons age 40–65. Amendments in 1978 raised the upper age limit to 70 but eliminated all age limits for most federal employees.

Deferred profit sharing plan   A plan in which the company's contributions are based upon business profits. Profits are credited to employee accounts to be paid at retirement or other stated dates or circumstances (for example, disability or death).

Defined benefit plans   Pension plans that state *before* retirement how much they will pay in benefits at retirement, benefits usually varying by years of service and/or earnings. These plans contrast with defined contribution plans that specify certain contributions to be made on an employee's behalf; the benefit is then determined at retirement on the basis of the total contribution accumulated.

Depreciation allowance   A charge against the current income of a business to reflect the using up or "wear and tear" on a certain amount of its assets—primarily buildings and equipment. This charge is not paid out to other businesses but is retained within the firm as a bookkeeping entry.

Depression   The recurrent ups and downs in the level of economic activity that extend over a period of years are referred to as the "business cycle." Depression usually refers to extreme low levels of economic activity extending over a long period (not seasonally). The Great Depression of the 1930s extended over almost a decade and resulted, at one point, in about one-quarter of the work force being unemployed.

Disregard   A term used to refer to provisions in means-tested financial support programs that exempt certain amounts of financial resources in determining benefit eligibility. For example, in the SSI program, $20 of social security benefits is disregarded in determining whether an applicant's total income falls below the level specified for payment of benefits.

ERISA   Employee Retirement Income Security Act of 1974. Federal legislation establishing participation, vesting, funding standards, plan-termination insurance, disclosure requirements, and Individual Retirement Accounts (IRAs).

Federal Reserve   A central banking system for the United States established in 1913. There are 12 district banks and a coordinating seven-member Federal Reserve Board of Governors in Washington. Appointed to the Board of Governors for 14-year terms, members constitute a body that has been purposely established as an independent monetary authority.

Fertility rate   The total fertility rate is the number of births that 1,000 women would have in their lifetime if, at each year of age, they experienced the birth rates occurring in the specified calendar year. The fertility rate is an annual (or percentage) measure, even though it is expressed as a hypothetical lifetime (or cohort) measure.

Fiscal policy   Action by the government to influence the economy (especially to promote employment and decrease inflation) through changing tax rates and expenditure levels.

Gross national product (GNP)   The dollar value of the total annual output of final goods and services in the nation.

Index(ing)   The use of mathematical ratios to make comparisons between two different periods of time (or comparisons between different locations, industries, nationalities, etc.). The Consumer Price Index is probably the most well-known index, comparing "average" prices in a given year with those in a predetermined base year.

Individual Retirement Account (IRA)   Originally, workers not covered by a retirement plan where they were employed could make tax deferrable contributions of 15 percent of earned income up to $1,500 per year to an individual account or annuity. Beginning in 1977, if there was a nonemployed spouse, the maximum was increased to $1,750. Funds in IRAs may be placed in a life insurance company, a bank, a mutual fund, or in certain special government bonds. There are penalties and immediate tax liability if funds are withdrawn prematurely. Since 1981, *all* workers can deposit up to $2,000 (plus $250 for a nonworking spouse).

Inflation   A general and widely diffused increase in the level of prices for various goods and services. The result is a loss in the purchasing power of money, customarily measured by various price indexes (e.g., the Consumer Price Index). Inflation hurts those whose incomes do not rise as fast as prices increase: people with fixed or slowly rising income and savers who lend money. A rise in the index of prices means that it will take more money to buy the *same* amount of goods and services.

Investment   *Economic* investment is an activity (usually by businesses) that uses the resources of a nation to maintain or add to its stock of physical capital (i.e., buildings and equipment). The main source of investment expenditure is the retained earnings and depreciation allowances of business. Expenditures, however, are also made possible by savings from households (a) by direct borrowing or by sale of new stock issues or (b) indirectly via financial institutions.

Joint and survivor option   A type of pension benefit that provides income to the surviving spouse in an amount equal to some percentage of the income payable during the time that the employee and spouse were alive. Typically the percentage is 50 or 100 percent. In the absence of this provision, the spouse often loses his or her interest in the pension benefit.

Life expectancy   A statistical measure of the average number of years persons born in a given year can be expected to live under the conditions prevailing in that year. Life expectancy is measured both at birth and at other stages of life.

Lifetime rate of return   The interest rate that equalizes the compounded value of total taxes paid over a lifetime and the "present value" of the expected stream of benefits. A less technical definition is the rate at which the total value of accumulated payroll taxes (increased for interest) is equated to the value of benefits (decreased for interest). The present value of a sum of money due at a future date is the amount which, put at compound interest at a given rate, will amount to the sum specified at the stated date. The present value of, say, $1,000 six years hence at 5 percent is $746.30, since that sum compounded at 5 percent equals $1,000.

Means test   A regulation stipulating that eligibility for aid and the amount of aid provided depend not, for example, on past employment or earnings but on specified amounts of income and/or assets of the persons (family) requesting assistance.

Median   A statistical measure that is often used instead of the mean to describe the center, middle, or average of a set of data. It is the value of the middle data item when the items are arranged in an increasing or decreasing order of magnitude. For example, the median of the data set 13 16 18 20 40 is 18.

Monetary policy   Action by the government to influence the economy by changing the demand for, and supply of, money.

National income accounting   A generally accepted methodology developed by economists to assist in describing and analyzing a nation's economy. Productive activity and income generated by that activity are measured and organized in a set of standardized tables called "the national accounts." Information from these accounts is used to derive specific economic measures, such as gross national product, national income, and personal income. The tables, and statistics based on them, are usually published by the governments concerned or international agencies such as the Statistics Division of the United Nations.

Negative income tax   A type of benefit proposed to deal with the problem of poverty. As the name implies, a negative income tax is an "income tax in reverse." Income tax programs collect revenues from individuals who have taxable incomes in excess of certain deductions, exemptions, and credits. In contrast, a negative income tax would require the government to make payments to individuals with incomes below some specified poverty level. Thus, such plans subsidize people with low incomes.

Net worth   An accounting measure of the value of assets minus the value of liabilities.

Pension   A fixed dollar amount that is paid *regularly* over time by a former employer or the government to a retired, disabled, or deserving person (or his dependents). The amount may be increased partially or fully in later years to compensate for inflation.

Portability   A type of **vesting** (defined below) mechanism that allows employees to take their pension credits with them when they change jobs. For credits to be portable they must be vested, that is, nonforfeitable. ERISA permits portability but only if both employees and the involved employers mutually agree.

Private pensions   Pensions obtained through employment in the nongovernment sector of the economy. See **pension**.

Productivity   An economic concept defined as the total output of a good or service divided by the total number of man-hours expended in producing the goods. Productivity is influenced by the level of technology, changes in capital plant and equipment, and the quality of the labor force.

Profit sharing plan   See **deferred profit sharing plan**.

Progressive tax   A tax that takes a larger proportion of income in taxes, the higher the income. The key to whether a tax is progressive or not lies in the increasing percentage of income paid in taxes, *not* in the increasing amount paid. Thus, the payroll tax is "proportional" up to the taxable earnings ceiling, but the federal income tax is progressive.

Recession   A "mild" **depression** (defined above).

Retained earnings   Business income after expenses that is not paid out in dividends or government taxes.

Transfer income   Income that results from government disbursements for which no products or services are received. Most government welfare expenditures fall into this classification—social security payments, unemployment compensation, etc. Transfer payments, in a sense, rechannel tax revenues of the public sector back into the hands of individuals and groups in the private sector.

Vesting   The pension rights of a terminating employee depend on the plan provisions. Vesting refers to the provision that gives a participant the right to receive an accrued benefit at a designated age, regardless of whether the employee is still employed at that time. Thus, vesting removes the obligation of the participant to remain in the pension plan until the date of early or normal retirement.

Wage index   A measure of the change in general wage levels. Such an index is used in the social security program to adjust recorded wages of workers before calculating benefits. Thus, if a worker earned $3,000 in 1956, retired at age 65 in 1984, and wage levels were, say, two and one-half times higher than in 1956, the indexing factor of two and one-half would be applied to the $3,000 and the index earnings would be $7,500 (see also **indexing**).

References

Aaron, Henry J. 1977. "Demographic Effects on the Equity of Social Security Benefits." In M. S. Feldstein and R. P. Inman, eds., *The Economics of Public Service.* New York: Macmillan, pp. 151–173.

_____. 1981. "Salvaging Social Security." *The Brookings Bulletin* 17 (Spring): 13–16.

_____. 1982. *Economic Effects of Social Security.* Washington, D.C.: The Brookings Institution.

Abbott, Julian. 1977. "Socioeconomic Characteristics of the Elderly: Some Black-White Differences." *Social Security* 40 (July): 16–42.

Ad Hoc Advisory Committee. 1975. "Social Security: A Sound and Durable Institution of Great Value." In U.S. Senate Special Committee on Aging. *Future Directions in Social Security—Unresolved Issues: An Interim Staff Report.* Washington, D.C.: U.S. Government Printing Office.

Adamchak, Donald J., and Eugene A. Friedman. 1983. "Societal Aging and Generational Dependency Relationships: Problems of Measurement and Conceptualization." *Research on Aging* 5 (September): 319–338.

Advisory Council on Social Security. 1979. *Social Security Financing and Benefits.* Reports. Washington, D.C.: mimeo.

Advisory Council on Social Security. 1975. Reports. Washington, D.C.: mimeo.

Ahart, Gregory J. 1978. Testimony. In Subcommittee on Social Security, U.S. House Committee on Ways and Means, *Disability Insurance Program: 1978.* Washington, D.C.: U.S. Government Printing Office, pp. 2–9.

Andrisani, Paul J. 1977. "Effects of Health Problems on the Work Experience of Middle-aged Men." *Industrial Gerontology* 4 (Spring): 97–112.

Arenson, Karen W. 1981. "The Low U.S. Rate of Savings." *The New York Times* (22 December): D1 and D7.

Aspin, Les. 1976. "The Burden of Generosity." *Harper's* 253 (December): 22–24.

Atchley, Robert. 1971. "Retirement and Leisure Participation: Continuity or Crisis?" *The Gerontologist* 11 (Spring, Part I): 13–17.

_____. 1976. *The Sociology of Retirement.* New York: Wiley/Schenkman.

Atchley, Robert C., and Judith L. Robinson. 1982. "Attitudes Toward Retirement and Distance from the Event." *Research on Aging* 4 (September): 299–313.

Ball, Robert. 1978a. "Income Security for the Elderly." In *The Economics of Aging.* A National Journal Issues Book. Washington, D.C.: The Government Research Corporation, pp. 1748–1753.

_____. 1978b. *Social Security Today and Tomorrow.* New York: Columbia University Press.

Bankers Trust. 1977. *Study of Employee Savings and Thrift Plans.* New York: Bankers Trust.

Barfield, Richard E., and James N. Morgan. 1978a. "Trends in Planned Early Retirement." *The Gerontologist* 18 (February): 13–18.

_____. 1978b. "Trends in Satisfaction with Retirement." *The Gerontologist* 18 (February): 19–23.

Barnes, Roberta, and Sheila Zedlewski. 1981. *The Impact of Inflation on the Income and Expenditures of Elderly Families.* Final Report to the Administration on Aging. Washington, D.C.: mimeo.

Barro, Robert J. 1978. *The Impact of Social Security on Private Saving—Evidence from the U.S. Time Series.* Washington, D.C.: American Enterprise Institute.

Bassett, Preston C. 1978. "Future Pension Policy and the President's Commission." *Employee Benefit Plan Review* 33 (December): 28, 30, 91.

Batten, Michael D. 1973. "Application of a Unique Industrial Health System." *Industrial Gerontology* (Fall): 38–48.

Berkowitz, Monroe; William G. Johnson; and Edward H. Murphy. 1976. *Public Policy Toward Disability.* New York: Praeger.

Binstock, Robert H. 1983. "The Aged as Scapegoat." *The Gerontologist* 23 (April): 136–143.

BNA. 1978. *Pension Reporter* 202 (August 21): A-9.

Bondar, Joseph. 1982. "Initial Effects of Elimination of the Dependency Requirement on Entitlement to Husband's and Widower's Benefits." *Research and Statistics Note* No. 2. Washington, D.C.: Office of Research and Statistics, U.S. Social Security Administration.

Borzilleri, Thomas C. 1978. "The Need for a Separate Consumer Index for Older Persons." *The Gerontologist* 18 (June): 230–236.

Boskin, Michael, and M. Hurd. 1982. "Are Inflation Rates Different for the Elderly?" Mimeo.

Boulding, Kenneth. 1958. *Principles of Economic Policy.* Englewood Cliffs, N.J.: Prentice-Hall.

Bradford, Kenneth. 1979. "Can You Survive Your Retirement?" *Harvard Business Review* (November/December): 103–107.

Bridges, B., and M. Packard. 1981. "Prices and Income Changes for the Elderly." *Social Security Bulletin* 44 (January): 3–15.

Brittain, John A. 1972. *The Payroll Tax for Social Security.* Washington, D.C.: The Brookings Institution.

Broder, David S. 1973. "Budget Funds for Elderly Grow Rapidly." *Washington Post* (30 January 1973): A-16.

Brown, J. Douglas. 1972. *An American Philosophy of Social Security.* Princeton, N.J.: Princeton University Press.

———. 1973. Memorandum. In U.S. Senate Special Committee on Aging, *Future Directions in Social Security.* Part 3. Washington, D.C.: U.S. Government Printing Office, pp. 220–221.

Browning, Edgar K. 1973. "Social Insurance and Intergenerational Transfers." *Journal of Law and Economics* (October): 215–237.

Buchanan, James M. 1968. "Social Insurance in a Growing Economy: A Proposal for Radical Reform." *National Tax Journal* (December): 386–395.

Burkhauser, Richard V., and Wilkinson, J. T. 1983. "The Effect of Retirement on Income Distribution: a Comprehensive Income Approach." *The Review of Economics and Statistics* 65 (November): 653–658.

Butler, Robert N. 1975. *Why Survive? Being Old in America.* New York: Harper & Row.

Califano, Joseph A., Jr. 1979. Testimony. In U.S. Senate Special Committee on Aging, *Retirement, Work, and Lifelong Learning.* Washington, D.C.: U.S. Government Printing Office.

Callahan, James. 1981. "How Much, For What, and For Whom?" *American Journal of Public Health* 71 (September): 987–988.

Callahan, James, and Stanley S. Wallack, eds. 1981. *Reforming the Long-Term Care System.* Lexington, Mass.: Lexington Books, D. C. Heath.

Campbell, Colin D., and Rosemary G. Campbell. 1976. "Conflicting Views on the Effect of Old-Age and Survivors Insurance on Retirement." *Economic Inquiry* 14 (September): 369–388.

Campbell, Rita Ricardo. 1975. Supplementary Statement. In *Reports of the Quadrennial Advisory Council on Social Security.* Washington, D.C.: U.S. Government Printing Office.

Cardwell, James B. 1976. Testimony. In Subcommittee on Social Security, U.S. House Committee on Ways and Means, *Disability Insurance Program.* Washington, D.C.: U.S. Government Printing Office, pp. 273–281.

Chen, Yung-Ping. 1984. "Economic Status of the Aged." In Robert H. Binstock and Ethel Shanas, eds., *Handbook of Aging and the Social Sciences,* 2nd ed. New York: Van Nostrand Reinhold.

Chen, Yung-Ping, and Kwang-Wen Chu. 1974. "Tax-benefit Ratios and Rates of Return Under OASI: 1974 Retirees and Entrants." *The Journal of Risk and Insurance* 41 (June): 189–206.

Clark, Robert L.; D. T. Barker; and R. S. Cantrell. 1979. *Outlawing Age Discrimination: Economic and Institutional Response to the Elimination of Mandatory Retirement.* Final Report to the Administration on Aging. Mimeo.

Clark, Robert, and Joseph Spengler. 1978. "The Implications of Future Dependency Ratios and Their Composition." In Barbara Pieman Herzog, ed., *Aging and Income.* New York: Human Sciences Press, pp. 55–89.

Clark, Timothy B. 1983. "Congress Avoiding Political Abyss by Approving Social Security Changes." *National Journal* (19 March): 611–615.

Cohen, Wilbur J. 1957. *Retirement Policies Under Social Security.* Berkeley: University of California Press.

Cohen, Wilbur J., and Milton Friedman. 1972. *Social Security: Universal or Selective?* Rational Debate Seminars. Washington, D.C.: American Enterprise Institute for Public Policy Research.

Colberg, Marshall R. 1978. *The Social Security Retirement Test—Right or Wrong?* Washington, D.C.: American Enterprise Institute for Public Policy Research.

Consultant Panel on Social Security. 1976. *Report on Social Security to the Congressional Research Service.* Washington, D.C.: U.S. Government Printing Office.

Cooper, Keith H. 1980. "Pensions, Inflation and Benefit Indexing." In Aspen Institute, *The Quiet Crisis of Public Pensions*. Conference Report. New York: The Institute.

Cottrell, Fred, and Robert C. Atchley. 1969. *Women in Retirement: A Preliminary Report*. Oxford, Ohio: Scripps Foundation.

Cowgill, Donald O. 1981. "Can We Afford Our Aging Populations?" Paper prepared for Conference on Economics of Aging, Kansas City, Missouri, April 1981. Mimeo.

Cowgill, Donald O., and Lowell D. Holmes. 1970. "The Demography of Aging." In A. M. Hoffman, ed., *The Daily Needs and Interests of Older People*. Springfield, Ill.: C. C. Thomas, pp. 27–69.

Cutler, Neal E., and Robert A. Harootyan. 1975. "Demography of the Aged." In Diana S. Woodruff and James E. Birren, eds., *Aging*. New York: Van Nostrand, pp. 31–69.

Dale, Edwin L., Jr. 1973. "The Young Pay for the Old." *New York Times Magazine* (14 January): 8ff.

Danziger, Sheldon; J. VanderGaag; E. Smolensky; and M. K. Taussig. 1982. "Implications of the Relative Economic Status of the Elderly for Transfer Policy." Paper prepared for the Brookings Institution Conference on Retirement and Aging, Washington, D.C.: mimeo.

_____. "The Life-Cycle Hypothesis and the Consumption Behavior of the Elderly." *Journal of Post Keynesian Economics* 5 (Winter): 208–227.

Davis, Karen. 1982. "Medicare Reconsidered." Paper prepared for the Duke University Medical Center Seventh Private Sector Conference on Financial Support of Health Care for the Elderly and Indigent. Durham, N.C.: mimeo.

Daymont, T. N., and P. J. Andrisani. 1983. "The Health and Economic Status of Very Early Retirees." *Aging and Work* 6: 117–135.

DeVita, Carol J. 1981. "Measuring Dependency in the U.S. and in Canada." Paper presented at the 34th Annual Meeting of the Gerontological Society of America, Toronto.

Diamond, P. A. 1977. "A Framework for Social Security Analysis." *Journal of Public Economics* 8 (December): 275–298.

Doctors, S. I.; Y. M. Shkop; K. C. Denning; and V. T. Doctors. 1980. "Older Worker Employment Services." *Aging and Work* 3 (Fall): 229–237.

Donahue, Wilma; Harold L. Orbach; and Otto Pollak. 1960. "Retirement: The Emerging Social Pattern." In Clark Tibbitts, ed., *Handbook of Social Gerontology*. Chicago: University of Chicago Press, pp. 330–406.

Dowd, James J., and Vern Bengtson. 1978. "Aging in Minority Populations." *Journal of Gerontology* 33 (May): 427–436.

Drazaga, Linda; M. Upp; and V. Reno. 1982. "Low-Income Aged; Eligibility and Participation in SSI." *Social Security Bulletin* 45 (May): 28–35.

DRI (Data Resources, Inc.). 1980. *Inflation and the Elderly.* Report to NRTA/AARP. Lexington, Mass.: mimeo.

Epstein, Lenore A., and Janet H. Murray. 1967. *The Aged Population of the United States.* Office of Research and Statistics, Social Security Administration. Report No. 19. Washington, D.C.: U.S. Government Printing Office.

Esposito, Louis; L. B. Mallan; and D. Dodoff. 1980. "Distribution of Increased Benefits under Alternative Earnings Tests." *Social Security Bulletin* 43 (September): 3–9.

Fairholm, Gilbert W. 1978. *Property Tax Relief Programs for the Elderly: A Review of Current Literature and Policy Implications for Virginia.* Richmond: Virginia Center on Aging, Virginia Commonwealth University, mimeo.

Federal Council on Aging. 1975. *Study of Interrelationships of Benefit Programs for the Elderly.* Appendix I: "Handbook of Federal Programs Benefiting Older Americans." Prepared for the Federal Council on Aging by the Human Resources and Income Security Project, The Urban Institute. Washington, D.C.: mimeo.

Feldstein, Martin S. 1972. "The Incidence of the Social Security Payroll Tax: Comment." *The American Economic Review* 42 (September): 735–742.

_____. 1974. "Social Security, Induced Retirement, and Aggregate Capital Accumulation." *Journal of Political Economy* 82 (September–October): 905–926.

_____. 1975. "Toward a Reform of Social Security." *The Public Interest* 40 (Summer): 80–81.

_____. 1977. "Facing the Social Security Crisis." *The Public Interest* 47 (Spring): 88–100.

Fitzgerald, Albert J. 1978. Testimony. In Subcommittee on Retirement Income and Employment, U.S. House Select Committee on Aging, *National Pension Policies: Private Pension Plans.* Washington, D.C.: U.S. Government Printing Office, pp. 486–494.

Fitzpatrick, Edmund W. 1979. "Evaluating a New Retirement Planning Program— Results with Hourly Workers." *Aging and Work* (Spring): 87–94.

Flint, Jerry. 1977. "Early Retirement Is Growing in U.S." *New York Times* (10 July): 1.

_____. 1980. "The Old Folks." *Forbes* (18 February): 51–56.

Flowers, Marilyn R. 1977. *Women and Social Security: An Institutional Dilemma.* Washington, D.C.: American Enterprise Institute for Public Policy Research.

Foner, Anne, and Karen Schwab. 1981. *Aging and Retirement.* Monterey, Calif.: Brooks/Cole.

Foner, Anne, and Karen Schwab. 1983. "Work and Retirement in a Changing Society." In Matilda White Riley, Beth B. Hess, and K. Bond, eds., *Aging in Society: Selected Reviews of Recent Research.* Hillsdale, N.J.: Lawrence Erlbaum Associates.

Fox, Alan. 1979. "Earnings Replacement Rates of Retired Couples: Findings from the Retirement History Study." *Social Security Bulletin* 42 (January): 17–39.

_____. 1982. "Earnings Replacement Rates and Total Income: Findings from the Retirement History Study." *Social Security Bulletin* 45 (October): 3–24.

Freiden, Alan; Dean Leimer; and Ronald Hoffman. 1976. *Internal Rates of Return to Retired Worker-Only Beneficiaries Under Social Security, 1967–70.* Studies in Income Distribution No. 5. Washington, D.C.: Office of Research and Statistics, Social Security Administration.

Friedman, Eugene A., and Harold L. Orbach. 1974. "Adjustment to Retirement." In Silvano Arieti, ed., *The Foundations of Psychiatry.* Vol. 1, *American Handbook of Psychiatry*, 2nd ed. New York: Basic Books, pp. 609–645.

Friedman, Joseph, and Jane Sjogren. 1981. "Assets of the Elderly as They Retire." *Social Security Bulletin* 44 (January): 16–31.

Friedman, Milton. 1971. "Purchasing Power Bonds." *Newsweek* (12 April): 86.

_____. 1972. "Second Lecture." In Wilbur J. Cohen and Milton Friedman, *Social Security: Universal or Selective?* Rational Debate Seminars. Washington, D.C.: American Enterprise Institute.

Galbraith, John Kenneth. 1958. *The Affluent Society.* Boston: Houghton Mifflin.

Gordon, Robert J. 1981. "The Consumer Price Index: Measuring Inflation and Causing It." *The Public Interest* (Spring): 112–134.

Goudy, Willis J. 1981. "Changing Work Expectations: Findings from the Retirement History Study." *The Gerontologist* 21 (December): 644–649.

Guttentag, Jack M. n.d. "Home Equity Conversion: A New Factor in Retirement Planning." In Philip Cagan, ed., *Saving for Retirement.* Washington, D.C.: American Council of Life Insurance.

Hartman, Robert. 1983. *Pay and Pensions for Federal Workers.* Washington, D.C.: The Brookings Institution.

Hayghe, Howard. 1978. "Marital and Family Characteristics of Workers, March 1977." *Monthly Labor Review* 101 (February): 51–54.

Heidbreder, E. M., and M. D. Batten. 1974. "ESAR II—A Comparative View of Services to Age Groups." *Facts and Trends* No. 4. Washington, D.C.: National Council on Aging.

HEW Task Force (on the Treatment of Women Under Social Security). 1978. *Report.* Washington, D.C.: U.S. Department of Health, Education and Welfare.

Hewitt, Edwin S. 1970. Testimony. In U.S. Senate Special Committee on Aging, *Economics of Aging: Toward a Full Share in Abundance*, Part 10B. Washington, D.C.: U.S. Government Printing Office.

Hollister, Robinson G., and John L. Palmer. 1972. "The Impact of Inflation on the Poor." In Kenneth Boulding and M. Pfaff, eds., *Redistribution to the Rich and Poor: The Grants Economics of Income Distribution.* Belmont, Calif.: Wadsworth, pp. 240–270.

Hudson, Robert. 1978. "The 'Graying' of the Federal Budget and Its Consequences for Old-Age Policy." *The Gerontologist* 18 (October): 428–440.

Institute on Poverty, University of Wisconsin. 1983. "The Relative Economic Status of the Aged." *IRP Focus* 6 (Spring): 1–4, 11–14.

Irelan, Lola M., and K. Bond. 1976. "Retirees of the 1970's." In Gary S. Kart and Barbara B. Manard, *Aging in America—Readings in Social Gerontology.* Sherman Oaks, Calif.: Alfred, pp. 231–251.

Jackson, J. J. 1970. "Aged Negroes: Their Cultural Departures from Statistical Stereotypes of Rural-Urban Differences." *The Gerontologist* 10 (Summer): 140–145.

Johnson and Higgins, Inc. 1979. *1979 Study of American Attitudes toward Pensions and Retirement.* New York: Johnson and Higgins.

_____. 1981. *Funding Costs and Liabilities of Large Corporate Pension Plans.* New York: Johnson and Higgins.

Juster, F. Thomas. n.d. "Current and Prospective Financial Status of the Elderly Population." In Phillip Cagan, ed., *Saving Retirement.* Washington, D.C.: American Council of Life Insurance.

Kahne, Hilda. 1975. "Economic Perspectives on the Roles of Women in the American Economy." *The Journal of Economic Literature* 13 (December): 1249–1292.

Kasschau, Patricia L. 1974. "Reevaluating the Need for Retirement Preparation Programs." *Industrial Gerontology*, new series 1 (Winter): 42–59.

King, Jill. 1976. *The Consumer Price Index.* Technical Paper V. The Measure of Poverty reports. Washington, D.C.: U.S. Department of Health, Education, and Welfare.

Kingson, Eric R. 1979. "Men Who Leave Work Before Age 62: A Study of Advantaged and Disadvantaged Very Early Labor Force Withdrawal." Ph.D. dissertation, Florence Heller Graduate School, Brandeis University.

Kotlikoff, Laurence J.; Avia Spivak; and Lawrence Summers. 1982. "The Adequacy of Savings," *American Economic Review* 72 (December): 1056–1069.

Kreps, Juanita M. 1977. "Age, Work, and Income." *Southern Economic Journal* 43 (April): 1423–1437.

Kreps, Juanita M., and Joseph J. Spengler. 1966. "The Leisure Component of Economic Growth." In National Commission on Technology, Automation, and Economic Progress. *Technology and the Economy.* Appendix 2: The Employment Impact of Technological Change. Washington, D.C.: U.S. Government Printing Office.

Krute, Aaron, and Mary Ellen Burdette. 1978. "1972 Survey of Disabled and Nondisabled Adults: Chronic Disease, Injury, and Work Disability." *Social Security Bulletin* 41 (April): 3–17.

Lapkoff, Shelly. 1981. "Working Women, Marriage, and Retirement." Chapter 42 in the Appendix of the President's Commission on Pension Policy. *Coming of Age: Toward a National Retirement Policy.* Washington, D.C.: The Commission.

Leavitt, Thomas D. 1983. *Early Retirement Incentive Programs.* Waltham, Mass.: Policy Center on Aging, Brandeis University.

Leimer, Dean R. 1979. "Projected Rates of Return to Future Social Security Retirees Under Alternative Benefit Structures." In *Proceedings of the Workshop on Policy Analysis with Social Security Record Files.* Washington, D.C.: Social Security Administration.

Lesnoy, Selig D., and D. R. Leimer. 1981. "Social Security and Private Saving: New Time Series Evidence with Alternative Specifications." Working Paper No. 22. Washington, D.C.: Office of Research and Statistics, Social Security Administration.

Leuthold, Jane H. 1975. "The Incidence of the Payroll Tax in the United States." *Public Finance Quarterly* 3 (January): 3–13.

Liang, J., and T. J. Fairchild. 1979. "Relative Deprivation and Perception of Financial Adequacy Among the Aged." *Gerontology* 34 (September): 747–760.

Lindblom, Charles E. 1977. *Politics and Markets—The World's Political-Economic Systems.* New York: Basic Books.

Lopata, Helena. 1977. "Widows and Widowers." *The Humanist* 37 (September–October): 25–28.

McConnel, Charles E., and F. Deljavan. 1983. "Consumption Patterns of the Retired Household." *Journal of Gerontology* 38 (July): 480–490.

McGill, Dan M. 1975. *Fundamentals of Private Pensions*, 3rd ed. Homewood, Ill.: Irwin.

Mallan, Lucy B. 1975. "Young Widows and Their Children: A Comparative Report." *Social Security Bulletin* 38 (May): 3–21.

Marcou, Ross A. 1978. "Comparing Federal and Private Employee Benefits." *Civil Service Journal* (October–December): 12–18.

Markides, Kyriakos S. 1981. Letter to the Editor. *Journal of Gerontology* 36 (July): 494.

———. 1983. "Minority Aging." In Matilda White Riley, B. Hess, and K. Bond, *Aging in Society: Selected Reviews of Recent Research*. Hillsdale, N.J.: Lawrence Erlbaum Associates.

Maxwell, James A. 1975. "Characteristics of State and Local Trust Funds." In David J. Ott, Attiat F. Ott, James A. Maxwell, and J. Richard Aronson, *State-Local Finances in the Last Half of the 1970's*. Washington, D.C.: The American Enterprise Institute, pp. 35–62.

Meier, Elizabeth. 1975. "Over 65: Expectations and Realities of Work and Retirement." *Industrial Gerontology* (Spring): 95–109.

Michael, Robert T. 1979. "Variations Across Households in the Rate of Inflation." *Journal of Money, Credit, and Banking* 2 (February): 32–46.

Minarik, Joseph J. 1981. Testimony before the U.S. Senate Special Committee on Aging. Hearings on "Social Security Oversight: Cost-of-Living Adjustments." Part 3. Washington, D.C.: U.S. Government Printing Office.

Mirer, Thad W. 1974. "The Distributional Impact of Inflation and Anti-inflation Policy." Discussion Paper 231-74. Madison: Institute for Research on Poverty, University of Wisconsin-Madison.

———. 1980. "The Dissaving Behavior of the Retired Aged." *Southern Economic Journal* 46 (April): 1197–1205.

Mitchell, Olivia S., and E. S. Andrews. 1981. "Scale Economies in Private Multi-Employer Pension Systems." *Industrial and Labor Relations Review* 34 (July): 522–530.

Mitchell, Olivia S., and G. S. Fields. 1982. "The Effects of Pensions and Earnings on Retirement: A Review Essay." In R. Ehrenberg, *Research in Labor Economics*, Vol. 5. Greenwich, Conn.: Jai Press.

Moeller, Charles. 1972. "The Role of Private Pension Plans in the Economy." In *Financing Retirement: Public and Private*. Conference Proceedings. New York: The Tax Foundation, Inc.

Morgan, James N. 1977. "An Economic Theory of the Social Security System and Its Relation to Fiscal Policy." In G. S. Tolley and Richard V. Burkhauser, eds., *Income Support Policies for the Aged*. Cambridge, Mass.: Ballinger, pp. 107–126.

———. 1978. "Intra-Family Transfers Revisited: The Support of Dependents Inside the Family." In G. Duncan and J. Morgan, eds., *Five Thousand American Families: Patterns of Economic Progress*, Vol. 6. Ann Arbor, Mich.: Survey Research Center, Institute of Social Research, The University of Michigan.

———. 1980. "Retirement in Prospect and Retrospect." In Greg J. Duncan and James N. Morgan, eds., *Five Thousand American Families—Patterns of Economic Progress*, Vol. 8. Analyses of the First Eleven Years of the Panel Study of Income Dynamics. Ann Arbor, Mich.: Survey Research Center, Institute for Social Research, University of Michigan.

Morgan, James N.; Katherine Dickinson; Jonathan Dickinson; Jacob Benus; and Greg Duncan. 1974. *Five Thousand American Families—Patterns of Economic Progress*. Ann Arbor, Mich.: Survey Research Center, Institute for Social Research, University of Michigan.

Morris, Robert, and Paul Youket. 1981. "The Long-Term Care Issues: Identifying the Problems and Potential Solutions." In J. J. Callahan and S. Wallack, eds., *Reforming the Long-Term Care System*. Lexington, Mass.: Lexington Books, D. C. Heath.

Morrison, Peter A. 1982. "Demographic Links to Social Security." *Challenge* 24 (January/February): 44–48.

Motley, Dena K. 1978. "Availability of Retired Persons for Work: Findings from the Retirement History Study." *Social Security Bulletin* 41 (April): 18–29.

Munnell, Alicia H. 1977. *The Future of Social Security*. Washington, D.C.: The Brookings Institution.

———. 1979. "Are Private Pensions Doomed?" *New England Economic Review* (March/April): 5–20.

———. 1982a. *The Economics of Private Pensions*. Washington, D.C.: The Brookings Institution.

———. 1982b. "Guaranteeing Private Pension Benefits: A Potentially Expensive Business." *New England Economic Review* (March/April): 24–47.

Musgrave, Richard. 1968. "The Role of Social Insurance in an Overall Program for Social Welfare." In Bowen et al., *The American System of Social Insurance*. New York: McGraw-Hill, pp. 23–45.

Myers, George C. 1984. "Aging and World-Wide Population Change." In Robert H. Binstock and Ethel Shanas, eds., *Handbook of Aging and the Social Sciences*, 2nd ed. New York: Van Nostrand Reinhold.

Myers, Robert J. 1970. "Government and Pension." In *Private Pensions and the Public Interest*. Washington: The American Enterprise Institute.

_____. 1975. *Social Security*. Homewood, Ill.: Irwin.

_____. 1982. "Prevalence of Elections of Joint-and-Survivor Annuities under Private Pension Plans." Memorandum No. 25 to the National Commission on Social Security Reform. Washington, D.C.: mimeo.

Myrdal, Gunnar. 1963. *Challenge to Affluence*. New York: Pantheon Books.

National Commission on Social Security. 1981. *Social Security in America's Future*. Report of the Commission to the President. Washington, D.C.: The Commission.

National Commission on Social Security Reform. 1983. *Report*. Washington, D.C.: U.S. Government Printing Office.

National Survey of the Black Aged. 1978. Summary Report. *Social Security Bulletin* 41 (July): 33–35.

NCOA (National Council on the Aging). 1975. *The Myth and Reality of Aging in America*. Washington, D.C.: NCOA.

_____. 1980. "Retirement Preparation: Growing Corporate Involvement." *Aging and Work* 3 (Winter): 1–26.

Nordhaus, W., and J. Tobin. 1973. "Is Growth Obsolete?" In *The Measurement of Economic and Social Performance*. New York: National Bureau of Economic Research, pp. 509–532.

Office of Personnel Management. 1981. "Federal Fringe Benefit Facts, 1980." Washington, D.C.: Office of Personnel Management.

Okonkwo, Ubadigbo. 1975. "Intragenerational Equity Under Social Security." Washington, D.C.: mimeo.

Okun, Arthur. 1975. *Equality and Efficiency—The Big Trade-Off*. Washington, D.C.: The Brookings Institution.

Orshansky, Mollie. 1978. Testimony. In U.S. House Select Committee on Aging, *Poverty Among America's Aged*. Washington, D.C.: U.S. Government Printing Office.

Palmore, Erdman. 1977. "Facts on Aging—A Short Quiz." *The Gerontologist* 17 (July): 315–320.

Palmore, Erdman; G. G. Fillenbaum; and L. K. George. 1984. "Consequences of Retirement." *Journal of Gerontology* 39 (January): 109–116.

Paltiel, Freda L. 1982. "Women and Pensions in Canada." *International Social Security Review* 35 (No. 3): 333–334.

Parnes, Herbert S. 1981. "From the Middle to the Later Years." *Research on Aging* 3 (December): 387–402.

Parnes, Herbert S., and Gilbert Nestel. 1979. "The Retirement Experience." In H. S. Parnes, G. Nestel, T. H. Chirikos, T. N. Daymont, F. L. Mott, and D. O. Parsons. *From the Middle to Later Years*. Columbus, Ohio: Center for Human Resources, Ohio State University.

Pechman, Joseph A.; Henry J. Aaron; and Michael K. Taussig. 1968. *Social Security: Perspectives for Reform*. Washington, D.C.: The Brookings Institution.

Pellechio, Anthony J., and Gordon P. Goodfellow. 1983. "Individual Gains and Losses from Social Security before and after the 1983 Social Security Amendments." Paper prepared for the Cato Institute Conference on Social Security. Mimeo.

Pension and Investment Age. 1983. "Top 1,000 Fund Assets Surge to $622 Billion" (24 January): 1.

Peter D. Hart Research Associates, Inc. 1979. *A National Survey of Attitudes toward Social Security*. A report prepared for the National Commission on Social Security. Washington, D.C.: mimeo.

Peterson, Peter G. 1982. "Social Security: The Coming Crash." *New York Review of Books* 29 (2 December): 34.

Poverty Studies Task Force. 1976. *The Measure of Poverty*. A Report to Congress as Mandated by the Education Amendments of 1974. Washington, D.C.: U.S. Department of Health, Education, and Welfare.

President's Commission on Pension Policy. 1981. *Coming of Age: Toward a National Retirement Income Policy*. Report of the Commission. Washington, D.C.: The Commission.

Profit Sharing Research Foundation. 1978. *Profit Sharing in 38 Large Companies*. Evanston, Ill.

Pursell, Donald E., and William D. Torrence. 1979. "Age and the Jobhunting Methods of the Unemployed." *Monthly Labor Review* 102 (January): 68–69.

Quinn, Joseph F. 1975. "The Microeconomics of Early Retirement: A Cross-Section View of White Married Men." *Journal of Human Resources* 12 (Summer): 329–346.

Radner, Daniel B. 1982. "Distribution of Family Income: Improved Estimates." *Social Security Bulletin* 45 (July): 13–21.

Reich, Murray H. 1977. "Group Preretirement Education Programs: Whither the Proliferation?" *Industrial Gerontology* 4 (Winter): 29–43.

Reno, Virginia. 1971. "Why Men Stop Working At or Before Age 65: Findings from the Survey of New Beneficiaries." *Social Security Bulletin* (June): 3–11.

Rich, Spencer. 1983. "Census Finds Elderly's After-Tax Income Higher than Average." *Washington Post*, 19 August.

Riley, Matilda White, and Anne Foner. 1968. *Aging and Society*, Vol. 1. New York: Russell Sage Foundation.

Robertson, A. Haeworth. 1977. "OASDI: Fiscal Basis and Long-Range Cost Projections." *Social Security Bulletin* 40 (January): 1–9.

_____. 1981. *The Coming Revolution in Social Security*. McLean, Va.: Security Press.

Robinson, Pauline; Sally Coberly; and C. E. Paul. 1984. "Work and Retirement." In Robert H. Binstock and Ethel Shanas, eds., *Handbook of Aging and the Social Sciences*, 2nd ed. New York: Van Nostrand Reinhold.

Rones, Philip L. 1978. "Older Men—The Choice Between Work and Retirement." *Monthly Labor Review* 101 (November): 3–10.

_____. 1983. "The Labor Market Problems of Older Workers." *Monthly Labor Review* 106 (May): 3–12.

Rosenblum, M., and H. Sheppard. 1977. *Jobs for Older Workers in U.S. Industry: Possibilities and Prospects*. Report to the U.S. Department of Commerce, Economic Development Administration. Washington, D.C.: mimeo.

Rowen, Hobart. 1978. "Rethinking That Bite in Social Security." *Washington Post* (16 February): A-19.

Russell, Louise B. 1982. *The Baby Boom Generation and the Economy*. Washington, D.C.: The Brookings Foundation.

Samuelson, Paul. 1958. "An Exact Consumption-Loan Model of Interest With or Without the Social Contrivance of Money." *Journal of Political Economy* 66 (December): 467–482.

Schieber, Sylvester J. 1978. "First Year Impact of SSI on Economic Status of 1973 Adult Assistance Populations." *Social Security Bulletin* 41 (February): 18–51.

Schmundt, M.; E. Smolensky; and L. Stiefel. 1975. "The Evaluation of Recipients of In-Kind Transfers." In I. Laurie, ed., *Integrating Income Maintenance Programs*. New York: Academic Press, pp. 189–207.

Scholen, Ken and Yung-Ping Chen. 1980. *Unlocking Home Equity for the Elderly.* Cambridge, Mass.: Ballinger.

Schulz, James H. 1977. "The Social Security Retirement Test: Time for a Change?" *The Urban and Social Change Review* 10 (Summer): 14–18.

———. 1978. "Liberalizing the Social Security Retirement Test—Who Would Receive the Increased Pension Benefits?" *Journal of Gerontology* 33 (March): 262–268.

Schulz, James H., and Guy Carrin. 1972. "The Role of Savings and Pension Systems in Maintaining Living Standards in Retirement." *Journal of Human Resources* 7 (Summer): 343–365.

Schulz, James H.; A. Borowski; L. Kelly; T. D. Leavitt; and W. Spector. 1980. *Private Pension Policy Simulations.* Final report to the U.S. Department of Labor. Waltham, Mass.: mimeo.

Schulz, James H.; T. D. Leavitt; L. Kelly; and J. Strate. 1982. *Private Pension Benefits in the 1970s.* Bryn Mawr, Pa.: McCahan Foundation for Research in Economic Security.

Schulz, James H., and T. D. Leavitt. 1983. *Pension Integration: Concepts, Issues and Proposals.* Washington, D.C.: Employee Benefit Research Institute.

Schulz, James H.; T. D. Leavitt; J. Strate; and M. Stubbs. 1984. *State, Local, and Teachers Pensions: Coping with Inflation Over the 1975–1982 Period.* Final report to the AARP Andrus Foundation. Waltham, Mass.: Policy Center on Aging, mimeo.

Schwab, Karen. 1976. "Early Labor-Force Withdrawal of Men: Participants and Non-participants Aged 58–63." In Social Security Administration, *Almost 65: Baseline Data from the Retirement History Study.* Washington, D.C.: Office of Research and Statistics, pp. 43–56.

Shanas, Ethel. 1977. *National Survey of the Aged.* Final report to the U.S. Administration on Aging. Chicago: mimeo.

Shanas, Ethel, and Philip M. Hauser. 1974. "Zero Population Growth and the Family Life of Old People." *Journal of Social Issues* 30: 79–92.

Shanas, Ethel; Peter Townsend; Dorothy Wedderburn; Henning Friis; Poul Milhoj; and Jan Stehouwer. 1968. *Old People in Three Industrial Societies.* New York: Atherton.

Sheppard, Harold L. 1978. "The Economics of Population, Mortality, and Retirement." In *The Economics of Aging.* A National Journal Issues Book. Washington, D.C.: The Government Research Corporation, pp. 1880–1883.

Sheppard, Harold L., and A. Harvey Belitsky. 1966. *The Job Hunt.* Baltimore, Md.: Johns Hopkins Press.

Shuchman, Carol. 1983. "Family Transfers and Household Living Arrangements among the Elderly." Paper presented at the Population Association of America Meetings, April 13–16. Mimeo.

Siegel, Jacob S. 1976. *Demographic Aspects of Aging and the Older Population in the United States*. Current Population Reports, Special Studies. Series P-23, No. 59. Washington, D.C.: U.S. Government Printing Office.

Siegfried, Charles A. 1970. "The Role of Private Pensions." In *Private Pensions and the Public Interest*. Washington, D.C.: The American Enterprise Institute.

Skolnik, Alfred M. 1975. "Restructuring the Railroad Retirement System." *Social Security Bulletin* 38 (April): 23–29.

Slavick, Fred. 1966. *Compulsory and Flexible Retirement in the American Economy*. Ithaca, N.Y.: Cornell University Press.

Smeeding, Timothy M. 1982. "Alternative Methods for Valuing Selected In-kind Transfer Benefits and Measuring Their Effect on Poverty." Technical Paper 50. Washington, D.C.: U.S. Bureau of the Census.

Sobel, Irvin, and Richard C. Wilcock. 1963. "Job Placement Services for Older Workers in the United States." *International Labor Review* 88: 129–156.

Social Security Administration. 1976. *Almost 65: Baseline Data from the Retirement History Study*. Washington, D.C.: Office of Research and Statistics.

_____. 1981. "Erroneous Public Perception of SSA Administrative Expenses." *Social Security Bulletin* 44 (September): 1.

_____. 1982. "Federal Civil Service Annuitants and Social Security." *Research and Statistics Note*, Report No. 6. Washington, D.C.: Office of Research and Statistics, Social Security Administration.

Soldo, Beth J. 1981. "The Living Arrangements of the Elderly in the Near Future." In S. B. Kiesler; J. N. Morgan; and V. K. Oppenheimer. *Aging: Social Change*. New York: Academic Press.

Solow, Robert M. 1975. "The Intelligent Citizen's Guide to Inflation." *The Public Interest* 38 (Winter): 30–66.

Staines, Graham L., and Robert P. Quinn. 1979. "American Workers Evaluate the Quality of Their Jobs." *Monthly Labor Review* 102 (January): 3–12.

Storey, James R. 1983. Testimony before the Health and Long-term Care Subcommittee, House Select Committee on Aging (May 5).

Streib, Gordon F., and Clement J. Schneider. 1971. *Retirement in American Society*. Ithaca, N.Y.: Cornell University Press.

Taggart, Robert. 1973. *The Labor Market Impacts of the Private Retirement System*. U.S. Subcommittee on Fiscal Policy, U.S. Joint Economic Committee. Studies in Public Welfare No. 11. Washington, D.C.: U.S. Government Printing Office.

Task Force on Women and Social Security. 1975. *Women and Social Security: Adapting to a New Era*. Prepared for the Special Senate Committee on Aging. Washington, D.C.: U.S. Government Printing Office.

Thompson, Gayle B. 1978. "Pension Coverage and Benefits, 1972: Findings from the Retirement History Study." *Social Security Bulletin* 41 (February): 3–17.

Thompson, Lawrence H. 1974. *An Analysis of the Factors Currently Determining Benefit Level Adjustments in the Social Security Program*. Technical Analysis Paper No. 1. Office of Income Security Policy, Office of the Assistant Secretary of Planning and Evaluation. Washington, D.C.: Department of Health, Education, and Welfare.

Thompson, Lawrence H., and Paul N. Van de Water. 1975. "The Short-Run Behavior of the Social Security Trust Funds." *Technical Analysis Paper*, No. 8. Washington, D.C.: Office of Income Security Policy, Department of Health, Education, and Welfare.

Thurow, Lester. 1976. "Tax Wealth, Not Income." *New York Times Magazine* (11 April): 32.

Tibbitts, Clark. 1977. "Older Americans in the Family Context." *Aging*: (April–May): 6–11.

Tilove, Robert. 1976. *Public Employee Pension Funds*. Twentieth Century Fund. New York: Columbia University Press.

Tissue, Thomas. 1978. "Response to Recipiency Under Public Assistance and SSI." *Social Security Bulletin* 41 (November): 3–15.

Torda, Theodore S. 1972. "The Impact of Inflation on the Elderly." *Federal Reserve Bank of Cleveland Monthly Review* (October–November): 3–19.

Torrey, Barbara Boyle. 1982. "Guns vs. Canes: The Fiscal Implications of an Aging Population." *American Economic Association Papers and Proceedings* (May): 309–313.

Turnbull, John G.; C. Arthur Williams, Jr.; and Earl F. Cheit. 1967. *Economic and Social Security*, 3rd ed. New York: Ronald Press.

Universal Social Security Coverage Study Group. 1980. *The Desirability and Feasibility of Social Security Coverage for Employees of Federal, State, and Local Governments and Private Non-Profit Organizations*. Report of the Study Group. Washington, D.C.: U.S. Department of Health, Education, and Welfare.

The Urban Institute. 1981. *The Future of State and Local Pensions*. Final Report to Department of Housing and Urban Development. Washington, D.C.: mimeo.

U.S. Bureau of Labor Statistics. 1966. *Retired Couple's Budget for a Moderate Living Standard*. Bulletin No. 1570-4. Washington, D.C.: U.S. Government Printing Office.

_____. 1967. *Three Standards of Living for an Urban Family of Four Persons*. Bulletin No. 1570-5. Washington, D.C.: U.S. Government Printing Office.

_____. 1980. *Employee Benefits in Industry: A Pilot Survey*. Report 615. Washington, D.C.: U.S. Department of Labor.

_____. 1982. "Retired Couple's Budgets, Final Report, Autumn 1981." *Monthly Labor Review* 105 (November): 37–38.

U.S. Bureau of the Census. 1983. "Money Income and Poverty Status of Families and Persons in the United States: 1982." *Consumer Income*. Current Population Reports, Series P-60, No. 140. Washington, D.C.: U.S. Government Printing Office.

U.S. Department of Health, Education, and Welfare. 1978. "Major Initiative: Long-Term Care/Community Services." Memorandum, Office of the Secretary. Washington, D.C.: mimeo, July 14.

_____. 1979. *Social Security and the Changing Roles of Men and Women*. Report to Congress. Washington, D.C.: U.S. Department of Health, Education, and Welfare.

U.S. Department of Justice. n.d. *The Pension Game: American Pension System from the Viewpoint of the Average Woman*. Task Force on Sex Discrimination, Civil Rights Division. Washington, D.C.: U.S. Government Printing Office.

U.S. Department of Labor. 1965. *The Older American Worker*. Washington: U.S. Department of Labor.

U.S. House Committee on Education and Labor. 1972. *Interim Staff Report of Activities of the Pension Study Task Force*. Washington, D.C.: U.S. Government Printing Office.

_____. 1978. *Pension Task Force Report on Public Employee Retirement Systems*. Washington, D.C.: U.S. Government Printing Office.

U.S. House Committee on Ways and Means. 1967. *President's Proposals for Revision in the Social Security System*. Hearings, Part 1. Washington, D.C.: U.S. Government Printing Office.

U.S. House Select Committee on Aging. 1977. *Federal Responsibility to the Elderly*. Washington, D.C.: U.S. Government Printing Office.

_____. 1978. *Poverty Among America's Aged—A Staff Review*. In U.S. House Select Committee on Aging, *Poverty Among America's Aged*. Hearings. Washington, D.C.: U.S. Government Printing Office.

U.S. Senate Special Committee on Aging. 1970. *The Stake of Today's Workers in Retirement Security*. Washington, D.C.: U.S. Government Printing Office.

Van De Water, Paul N. 1979. "Disability Insurance." *American Economic Review* 69 (May): 275–278.

Viscusi, W. Kip. 1979. *Welfare of the Elderly*. New York: Wiley-Interscience.

Walker, James W., and Daniel E. Lupton. 1978. "Performance Appraisal Programs and Age Discrimination Law." *Aging and Work* 1 (Spring): 73–83.

Wallich, Henry. 1969. "Adjustable Bonds: Purchasing Power Bonds." *Newsweek* (24 November).

Wander, Hilde. 1978. "ZPG Now: The Lesson from Europe." In Thomas Espenshade and William Serow, eds., *The Economic Consequences of Slowing Population Growth*. New York: Academic Press.

Weaver, Warren, Jr. 1981. "Goal of Retiring at 65 Recedes under Economic Pressure and Population Curve." *New York Times* (9 March): 21.

Wellington, H. H., and Ralph K. Winter, Jr. 1971. *The Unions and the Cities*. Washington, D.C.: The Brookings Institution.

White House. 1983. White House Fact Sheet on President Reagan's Health Care Incentives Reform Proposal. Washington, D.C.: mimeo, February 28.

Zook, C., and F. Moore. 1980. "High-Cost Users of Medical Care." *New England Journal of Medicine* 302 (May): 996–1002.

Index